DENIAL OF THE SOUL

ALSO BY M. SCOTT PECK, M.D.

The Road Less Traveled

People of the Lie

What Return Can I Make?
(with Marilyn von Waldner and Patricia Kay)
(reissued as *Gifts for the Journey,* with Marilyn von Waldner)

The Different Drum

A Bed by the Window

The Friendly Snowflake (illustrated by Christopher Peck)

A World Waiting to Be Born

Meditations from the Road

Further Along the Road Less Traveled

In Search of Stones (illustrated by Christopher Peck)

In Heaven as on Earth

The Road Less Traveled and Beyond

DENIAL OF THE SOUL

*Spiritual and Medical Perspectives
on Euthanasia and Mortality*

M. SCOTT PECK, M.D.

SIMON & SCHUSTER
A VIACOM COMPANY

The names and some of the superficial circumstances of all of my patients as well as those of some other patients and their physicians have been altered to protect their confidentiality.

Grateful acknowledgement is made to:

G. P. Putnam's Sons for permission to reprint an excerpt from *Dying Well: The Prospect for Growth at the End of Life* by Ira Byock. Copyright © 1997 by Ira Byock. Reprinted by permission of
G. P. Putnam's Sons.

W.W. Norton & Company, Inc., for permission to reprint an excerpt from *Death and Dignity: Making Choices and Taking Charge* by Timothy E. Quill, M. D. Copyright © 1993 by Timothy Quill. Reprinted by permission of W.W. Norton & Company, Inc.

The New England Journal of Medicine for permission to reprint information from "Death and Dignity: A Case of Individualized Decision Making" by Timothy E. Quill, M.D., *The New England Journal of Medicine*, vol. 324, March 7, 1991, pp. 691-4. Copyright © 1991 Massachusetts Medical Society. All rights reserved.

The author also wishes to acknowledge:

"A Death of One's Own" by Andrew Solomon, *The New Yorker*, May 22, 1995

A Chosen Death: The Dying Confront Assisted Suicide by Lonny Shavelson (New York: Simon & Schuster, 1995)

Arguing Euthanasia: The Controversy over Mercy Killing, Assisted Suicide, and the "Right to Die", Jonathan D. Moreno, ed. (New York: Simon & Schuster, 1995)

First published in the US by Harmony Books, a division of Crown Publishers, Inc, 1997
First published in Great Britain by Simon & Schuster Ltd, 1997
A Viacom company

Simon & Schuster Ltd
West Garden Place
Kendal Street
London W2 2AQ

Simon & Schuster Australia
Sydney

A CIP catalogue record for this book is available from the British Library

ISBN 0-684-81791-82146-X

Printed and bound in Great Britain by
Butler & Tanner Ltd, Frome and London

To
the ministry
of the
employees and volunteers
of Hospice

ACKNOWLEDGMENTS

This book could not have come into being without the assistance of a large number of people. I regret I cannot thank them all, but some deserve special mention.

First, my basic support system that continues to keep me going: our office manager, Susan Poitras, who typed the book's drafts; our program director, Gail Puterbaugh, who organizes our lives; our assistant, Valerie Duffy, who picks up after us; and my beloved wife, Lily, who is their general manager and mine.

Next, the publishing professionals who have made the book a public reality: Jonathan Dolger, my long-term agent and champion; Leslie Meredith, simultaneously the book's acquisition editor, broad-brush editor, and line editor; and her talented assistant editor, Andrew Stuart.

More than any of my other books, this one has required the assistance of medical colleagues. I wish to thank Lucy Waletzky, M.D., whose early concern with its central issue helped inspire me to address the subject and who continued to encourage me after reading its first draft; Morris Clark, M.D., our generous and wise family physician for over two decades, who offered me his perspectives from internal medicine; and John Battista, M.D., who brought me up to date on some of the psychiatric aspects.

Andrew Solomon not only courageously provided me with the most central of all the cases in this book but also took the time to vulnerably and personally discuss with me those essential details that were initially unclear.

I would also like to take this opportunity to thank belatedly in print a person who has lurked behind the scenes of every book I have ever written: Sister Ellen Stephen, O.S.H. A nun, teacher, community leader, and anthologized poet, E.S. has been my primary spiritual director for the past twenty years. To her consistent friendship and sometimes gentle, sometimes confrontational guidance, I owe a large portion of whatever wisdom and sanity I possess.

All of the above are responsible for making this a better book than it would otherwise have been. They are not responsible, however, for any of its deficiencies. That responsibility is entirely my own.

Finally, I would like to express my particular gratitude to someone already mentioned: Gail Puterbaugh. Beyond the responsibilities of her employment and family, she has served for many years as a dedicated hospice volunteer. From the word go, she was a source not only of information but of boundless enthusiasm for this work at every stage of its evolution. She is an exemplary representative of those to whom this book is dedicated. Thank you.

While it is not necessarily our lot in this age that we should suffer physically to the end of our endurance, it is still our lot that we should so suffer emotionally. The denial of this fact of life is the central defect of the age.

CONTENTS

DENIAL OF THE SOUL

INTRODUCTION

This is an age where every possible issue seems to be coming out of the closet, which, I suspect, is generally to the good. One such issue is the topic of euthanasia. I have no desire to see it thrust back into the closet. I believe it a proper matter for public debate. Currently, however, the debate strikes me as strangely skewed, incomplete, and, in some quarters, passionless. This book is an attempt to rectify the situation—not to dampen the debate but to enlarge it and heat it up.

My motivation for the attempt is a sense of alarm that the subject of euthanasia is not being given the importance it deserves, almost as if it is being lost among the myriad of other issues that have come out of the closet or been on the table for some time. The issue of euthanasia may be more critical than all the others. Indeed, it is possible we may need to reach a national consensus about it *before* all the other issues can be more satisfactorily resolved.

———

Of course we've always known about the existence of euthanasia. Just because it was in the closet doesn't mean that we had no awareness of it, only that we didn't want to bring it into the living room for serious discussion.

In 1950, when I was fourteen, I began to think seriously about death. It occurred to me that perhaps the most important thing about my existence was that it was limited. Along with everybody else, I was going to die. Thinking for myself as well as others, it seemed to me that if someone was clearly dying there was no reason for that person not to hasten the process, if she or he so desired, to avoid the unpleasantness involved. I knew perfectly well what the word "euthanasia" meant, and I believed in it. I was very rational back in those days.

A generation later, in 1975, a very prominent American theologian, Dr. Henry Van Dusen, and his wife executed a suicide pact together in their New York City apartment, leaving behind them a most rational and public letter explaining that they were motivated by their desire to avoid the inconveniences of old age and natural death. I found myself mildly shocked. Had a more ordinary elderly couple made a suicide pact for the same reasons I wouldn't have been in the least surprised. But because Dr. Van Dusen had been a famous religious leader I was disquieted. Somehow it seemed that religion or spirituality was an aspect of the euthanasia issue, although I had no idea at the time of the nature of that aspect.

Since then, however, I have had enough life experience, including professional experience in medicine, psychiatry, and theology, to believe I can sufficiently understand the complexities of euthanasia so as to be able to make a clarifying contribution to its debate.

———

The current debate over euthanasia is often simplistic. That is hardly surprising, since the process of debate is usually construed as a win-or-lose activity in which one party will eventually be declared "right" and the other "wrong." It is also not surprising, since even the well educated tend to think simplistically about all manner of issues ranging from abortion and homosexuality to war and the "right" diet. But we do not live in a black-and-white world, and for some years I have been engaged in a crusade against simplistic, one-dimensional thinking.

The subject of euthanasia is complex. We don't even have a generally agreed-upon definition of the word. Is euthanasia solely an act committed by someone—a physician or family member—on someone else who is ill or dying? Or can the term also be used for someone who is ill or dying who kills himself without the assistance of another? Does euthanasia require the patient's consent? The family's consent? Is it separable from other forms of suicide and homicide? How does it differ from simply pulling the plug? If one type of euthanasia consists of refraining from the use of heroic measures to prolong life, how does one distinguish between those measures that are heroic and those that are standard treatment? What is the relationship between euthanasia and pain? Is there a distinction to be made between physical pain and emotional pain? How does one assess degrees of suffering? Above all, why are ethical issues involved, and what might they be?

—————

The first part of this work addresses issues of pain and death that are primarily medical in nature. Although sometimes complex, these issues are well within the understanding of any layperson. The discussion of them will provide information that is not only needed by the general public but is required before we can even arrive at a definition of euthanasia that is adequate for the last years of this century and the decades to come. Part I will conclude with such a definition.

Part II addresses primarily spiritual issues of the nature of secularism, the soul, and the meaning of living and dying. Here it will become clear why the book is entitled *Denial of the Soul*. More than anything else, it is our differing beliefs about the existence or nonexistence of the human soul that make euthanasia a subject for passionate ethical and moral debate.*

—————

* I have never before written on the topic of euthanasia. Consequently most of this work is completely new material. However, toward the very end of Part I and in the earlier chapters of Part II, where I deal with psychospiritual subjects, I am, by necessity, at times covering matters I wrote extensively about in one or more of my previous books. Readers of those books may therefore find some of what I have to say here old hat. In this instance, please feel free to skim or to skip ahead with my apologies for not knowing how to do it differently.

In Part III, I speak of those aspects of euthanasia that are primarily legal and social. In the end I point out how the euthanasia debate—if it is handled well—can ultimately be of great benefit to our civilization.

———

Although it might be bad literary form, I believe it is good taste in this particular instance to give away the punch line from the start. The position I shall reach at the end is one that dictates against a laissez-faire attitude toward euthanasia, or what could be termed "euthanasia on demand."

While I am passionate about this position forged out of complexity, I am also profoundly aware that I may not yet have the whole truth. I have experienced a number of the vicissitudes of aging, but hardly all of them. I am obviously dying—I can even feel it—but I do not know personally what it is like to be totally and permanently incapacitated or to live under a death sentence as a result of a very specific disease with a rapidly deteriorating course. In other words, I have not been there. I may yet change my mind. All that I write here, therefore, should be taken with at least that much of a grain of salt.

Finally, while my conclusion may suggest that some who have practiced euthanasia, like Dr. and Mrs. Van Dusen, should have done it differently, I do not condemn such people. In my declining years, my deepest desire is to praise the God who is mostly beyond my definition. Praising God is usually something qualitatively very different from condemning anyone.

Part I

FROM CONFUSION TO DEFINITION

———✦———

THE MEDICAL AND PSYCHIATRIC PERSPECTIVES

Chapter 1

PULLING THE PLUG

At age seventy-nine my paternal grandmother, Juliet, a tart-tongued tiny lady, became whiny and demanding, tremulous, humorless, and totally self-centered. "Well, this is going to be my last Christmas," she would pronounce annually. Or Easter. Or Thanksgiving. "You boys aren't going to have your old grandmother around much longer," she would add for the benefit of my brother and me. Although probably not diagnosable as senile exactly, she was hardly an uplifting presence.

Shortly after reaching eighty-four, she developed an intestinal obstruction one evening and was rushed to the hospital. Relatively easy abdominal surgery healed her of the problem but gave her a far worse one: staphylococcal septicemia. She was one of the early victims of a new breed of bacteria that had become resistant to penicillin, specifically one that had begun to flourish within hospitals and was known as staph 80/81, or hospital staph. It was a devastating disease. For over two weeks she was on the critical list, more or less in coma, while intravenously being fed massive doses of virtually every experimental antibiotic available. Each day my grandfather was informed, "Tonight is probably when your wife will die."

Then a college student, I visited my grandmother in the hospital once during this period. Since she was comatose, that visit consisted simply of my sitting in the room with her for five minutes. She had been reduced to a body—a maimed body. Back then, when physicians ran out of superficial veins into which they could insert their needles, they did cutdowns, minor surgery to expose for their ministration the deep veins in the ankles and armpits.* Both of my grandmother's ankles and armpits had been used or were being used for that purpose. Putting myself in the role of resident physician in charge of the case, I could only wonder, "Why in God's earth should I bother to try to stick a needle in yet another vein in this poor eighty-four-year-old woman who's apparently senile, who probably won't survive anyway, and who, if by some miracle she should survive, clearly won't be any good for anything anyway?" It seemed to me at the time of my visit that they should have pulled the plug.

It so happened, however, that my grandmother did survive . . . physically. After two and a half weeks her temperature came down, the bacteria cleared from her blood, and she became alert enough to take nourishment by mouth. There was only one problem: she was stark raving mad—hallucinating night and day, making no sense whatsoever. The doctors told my parents and grandfather not to be alarmed. "It is quite common," they explained, "for someone after such a massive infection to have what we call an organic brain syndrome. It's usually temporary and goes away in a week or so."

But it did not go away. One week passed, two weeks passed, three weeks passed, and my grandmother was still hallucinating around the clock. The doctors opined that her brain syndrome was chronic and she would probably not recover. My parents began vigorously searching for the best nursing home available.

At this point I visited my grandmother in the hospital a second time. Now she was a little more than just a body. But she didn't seem to recognize me and didn't talk to me. She only rambled on about nonexistent pictures on the wall. Nonetheless, although I hadn't yet had any medical, much less psychiatric, training, when I returned home I told my parents, "I'm not sure she's as crazy as she

---

* Today the placement of deep intravenous catheters, or leads, has rendered cutdowns obsolete.

looks. It's not so much that she couldn't talk to me as she wouldn't talk to me. It's like she *refused* to recognize me. Somehow I sensed that she's very angry."

Regardless, the fact remained that she was essentially non compos mentis, and plans went ahead for a nursing home placement. Five weeks after the recovery from her infection, she was scheduled on a Monday morning to be transferred from the hospital to the nursing home.

On Saturday morning, two days before this well-planned transfer, in the midst of a visit by my parents and my grandfather, my grandmother sat up straight in her hospital bed and announced, "I'm going home today."

I was told the ensuing dialogue went something like:

"But, dear, you've been very, very sick for a long time."

"I know I've been sick," my grandmother responded, "but I'm not sick any longer."

"Still, it would be better for you to go to a place that provides less intensive care. We've chosen such a place. It's most comfortable and will offer you the opportunity for transition."

My grandmother said, "I'm quite aware you have a nursing home picked out for me. You want to send me there Monday, but I'm not going there. I'm going home."

"Do you realize you've been emotionally disturbed for weeks?"

"Of course I realize it. I've been crazy. I am not, however, crazy now, and I am going home. *Today*."

She went home that very afternoon.

For the next five years my grandmother never trembled, whined, or complained. She seemed unfailingly happy. Her wit and her sense of humor were sharper than they had ever been.

Then, toward the end of her eighty-ninth year, she began to become tremulous and petulant once more. Gradually she faded away, dying peacefully in her home at the age of ninety-one. She had survived to meet four of her six great-grandchildren.

So I am glad the doctors did all those cutdowns and used what seemed to me at the time heroic measures to keep her alive.

I am not just glad in the abstract. I have a very personal reason for my gladness. During her five years of lucid happiness, Lily and I became engaged to be married. My parents basically went bonkers over this because my bride-to-be was Chinese. During Thanksgiving 1959, a month before our wedding, Lily and I went to visit my grandparents. At that visit my grandmother said of our marriage, "I can't say that I approve of it, because I don't. But then, it's none of my damn business, and that's the last you'll ever hear me say about it."

Her pronouncement could hardly be construed as a blessing. Nonetheless, given the fact that it was the sole sane response I had received from my family, it almost felt like one.

———

Tony and I met in the early summer of 1965, toward the end of my first year of resident training in psychiatry at Letterman General Hospital, then a large military medical center in the Presidio of San Francisco. Tony was a thirty-two-year-old sergeant in the air force. Previously an alert and competent career enlisted man of Italian extraction, he had recently been making numerous small mistakes in his work and seemed to be mildly confused. He was referred from the mental health clinic of his air base for inpatient psychiatric evaluation and assigned to my care for that purpose.

From my point of view, it was a simple evaluation. Although he appeared physically robust and healthy as well as handsome, mentally he was obviously not all there. In fact, he was hardly there at all. He did not know where he was. He kept drifting off to sleep during my one interview. When I prodded him awake he was unable to answer most of my questions. While I could discover nothing distinctly abnormal in a brief, traditional neurological exam—his arms, legs, eyes, and tongue all seemed to be working perfectly well—in no way did his condition resemble a typical psychiatric disorder. My sense was that physically something was terribly wrong with his brain. Specifically, I suspected he had a brain tumor. I requested an urgent consultation by the neurology service.

Tony was seen by the neurologists the next morning. They too suspected a brain tumor and agreed to his transfer to the neurology ward for further workup: skull X rays, electroencephalogram, arteriogram, and so forth. I told Tony what was happening to him, but he appeared beyond apprehension and, for that matter, unaware of any relationship with me. I assumed we would not meet again. He was no longer under my care, and I quite forgot about him. Case closed, as far as I was concerned . . . or so I thought.

Approximately ten weeks later I completed my first year of the three-year psychiatry residency training program and was immediately rotated to a mandatory two-month stint on the neurology service. In that service I reinherited Tony as my patient. A great deal—or very little, depending upon how you looked at it—had happened to him in the meantime. Tests had, in fact, demonstrated a massive brain tumor primarily involving his frontal lobes. He was transferred to the neurosurgery service. At surgery the tumor proved to be inoperable. Biopsies showed it to be a highly malignant astrocytoma. Following his immediate recovery from surgery, Tony was transferred back to the neurology service for radiation treatment. The radiation was utterly ineffective. Tony's condition rapidly deteriorated. A week before I arrived on the neurology service he slipped into a coma. A few days thereafter, because he was having great difficulty breathing, someone had decided to do a tracheotomy and plug him up to a respirator. His family had been notified that he was terminal, and one member or another was at the hospital around the clock.

It was at this point that Tony reentered my life. Initially there was nothing for me to do other than monitor his intravenous fluids and see to his electrolyte balance. I was not supposed to have any responsibility in regard to his family. I spoke to them only casually. I was under the impression that it was a difficult time for them. They seemed almost desperately to want to know the hour or day of his death—information, of course, that I could not provide. Despite the ways in which my grandmother's case had taught me a certain appreciation for heroic measures, I nonetheless wondered how and why the decision had been made to place Tony on a respirator. But it had been made; it was past and not my place to question it.

Four days after I took over his care, Tony's blood pressure dropped to dangerously low levels. He was in shock not because of any apparent infection but probably because his cancer directly or indirectly was now affecting the deep part of the brain that was involved in blood pressure control. I ordered levophed, the strongest form of adrenaline available, added to his IV infusion in small amounts. His blood pressure returned to normal. I called the chief of neurology to inform him of what I'd done. He commended me. "But, Colonel," I said, "I did it on the spot simply to keep him from dying. Frankly, I'm not sure it's the right thing to do. We can't hold back the sea. He's going to die, and it seems to me that his family's in agony waiting for it to be over." The chief reassured me I'd done only what was appropriate and necessary.

Each succeeding day I had to double the dose of levophed flowing into Tony's veins to keep his blood pressure going. By the fifth day he was on a higher dose than I'd ever known to be used before. His dilated pupils did not react to light. He had started to develop massive bedsores despite frequent turning. But what disturbed me more than anything was the copious amount of frothy light brown liquid that had begun to ooze out along the edges of his tracheotomy. It seemed to me that Tony's body had clearly begun to rot. I called my chief again to tell him of my impression and my opinion that we ought to stop the levophed.

"I'll tell you what," the chief said. "I'll come down tomorrow morning to the ward with the portable electroencephalogram machine, and we'll see if he's got any brain-wave activity left. There are starting to be articles in the literature that it's okay to terminate life-support systems when a patient is brain-dead."

When I came in early the next morning Tony's blood pressure was once again seriously faltering, and once again I doubled his dose of levophed, now to astronomic levels in an intravenous flow that was no longer dripping but pouring into him. I eagerly awaited the arrival of my chief with his machine. He came on schedule. When the static was finally controlled by complicated grounding measures, the machine indicated that Tony had an occasional distorted brain wave. "There's still electrical activity," my chief pronounced. "Not much, but some," and he started packing up.

I showed him the signs of rot in Tony's body. "Yes," he acknowledged. "The fact remains, however, that he's not yet certifiably brain-dead."

After my chief left with the machine I sat looking at Tony for perhaps a quarter of an hour. Then I stood up and twisted the clamp on the IV tubing to cut the flow in half from a pouring stream to a rapid drip. After that I went to the doctors' lounge, where I smoked a single cigarette. In no more than ten minutes I returned to find Tony dead. I informed the nurses and from there went to the waiting room to tell the family that Tony had expired. They wept, speaking to each other in Italian. I could not tell whether they were weeping in grief or relief. Probably both.

I had the presence of mind, of course, not to tell anyone what I had done. It amazes me somewhat, looking back on the event, that I never consciously considered the fact that, in addition to everything else, I was probably disobeying the order of a medical superior and much higher ranking military officer. All I can remember is the simple sense I had that I was halting an abomination.

———

Most physicians could come up with a similar pair of opposing cases from their experience. Recently another physician, Francis D. Moore, published his pair in an article in *Harvard Magazine* entitled "Prolonging Life, Permitting Life to End."*

One case is of a sixty-five-year-old woman who went into total body failure following the fracture of a hip and was for several weeks maintained on almost every modern technical life-support

———

* July–August 1995, pp. 46–51. Excerpted from Francis D. Moore, "Ethics at Both Ends of Life," in *A Miracle and a Privilege: Recounting a Half Century of Surgical Advances* (Washington, D.C.: Joseph Henry Press, 1995).

system imaginable. At one point the patient's family actually asked Dr. Moore to terminate these heroic measures. He told them, in essence, that he did not *know* why she was in such a drastic condition and hence did not *know* that she couldn't recover. He asked them to hang in for a few days. In fact, the patient did recover to become a particularly vibrant human being within a week or two, and six months later the family came back to thank Dr. Moore tearfully for gently refusing to pull the plug.

His other case was of an eighty-five-year-old woman who had suffered a severe burn to a relatively small but vulnerable area of her body: her nose, mouth, and airway. No family was available. In Dr. Moore's immense experience such burns in the elderly were invariably fatal. "When she complained of pain, we gave her plenty of morphine," he wrote. "A great plenty. By the clock. Soon she died quietly and not in pain."

Although Dr. Moore's and my two cases differ dramatically in their particulars—including the factor of age—the pairs have one essential feature in common. In the case of my grandmother and Dr. Moore's younger patient, no one knew what the outcome of heroic treatment would be. In the case of my young patient with brain cancer and Dr. Moore's elderly patient with burns, we had no doubt that we were faced with an inevitable and rapid fatal outcome, regardless of treatment.

The moral would seem to be that the cessation—the termination—of artificial, extraneous life-support systems or heroic medical measures is not only justified but actually decent and positive when there is no longer any doubt that the patient's condition is fatal. There is no point in attempting to prolong the life of a person who is in the agony of his unredeemable death throes, and there is every reason to minimize such agony.

No Doubt?

How can I say there was no doubt that Tony would have rapidly expired even if I hadn't cut down the amount of medicine being used to maintain his blood pressure? Are there not spontaneous remissions from cancer? Miracle cures? Unexplainable healings of all manner of diseases?

Yes, there are such things. But they tend to occur relatively early in the course of the disease. I have never heard of the healing of a disease that had progressed as far as Tony's cancer.

Still, I have learned to distrust the human capacity to predict almost anything *absolutely*. I believe there is always doubt. That is why when I twisted the clamp on Tony's IV ever so gently that morning over thirty years ago I did so in fear and trembling. I desperately wished I could have shared the decision. I do not think that such a decision should be made by a physician acting alone, unless no other option exists.

I am glad to say that the climate for such decision-making has improved dramatically over the past thirty years. It is now routine to question the use of heroic measures in cases such as Tony's and to involve the family in the decision to use or not to use them. In 1965 it was not. The routine then was to use our medical technology to its limits, to fight death to the end, and never even to consider the possibility that the family should have a voice in such matters. Today, as a matter of course, I would discuss the issues with most families. Back then, had I indicated to Tony's family that there was a choice to be made, I would have opened myself to court-martial for unacceptable medical behavior.

Moreover, many hospitals these days have ethics committees for the purpose of sharing the responsibility for difficult medical decisions. So it is a very different and much better ball game now. Now my chief would be much more open to pulling the plug on Tony. He would expect me to involve the family in the decision unless there was clear reason not to. And if matters were still murky we would have other professionals with whom we could wrestle toward clarification. I would not have to act alone.

No Formulas

My chief would have been willing to terminate Tony's mechanical life support had our patient been certifiably brain-dead by the new formula of the day. Actually the development of that formula was one of the early steps forward in the liberalization of the climate so that pulling the plug became a subject for legitimate debate.

It is still a useful formula in at least one circumstance: it is accepted procedure for organ donors who have suffered massive head trauma and are still alive to be sacrificed so that their organs can be harvested for transplant recipients—if there is no longer any electrical activity in the donor's brain.

But note that I pulled the plug on Tony even though there was brain-wave activity. I did so because it seemed to me that while he was not yet certifiably brain-dead, he was in essence "body-dead." In other words, I believed that the brain-dead formula was not an appropriate one in his case. I suspect the vast majority of authorities today would agree.

Then what is the appropriate formula? There isn't one in most cases.

This answer may go against the grain. In regard to virtually every aspect of existence, the most frequent request I receive is for a formula. "Tell me, Dr. Peck, how can I know when I'm being loving and when I'm being a doormat? How do I know when to intervene in my child's life and when to leave him alone? Please give me a formula so that I can know that I'm doing the right thing!" It almost seems to be a human instinct to desire formulas that will totally relieve us of uncertainty and the necessity to agonize over important decisions.

But seldom are there such formulas, and the complex discernment of when the use of heroic medical measures is appropriate and when it is excessive is usually no exception. Too many factors need to be considered: not merely the nature of the disease and its prognosis but family feelings and the patient's own desires, if they are known. There is no mathematical formula that *should* relieve physicians from the responsibility of judgment. This is why I did not follow the lead of my chief in Tony's case; I believed my chief was trying to substitute a formula for judgment. I believe there is usually something subtly unethical about such abdication. It is quite possible for a computer to make the decisions about when to pull the plug; allowing a computer to do so, however, strikes me as inherently inhumane.

Quality of Life: Beware!

With my twenty-year-old wisdom I believed the doctors were employing excessively heroic measures to save my grandmother's life. This assessment was based not only upon her age but also on her seeming unhappiness and her apparent senility. In other words, I had written her off because the quality of her life struck me as poor.

Later I shall speak in great depth about the dangers of assessing the quality of one's own life. Making life-or-death judgments about the quality of other people's lives is even more dangerous.

We human beings—including physicians, psychiatrists among them—have a great tendency to write a great many people off in a great many ways for a great variety of reasons: sex, age, skin color, religion, mental retardation, psychiatric illness, and so on and on and on. Let me speak only briefly about just one such reason: senility.

Because she was elderly, when my grandmother first became whiny and self-centered, my family and I simply assumed she was going senile. No one stopped to consider that she might have been depressed. When she was hallucinating after recovering from the infection, the physicians assumed that she was brain-damaged. In retrospect and with a good deal of psychiatric experience under my belt, it is clear to me that my grandmother was never senile or brain-damaged. She was not an isolated case. A significant number of elderly people are misdiagnosed as having untreatable senility when their true condition is one of potentially treatable depression.

Although probably the most common cause for the misdiagnosis of senility, depression is not the only cause by any means. I once worked in depth with an elderly woman who had faked senility because she wanted to be in a nursing home, and she succeeded for many years in getting her wish. Although seldom so blatant, there is an element of choice in most cases of senility. Anyone who has worked in nursing homes can tell tales of how well many seemingly demented patients can pull themselves together "when they have a mind to"—when they have some compelling motivation. In fact, we don't really know in a scientific sense what most senility really is.*

Nonetheless, we assume that the quality of life of anyone who is senile must be miserable. Among other reasons for this assumption, we think that anyone whose intellect appears to be deteriorating must also have a deteriorating spiritual life. But this is a misidentification of the intellect with the soul.

My mother-in-law spent the last seven years of her life in a nursing home because of senility, diagnosed as accurately as possible by other psychiatrists as well as by me. She appeared at least as happy during that period as she had for the preceding two decades when she was not senile. Most of the time in the nursing home she wouldn't talk. Lily refers to that period as her mother's "silent years." It wasn't that her mother couldn't talk but that she had chosen not to. Since she wouldn't talk about her choice to keep silent, we have no idea why she made it. We do know, however, that some groups of people over the centuries have chosen silence: certain monks and nuns who have voluntarily withdrawn from the world in order to facilitate their own spiritual growth.

The point is that we should never judge the quality of someone else's life. We know about that which is physical. We are often in a position to assess how, why, and when the body is likely to die. On that basis we are often in a position to make accurate judgments about whether or not to take heroic medical measures. But if we make such judgments on the basis of assumptions about quality of life, which can only be assumptions, we will be on very shaky ground.

In this regard, it might help us to bear in mind that the Holocaust did not begin in 1941. It began in 1939 when the Nazis quietly began to put to sleep the institutionalized mentally retarded. Then they went on to exterminate German schizophrenics. After that the

---

* I am delighted to refer readers interested in further exploring the ambiguities of senility to my book *A Bed by the Window: A Novel of Mystery and Redemption* (New York: Bantam Books, 1990), which is set in a nursing home.

senile. Only after taking these measures did they finally turn their technology of death to the Gypsies and the Jews.

In exterminating their schizophrenics, retarded, and senile, the Nazis were primarily motivated, I believe, by an excessive sense of efficiency and economics. I imagine, however, they were helped in justifying their ruthlessness by an assumption that the quality of life of the victims was so poor that killing them was an act of mercy. Indeed, they called the project the Euthanasia Program.

I am generally against the use of heroic measures to prolong the life of a person who is in the terminal stage of a clearly fatal illness. I am against initiating such measures in the first place. Once initiated, I am in favor of gently stopping them. In other words, I am distinctly liberal when it comes to this matter of pulling the plug for medical reasons. But only for medical reasons. Assumptions about the quality of a patient's life do not constitute medical reasons. Pulling the plug solely on the basis of such shaky assumptions is potential murder, and doing so as a matter of policy is not only dangerous to the souls of medical practitioners but gravely dangerous to the whole society of which they are a part.

What Are Heroic Measures?

Some medical treatments are obviously heroic measures, and in my opinion, in obviously terminal patients like Tony, such treatments are unnecessarily, foolishly, even inhumanely heroic. Placing him on a respirator was such a measure. In his circumstances, maintaining his blood pressure was another. There could have been still others. Seeing to his nutrition through nasogastric feeding would have been one. Starting him on dialysis had his kidneys failed would have constituted a further abomination. I could go on, but it is not my purpose to detail the entire medical armamentarium.

Other treatments are more ambiguously heroic. Chemotherapy and radiotherapy for the treatment of cancer are examples. These treatments almost always have side effects, and not infrequently these side effects are extremely unpleasant or debilitating. If such treatments are likely to produce a cure or a lengthy remission they would not generally be considered heroic. But if they might result in only a brief remission, then these treatments certainly fall into the heroic category.

Here we are usually—but not always—dealing with patients who are not only conscious but competent to make decisions on their own behalf. When he was given radiotherapy for his highly malignant brain tumor, Tony was still conscious, but I would not have considered him competent to decide about the matter. Nor would I have considered that radiotherapy to be excessively heroic. Although it proved to be utterly ineffective, his physicians could not have predicted that; the therapy was untried at the time and might have been strikingly efficacious.

In refusing radiotherapy or chemotherapy, mentally competent cancer patients might be thought of as pulling their own plug. If a treatment is unlikely to be effective I would wholeheartedly support such a patient's decision. Were a treatment likely to be significantly effective I might be very strong in urging the patient to reconsider. In the end, however, I would still support the patient's decision, albeit ambivalently. In relation to cancer we are not talking about a minor illness, and in relation to these therapies we are not speaking of innocuous treatments. People have a *right to die* in these circumstances.

But there are other lifesaving or life-prolonging treatments that are relatively innocuous. Antibiotics are a prime example. Does a patient have the right to refuse antibiotics? Sometimes yes, in my opinion, and sometimes no. Let me use the cases of two hypothetical thirty-year-old men, James and Ted, to illustrate the ambiguity.

James at thirty is dying from AIDS. He has been symptomatic for almost five years. His body is wasted. He is admitted to the hospital with his fifth episode of pneumonia in the past thirty months. Because he refuses antibiotics, his attending physician asks me for a psychiatric consultation. James tells me he is infinitely tired and feels ready to die. After posing some questions, I believe it is clear he has made peace with his family. We speak of the afterlife. He welcomes my suggestion that he see the hospital chaplain for confession and last rites but persists in refusing antibiotics. I call the chaplain and promise to visit James daily. In writing I strongly urge the attending physician to respect totally James's refusal of antibiotics.

Ted, on the other hand, is admitted to the ICU unconscious from an overdose of sleeping pills he stole from his mother's medicine cabinet. After he recovers consciousness he is transferred to the psychiatric ward. Although he is suffering from no chronic physical illness, I find him to be seriously depressed and still suicidal. A day after his transfer to my care he develops a cough and sudden high fever. The internist I call for consultation diagnoses acute pneumonia, probably the result of aspiration during unconsciousness, and recommends IV antibiotics. Ted refuses them. Together with the internist and aides, at my order, we strap Ted into restraints and start the antibiotics against his will. Leaving him in the constant attention of an aide, I go to the nurses' station where, after documenting what I have done on an emergency basis, I fill out papers certifying Ted as representing a severe danger to himself and in need of involuntary commitment. I call the state psychiatric hospital and arrange for his transfer to their locked "involuntary" ward—transfer by ambulance in restraints with his antibiotic IV drip in place.

There is very little in this world that is absolute.

It is not my purpose to exhaust the discussion of heroic measures but simply to make two points. One is that there is—as in virtually any matter of grave importance—often a large middle ground where things can get ambiguous in determining when medical treatment is ordinary, heroic, or excessively heroic.

My other point is that within this middle ground of ambiguity I generally believe that the patient's wishes, when known, should be respected. So does my wife, Lily. This is why we each have a living will: to make our wishes known to the maximum possible extent, even if we are unconscious or speechless. We are not so naive as to think that such a document can eliminate ambiguity and that our wishes will inevitably be respected. A living will can be broken or violated, properly or improperly, by physicians, family members, or both in collusion. Nonetheless, we have voiced in legal written language our hope that modern medical technology, which thus far has blessedly prolonged our lives, will not, in the future, be used to do so at the expense of our humanity by maintaining us as "vegetables."

Helping Patients Decide to Die

Malcolm Morrison was not a hypothetical case.

I was asked to consult on the case in the early 1980s, toward the conclusion of my psychiatric practice. The formal request came from the oncologist at the hospital where Malcolm was an inpatient, but I was informed it was actually initiated by Malcolm's wife, Betty.

Malcolm had been diagnosed as having inoperable cancer of the lung two years previously when he was sixty-five. At the time I was asked to see him, he was undergoing his third course of radiation therapy, and the radiologist had reported that his massive tumor had possibly begun to shrink slightly once again in response. Only Malcolm had almost stopped eating. The oncologist explained to Betty that, despite the equivocally positive radiology report, Malcolm would die if he couldn't become better nourished. She asked if a psychiatrist could be called in to discover why he wasn't eating.

There is a medical term for the wasting of the body that so often accompanies cancer and a few other conditions: cachexia. Literally it means "bad disease." It is as if the cancer has run wild and is consuming all the patient's nutrition and sapping the healthy tissues as well. Cachexia may range from mild to severe. When mild, the patient may look perfectly well nourished, but there is a certain slight sunkenness to the cheeks and a subtle sense of shadow descending upon the body. When severe, the patient has wasted away to little more than a skeleton. I began my consultation simply by looking at Malcolm lying in bed from the distance of his hospital room doorway. I'd never seen a human being more cachectic. I'd also never known a cancer patient so cachectic to survive.

Since she had been the one to request my services, I next went to talk to Betty in the waiting room, aware that there were at least three possible purely physical reasons why Malcolm wasn't eating that had nothing to do with psychiatry. Betty was a robust, deeply caring woman in her sixties. I took an instant liking to her. Interspersed between her comments on the details of the case, she said, "It's been a long battle, but we'll win it yet. I know it looks bad right now, but Malcolm's a fighter. Together we're going to beat this thing. Neither of us is a quitter." The military analogies went on and on.

Finally I said with trepidation, "Betty, it's clear to me that your fighting spirit, in conjunction with Malcolm's, is what has kept him alive for so long. You've done a wonderful and heroic job. But I'm not sure that now is the time for fighting. I wonder if the most loving thing you could do for Malcolm at this point wouldn't be to give him your permission to die, if that's what he wants. Is that something you'd be willing to consider?"

Clearly this was a shock to her, but yes, Betty said, it was something she would think about. It was now Monday noon; I made an appointment to meet her at the hospital again early Wednesday morning.

Next I went to talk with Malcolm. It was painful to look into eyes so sunken, and difficult to understand a voice so weak. But he was quite lucid. He didn't really know why he wasn't eating, he explained. He didn't actually feel an obstruction; he simply had no appetite. No, it was worse than that. That he could overcome. But whenever he forced himself to take a mouthful of food he felt absolute repugnance at the thought of taking a second.

"You must be tired," I said.

He acknowledged he was.

"Would you like to die?" I asked. "Do you feel like giving up?"

A spasm of fear, almost panic, crossed Malcolm's face. "No," he exclaimed, "I don't want to die. I'll eat. I'll make myself eat. I'm not a quitter."

"You sound as if it's bad to quit," I commented.

Those sunken eyes looked up at me with such surprise it was almost like a glimmer of light. "Isn't it?" he asked.

"Isn't it bad to quit?" I repeated.

"Yes. Isn't it?"

"Sometimes yes, sometimes no," I answered him. "When I was fifteen I quit a school where I'd been very unhappy for over two years. At the time I felt guilty for not toughing it out, but now when

I look back on it I think it was the best decision I ever made in my life. I'm also here seeing you today as a country psychiatrist only because ten years ago I quit a government job in Washington. Although I was exhausted, I again felt guilty—this time for letting the government down. But the government could go on without me, and I'm glad I did it, and I'm glad I'm here with you now.

"I'm not saying that quitting is good, Malcolm," I continued. "It might just be the wrong thing to do. And I can't tell you what to do in your case. It's a terribly difficult decision, and it's entirely yours to make. All I can tell you is that it's not necessarily bad to quit."

With that I left.

When I returned to see her on Wednesday morning, Betty said, "Malcolm and I have done a lot of praying and crying together these past thirty-six hours. We've decided to go home today. In fact, they're preparing Malcolm now." I told her I thought it was a courageous decision.

Early Friday evening Betty called to tell me Malcolm had died peacefully at home that morning. I wrote her a note of condolence. Two weeks later I received a note back from her thanking me for my service. I felt as proud of that brief service as any other in my career as a psychiatrist and physician.

A Red Herring

In this chapter I have defined "pulling the plug" as the process of allowing a terminal patient to die a *natural* death without prolongation by medical technology. I have made it clear that the subject is fraught with ambiguities. Certain decisions have to be made as to whether a patient is or is not truly terminal. Indeed, certain decisions even have to be made about how to make such decisions. What constitutes heroic medical measures varies from case to case. In fact, I have not yet fully clarified the distinction between natural and unnatural death—a clarification we shall further struggle with in a later chapter.

But while this chapter has its ambiguities, it has also made clear, I hope, that the subject is not entirely murky. I see the following firm guidelines in determining when it is appropriate to pull the plug. This decision:

1. Should relate only to cases of clearly fatal illness wherein the patient is in a relatively terminal or final stage.
2. Is ultimately a medical decision involving physical factors and not involving an assessment of the patient's quality of life beyond physical factors of the terminal disease.
3. Being ultimately a medical decision, requires the physician to play a critical role, but wherever possible both patient and family should have equally critical roles, as should a medical ethics committee in cases of particular ambiguity or conflict between the involved parties.
4. Should seldom be made according to a formula without benefit of human and humane judgment.

Euthanasia literally means "good death." In that sense, pulling the plug is very much a euthanasia issue, and within the guidelines just given, I am very much for it. I believe that Malcolm, who expired quietly at home, died a good death, just as I believe that Tony with his brain cancer, while he was kept on a respirator and massive doses of blood pressure medicine, was not allowed to die a good death with dignity.

A $28 million study of over 9,000 chronically and seriously ill patients at five different U.S. medical centers over the course of ten years (sponsored by the Robert Wood Johnson Foundation and published in the November 22, 1995, issue of the *Journal of the American Medical Association*) reported that a distressingly large number of the studied patients endured unnecessarily prolonged and often painful deaths as a result of unjustified heroic measures. On the one hand, the study clearly demonstrates we have a good way to go in many medical settings. On the other hand, the conduct of the study itself and the major attention it immediately received by the American Medical Association demonstrates how far we have come.

I have said that the decision as to when and when not to employ heroic medical measures to prolong life is, in the strict sense of the word, an issue of euthanasia—that is, helping someone to die as good a death as possible. This does not mean, however, that such decisions should *currently* be considered part of the euthanasia debate. Thirty years ago when pulling the plug was an unspoken and taboo act, they were. The act was then highly debatable. Today it is not. As the Johnson study just mentioned indicates, in some quarters medical professionals need to become much more comfortable with the ambiguities involved. Greater nurse and physician training is required. Nonetheless, I believe we have reached a national consensus on the subject. Discontinuing heroic medical measures—or refraining from their use at all—is not now taboo. The ambiguities are resolvable and are best resolved on a case-by-case basis, not according to a formula, by the people most directly involved. Whether pulling the plug is permissible or not no longer needs to be a matter for public debate. The verdict is in. It is permissible within the guidelines I've offered. Indeed, it is not only permissible but often ethically mandated. It is simply a matter of the practice of good medicine.

I deliberately began this book with this subject for the purpose of clarification. In the minds of much of the public the issue of pulling the plug remains a part of the euthanasia debate even though the whole climate has changed. Keeping it part of the current debate serves only to obscure the issues. As a matter of debate it has thankfully evolved into a red herring. It can be put to rest. Let us now move on toward deeper and still truly debatable issues.

Chapter 2

PHYSICAL PAIN

The greater fear of most people is not that they will die hooked up to life-support machinery. It is that they will die in protracted physical agony—an agony prolonged by such machinery or by some other form of medical mismanagement. Nothing fuels the euthanasia debate so much as this fear of intractable physical pain.

At this point in time that fear may be either realistic or unrealistic. To understand how it is an either-or situation, it is necessary to understand in some depth the nature of physical pain and the problems associated with its treatment.

Blessing and Curse

Throughout much of history the now treatable disease of leprosy was the most dreaded of medical afflictions. The reason for this dread was not that leprosy was a rapidly fatal disease, or even that it was fatal at all, but that it inexorably caused ghastly and chronic disfigurement or deformity.

The cause of leprosy, Hansen's bacillus, is a kind of bacteria that, when it infects a person, has a certain predilection for taking up habitation along the patient's nerve fibers and specifically for destroying those microscopic fibers that carry the sense of pain. A leper may break his ankle and continue to walk on it as if nothing has happened because he is not aware that anything has happened; the leprosy has destroyed the pain sense in his ankle. The signal that something is wrong doesn't get through to his brain, and continuing to walk on his ankle will shortly cause severe, degenerative arthritis and deformity of the joint. Or a leper may lay her hand on a hot stove and, after a few minutes, begin to enjoy the aroma of what she thinks is a roast in the oven when actually it is her own hand that is roasting and being destroyed.

For ages it was thought that the dreadful deformities of leprosy were a direct result of the infection. When a leper's eye began to ooze pus and eventually become blind, no one realized he might have gotten a large cinder in his eye and been unable to feel it. It was only a few decades ago that the great American missionary surgeon Paul Brand, working in India, discovered that most—not all, but most—of the devastation of leprosy is caused by a localized absence of pain.

Thank God for pain.

Most of life's blessings, in my experience, are potential curses. And vice versa. So it is with physical pain.

Acute short-term physical pain, whether mild or severe, is virtually always a blessing. It is a signal that something is wrong with the body, something that needs attention. Without that signal our lives would quite quickly become devastated.

But pain is useful *only* as a signal that something is wrong, be it a broken ankle, a burn, or a cinder in the eye. Once the problem is diagnosed and is being appropriately treated, there is no reason for the signal to continue. Pain has lost its utility. If the pain does continue, the blessing has become a curse.

Fortunately, there is a plant, the opium poppy, from which can be derived medicines to relieve pain. All the strong pain relievers, such as morphine, are either derivatives of opium or synthetic look-alikes.

Physical pain can be divided into four types: mild, moderate, severe, and excruciating. Mild pain can either be lived with or adequately relieved by over-the-counter medicines such as aspirin, Tylenol, or Motrin. Moderate pain can be lived with for hours or days but generally shouldn't be; it saps the body and mind and should be treated with low-grade, only debatably addictive opiates, like codeine. The more serious the pain, the more it will require stronger opiates in higher doses. Truly severe or excruciating pain can generally be relieved only by morphine.

Pain can also be categorized as either acute or chronic. It is important to bear in mind that acute, short-lived pain should not generally be treated by pain-relieving medication until its cause has been discovered and appropriate treatment begun. A patient with sudden severe abdominal pain does not need a shot of morphine; he needs to see a physician. Morphine would only mask his disease so as very possibly to result in an otherwise preventable death from a ruptured appendix or similar condition.

Chronic or acute pain for which the cause is known is another matter entirely. Failure to treat adequately such moderate, severe, or excruciating pain with pain-relieving drugs is medical malpractice.

Mild chronic pain, as I have suggested, can be lived with. I, like many other arthritis sufferers, have done so for years—which is not to imply that the pain of arthritis is always mild; it may be moderate or, occasionally, severe, and it may at times lead to secondary conditions that are excruciating. Beyond the stage of mildness, however, the longer pain lasts, the worse it becomes. People do not get used to it. To think that they should is sadism.

Severe or excruciating pain represents a medical emergency. A patient in such pain should not be kept waiting. The necessary diagnostic procedures should be begun immediately and completed as rapidly as humanly possible. And as soon as the diagnosis is made and pain-relieving medicines can be safely used, these medicines should be given instantly in adequate doses as frequently as is necessary. When medical personnel unnecessarily allow a patient's severe or excruciating pain to be prolonged they are guilty of torture.

The Most Prevalent Crime of Medicine

Torture? Malpractice? Sadism? These are harsh words, and now I add another: crime.

We have all been horrified by accounts of men being beaten or women raped in the street while people look on, doing nothing. To my knowledge, no onlooker has ever been prosecuted for the crime of passivity. To commit a crime, one must *do* something. People have been prosecuted for abetting a crime, but only because they have more or less actually participated in it from the sidelines. Passive onlookers are not participants. Nonetheless, in our guts we sense that these witnesses are guilty and that some of them, at least, could appropriately be punished.

When queried, passive onlookers generally offer two reasons for their inaction. One is the fear that they themselves might have been hurt or even killed if they had attempted to intervene. Sometimes this fear is reasonable. They might indeed have put themselves at risk. But often the risk is so minimal that their excuse of fear seems flimsy indeed. Then they will offer their other excuse: they simply didn't want to get involved.

Medical professionals who stand by in hospitals watching patients writhe in the agony of severe or excruciating pain without lifting a finger to relieve the pain do not have these excuses. They may not want to get involved, but the fact is they *are* involved. As medical professionals it is their *responsibility* to be involved. Moreover, in properly medicating patients for pain, they are in no way putting themselves in danger or at risk. Nevertheless, at this very moment, across the country, hundreds upon hundreds of doctors and nurses are literally turning their backs on patients in physical agony when that agony could be quickly, easily, and safely relieved.

Failure to medicate adequately for pain is the most prevalent crime in medicine today.*

In calling this a crime—which I truly believe it is—I have no

---

* See Ronald Melzack, "Tragedy of Needless Pain," *Scientific American,* February 1990, pp. 27–33.

desire to see police or malpractice lawyers routinely prowling through the corridors of our hospitals. My only desire is to see the crime stopped. I would like to see it stopped peacefully by a change of climate regarding the issue of pain relief in our hospitals—a change like the one that has already mostly occurred regarding the issue of pulling the plug. I am not aware of any case where a doctor or nurse has been prosecuted for improperly withholding pain relief. Despite my distaste for litigation, if the climate does not change, I do believe such prosecution would be justified in helping it to change. I do hope, however, that this book, along with the work of others, will serve rapidly to bring about the needed change without resort to the legal process.

One reason I am optimistic is that the climate already has changed on many wards and throughout many hospitals in many communities. Yet there remain at least an equal number of specific wards or entire hospitals—quite often university "teaching" hospitals with the highest reputations—where the climate has not changed, where the treatment of pain remains almost back in the Dark Ages. I write this on a sunny early autumn day with the full knowledge that on this day thousands of hospital rooms are functioning in part as torture chambers.

Why? How can this be? We psychiatrists say that this phenomenon, like so many diseases of our society, is "overdetermined," meaning that it has multiple causes. I will now analyze, each in turn, what I see as the five major causes of this most prevalent crime in medicine.

Misunderstanding of Addiction

All of the stronger opiates are addictive, as are most of the sedatives that can be used to enhance their efficacy. Modern pharmacology has not yet succeeded in developing a strong pain reliever that isn't addictive, although this failure is not for want of trying.

What is meant by addiction? Two things. One is that prolonged administration of an addicting drug, such as morphine, produces a condition of the body where gradually higher and higher doses of the drug must be given to achieve the same result. The other is that when the drug is stopped, even though the cause of the pain has been eliminated, the addicted patient will experience a temporary painful condition known as withdrawal.

All addicting drugs, as well as many others, are habituating—in other words, they have a tendency to be habit-forming. This is particularly true of opiates, the strongest of which is heroin. Opiates not only relieve physical pain but produce in most people a feeling of euphoria where they are also relieved of all emotional pain. They produce a high that tends to be quite enjoyable. Anything that is enjoyable, whether morphine, golf, or rose gardening, is potentially habit-forming.

Because these drugs are both habituating and addicting, a small percentage of people who are otherwise physically well (perhaps as many as 2 percent) are hooked on these strong pain relievers. They are either frankly addicted to them or will use them "recreationally." They may lie, cheat, malinger, steal, and sometimes even kill to obtain them. For this reason these drugs are tightly controlled by law. They are manufactured and stored under lock and key. Even physicians must have a special license to prescribe them. All this is quite proper. I would not change a single one of the laws that regulate these potentially dangerous drugs.

The problem is that the dangers are *grossly* exaggerated in the minds not only of the general public but also in the minds of the majority of medical professionals, who should know better.

This first gross exaggeration pertains to the habituating potential of even the strongest of the painkillers. As I wrote in a chapter on addiction in *In Search of Stones:*

> Addictions are over-determined. In 1970–71 approximately half of the American troops in Vietnam tried heroin at least once. This statistic became a hot political issue. Inexperienced about such matters, members of Congress and other government officials assumed most of the soldiers would return to the United States as confirmed heroin addicts. My boss and I, representing military psychiatry in Washington during those years,

doubted it. We had reason to suspect that much more than a simple exposure to the drug was required to create an addict. Time proved us correct. A small minority did develop a real passion for it. But the vast majority, as soon as they were out of Vietnam, never sought after heroin again. In addition to the drug itself, sociological, psychological, spiritual, and biological factors are involved. Addictions are over-determined.*

To illustrate how the minds of physicians are often as ill informed as those of congressmen, I will speak of diagnostic procedures. A number of such procedures can be extremely stressful and painful for the patient. Indeed, they can't even be performed without the use of a combination of sedatives such as Valium and painkillers such as Demerol. Without them the patient would be thrashing around in agony and his or her internal organs would go into such spasm that the procedure would become impossible. The question in such procedures is not whether to employ these medicines but how much of them to employ. Let me use as an example the procedure known as endoscopy in which a flexible tube is passed either through the mouth, esophagus, stomach, and duodendum (and possibly even the pancreatic duct) or through the anus for the entire length of the colon. The physician can look through this tube under magnification projected onto a screen and can, if necessary, use it to make biopsies of the tissue in questionable areas.

To help the patient be comfortable during an endoscopy, the physician can give her sufficient sedatives and painkillers intravenously before beginning the procedure and throughout it so she never experiences significant discomfort. She will never be unconscious. She will be able to answer simple questions during the procedure, but otherwise she will drowse through it in its entirety. Afterward she will be able to comprehend basic instructions before she is driven home by a friend or relative. For the remainder of the day she will either nap or feel pleasantly relaxed: beyond that, there will be no aftereffects. If she has to undergo such a procedure again,

* *In Search of Stones* (New York: Hyperion, 1995), p. 43.

as she likely will, she will not look forward to all the inconvenience involved, but in no way will she dread it.

The same procedure conducted by another physician, Dr. X, might unfold very differently. Dr. X gives his patient the exact same medications but in approximately half the dosage used in the previously described case. This smaller dosage is just sufficient to permit the procedure to proceed, but his patient is uncomfortable throughout, experiencing mild to moderate pain for an hour with occasional spasms of severe pain. If you ask Dr. X why he allows this discomfort, he will answer that he is just practicing good medicine. For one thing, he will tell you, he doesn't want to mask any of his patient's symptoms should something go wrong with the procedure. (We shall shortly speak more about this issue of masking.) For another, he will pronounce a general principle: "The less medicine you can get by with, the better." Particularly, he will think, with these narcotics that can give the patient a high. God forbid she might *enjoy* a medical procedure! He is not going to be responsible for hooking a patient, starting her on the road to a habit and addiction. He doesn't realize, however, that his patient is likely to spend the rest of the day crying because she feels as if she has been violated, almost as if she's been raped. Or that the next time she needs such a procedure she will not go for it until it is too late, until her treatable disease has become untreatable. Even if he knew this, he might feel that it's her responsibility, not his.

If it is rare that a soldier who has taken heroin and experienced a far greater high becomes hooked, then the likelihood of a patient becoming hooked as a result of exposure to far milder narcotics during a medical procedure is infinitesimal. I'm not saying it could never happen. What I can say, however, is that if such a patient does become hooked it is because she has such a predisposition to addiction that she will almost undoubtedly become hooked on narcotics sooner or later even without medical assistance.

Unfortunately it is not just the procedure rooms that often serve as torture chambers in hospitals; even more frequently it is the ordinary bedrooms on the wards for the same reasons. There too, because they are so terrified of addicting patients, physicians will prescribe the lowest possible doses of opiates with the least frequency. Their prescriptions are usually carried out by nurses on written schedule—every three hours, perhaps, or four hours or six hours. As I write this, I also know at this very moment across the country patients in their hospital rooms are screaming in genuine agony for their pain medication and a nurse is saying to them, "But you're not due for your shot for another hour. You'll just have to wait."

I said that this climate is fortunately beginning to change. The single greatest reason for this change, I believe, was the invention about a decade ago of a machine that is sometimes called a morphine pump, although it may also be used to dispense other medications. Physicians refer to it as a patient-controlled analgesia (PCA) machine. Using this machine, which is attached to an intravenous drip, the patient, simply by pushing a button, can administer morphine to herself as frequently as she wishes within a certain limit of amount for which the machine is set. Allow a patient to give herself her own strong pain reliever on her own schedule? Such a thing was unheard of at the time. I salute those who designed this machine and first dared to use it.

Since then researchers have discovered in study after study that patients—most commonly postoperative or cancer patients—who are on the pump, with only rare exceptions, will actually use less morphine than if it was given to them according to the nurses' and doctors' schedule. Often a great deal less. How can this be?

The reason is fear, which gets worked out in two ways. Patients are terrified of severe pain and become fanatical clock-watchers. If they know that their next dose of morphine is due at 2:00 P.M., they will ask for it at 1:50 P.M., even if they are not in the least bit of pain at the time. They are smart to do so because they know that if they wait to ask until their pain begins again—let's say at 2:20 P.M.—they may have to wait for at least twenty minutes or more until the nurse gets around to giving them their shot, by which time they will be writhing in agony. The morphine pump totally relieves patients from all this panicky clock-watching . . . and also happens to make life easier for the nurses.

The other reason is that fear and physical pain are synergistic. Severe pain produces the fear of pain, and that fear—any fear, but particularly the terror of severe physical suffering—also actually increases the intensity of pain. Some medical professionals scoff at this fact and think that their patients are just a bunch of chickens. But let them experience severe physical pain and they will discover themselves to be chicken too. The synergy of pain and fear is simply a fact of human nature. And a patient who knows that he can give himself a tiny dose of IV morphine just by pushing a button whenever the pain begins and experience almost instant relief is a patient relieved of fear. Hence less pain. Hence still less morphine.

PCA machines are in relatively common use now. Yet physicians are not infrequently too quick to unhook their postoperative patients from them and to substitute less potent painkillers by injection or by mouth. Why? Other reasons, some of them valid, can be given, but the most common is the bugaboo of addiction. They are afraid of addicting their patients. But remember I said that addiction is a gradual process. It doesn't happen quickly, but physicians are usually unaware of this. Indeed, they may unhook the pump against a patient's wishes for this reason even when the machine tells them mathematically that the patient used half as much morphine as the day before. Such a patient is not addicted.

Although not justifiable, some of this is understandable. It relates to the first thing a physician in training is taught: "Do no harm." Part of physicians' fear of causing addiction is their terror of precipitating a withdrawal syndrome. Much of this terror comes not from professional literature but from the theater and the embellished accounts of heroin addicts who have depicted opiate withdrawal as horrifying beyond imagination. Actually I have been told repeatedly by honest heroin addicts that cold turkey withdrawal from full-scale heroin addiction was easier for them than withdrawal from cigarettes. Still, it is unpleasant and even dangerous for someone in poor health. A variety of drugs can be used in decreasing doses to ease greatly the withdrawal process, but often they are not used. Physicians frequently think, "Well, if his withdrawal is really unpleasant, he'll be less likely to get himself readdicted." There is absolutely no evidence to support that supposition . . . and a fair amount of psychiatric theory to make one suspect that the opposite is true.

Until now we have been talking primarily about the management of acute pain, like that which results from medical procedures or surgery, a self-limited pain. But what about chronic physical pain that is not self-limited, that is not curable, that is severe and intractable? Here we are talking most commonly about patients who are fatally ill with inoperable cancer—although, of course, not all patients dying from cancer are in pain. And nowhere is the bugaboo about addiction more absurd. I have known physicians to undermedicate dying patients for pain—to prolong their agony—because they didn't want the patients to become addicted. This would be laughable were it not in reality atrocious and atrociously sad.

Other Side Effects

Even relatively mild pain relievers can have side effects. Codeine, for instance, is usually constipating, but in a patient with normal bowel functioning, this effect usually goes away after a couple of days, even though the pain-relieving effect of the codeine persists. It also dramatically suppresses the cough reflex. This suppression may create in a patient a slight predisposition to pneumonia. The same effect, however, may be profoundly useful in actual cases of pneumonia or other diseases that would otherwise cause intractable and useless coughing.

Such side effects are generally of no consequence during brief procedures such as endoscopy. They may be of greater consequence during postoperative recovery. For example, abdominal surgery almost invariably causes temporary paralysis of bowel functioning—a condition physicians call ileus. The longer and more traumatic the abdominal surgery, the longer the ileus is likely to persist. It can be worrisome. There is reason to believe that pain-relieving medications may contribute to prolonging ileus in these cases. The physician is then faced with a trade-off, which is generally made in favor of combating ileus and against providing adequate pain relief. Without wishing to diminish the reality of such tough decision making,

I believe that this balance is usually mistaken. Patients without major pain are likely to recover more quickly, regardless of side effects, than those who are significantly suffering.

Moreover, many of these side effects are preventable. The ill effects of ileus can be greatly delayed by strictly limiting the intake not only of food but also of fluids by mouth. Yet I have known patients following abdominal surgery who were actually encouraged to drink water before the return of bowel sounds. Beyond this there are medicines that serve to stimulate bowel functions. I have also known patients who have been allowed to suffer greatly because of less than adequate pain relief designed to "treat" their ileus when their doctors had not even considered adding a bowel stimulator while maintaining the pain relief. Yes, "the fewer medications the better" isn't a bad rule of thumb, but when it is made into an ironclad dictum, physicians sometimes seem to be members of the Inquisition.

The one side effect of potent painkillers that physicians perhaps worry about the most is not properly a side effect at all; painkillers "kill" pain, bringing about the problem of masking. For instance, a patient who is on morphine immediately following orthopedic surgery on his ankle might simultaneously develop an abscessed tooth. The only problem is, he doesn't know that he has an abscessed tooth—nor do his physicians—because not only is he feeling no pain in his ankle, he's not feeling any pain in his jaw either. He has become like a temporary leper. His painkillers have masked the onset of a new disease.

The problem of masking is very real, although generally of little consequence. As his pain medicine is reduced, the patient will likely report, "My ankle only throbs a bit, but I've got a hell of a pain in the middle of my left upper jaw." But then the physician simply has to go to work again—as she would anyhow—and ask for a dentist to see her patient. I don't want to whitewash the problem totally. In fact, the abscess may kill the nerve before the patient feels pain, and he will be left with a problem he doesn't know about—until pus starts dripping out of a small hole in his jaw. The problem of masking is rare, but it does exist.

In cases of relatively acute—such as postoperative—pain, physicians usually strike the right balance, deciding in favor of relieving severe pain as opposed to the relatively minimal, temporary dangers of masking. Where they more frequently fall down is in the management of chronic pain. One way is a failure to instruct the patient clearly. For example, they may properly prescribe codeine or even Percodan in regular doses for years to a patient with severely painful arthritis but neglect to tell the patient that she ought to see her dentist for more frequent X rays and checkups. The patient is entitled to participate in the problem of masking.

The worst neglect, once again, is to undermedicate for pain so that a patient is allowed to suffer interminably lest he develop some new disease unnoticed. Once again, patients requiring prolonged treatment with powerful painkillers are usually terminally ill. Yet over and over I have heard doctors say to relatives, "I can't give your mother any more morphine. If I do it will mask her other problems." Or even more commonly, "It will predispose her to pneumonia."

Terminal patients usually die from a secondary disease such as pneumonia instead of as a result of their primary disease, like cancer, whether they are well medicated for pain or not. The possibility of hastening death as a secondary result of adequate pain relief is referred to as the "double effect." It will be mentioned again. For the moment I shall acknowledge that allowing a terminal patient to writhe in physical agony to avoid the double effect might prolong his life a week or two. To my mind, however, engaging in such prolongation of life is almost invariably to become an actor in the theater of the absurd. I would counsel, rather, "Let my people go, Lord, oh, let my people go."

Formulas and Schedules

Physicians' minds are filled with formulas, whether they are aware of them or not. Many of these formulas have to do with pain and its management. Many of them are also often wrong: "Arthritis can cause mild or moderate but not severe pain." "A broken bone will cause severe pain but, if properly casted, for no more than two days." "Passage of a kidney stone through the ureter causes the most severe pain there is." "Demerol is a stronger pain reliever than codeine." "The effect of Demerol lasts for three hours."

Doctors translate such formulas into prescriptions and nurses' orders. A typical order will read "Demerol, 50 mgm IM q3h prn," which translates, "Demerol, 50 milligrams intramuscularly every three hours as needed." The nurse will further translate this order to mean: "I cannot give the patient another injection of Demerol until at least three hours after her last shot and then only if she specifically asks for it."

The problem is that individual patients frequently do not conform to formulas. Their diseases don't conform. The ways they respond to different medicines often don't conform. The duration of their pain relief may not conform. Let me use some personal examples.

One morning a few years ago while writing in my office I experienced the sudden onset of moderate pain in my left abdomen. At first I thought it was gas. But it was different and more persistent. I wondered what else it might be. The possibility that I was passing a kidney stone occurred to me. It didn't fit the formula, however: this was only moderate pain. Fifteen minutes later, unable to make any other decent guess, I thought, "Maybe I really am passing a kidney stone. If it lasts another fifteen minutes I think I'd best hop in the car, drive down to the emergency room, and let them have a look." Within five minutes my pain stopped. I resumed writing and forgot about the incident.

Two weeks later I began to have burning whenever I urinated. After a couple of days I went to the lab and had a urinalysis. It showed a lot of microscopic blood in my urine. I was terrified I had cancer. Fortunately, X rays revealed the true cause: a relatively small kidney stone stuck in the juncture between my bladder and left ureter, easily treatable by drinking a gallon of water very quickly.

Yes, the passage of a *large* kidney stone is indeed usually a nightmarish event to remember. The passage of a tiny one may be totally painless. Or the passage of a relatively small one like mine may cause only temporary discomfort that is quickly forgotten.

Another kind of example is even more common: tooth abscess. An abscess may kill the nerve of a tooth so gradually that the process is painless. Or it may cause daily flashes of excruciating pain that last no more than a second but continue to occur over months—presenting a most difficult diagnostic problem—before the nerve dies. Or it may cause severe unrelenting pain for an entire night until the nerve dies. Such pain alone represents a dental emergency—not that one can necessarily locate a dentist in the middle of the night to treat it.

Psychiatrists quickly become accustomed to the fact that the effective use of psychoactive drugs is much more of a hit-and-miss affair than a fail-safe formulistic approach. Patients A and B both have depressions that look *exactly* the same. Patient A may not respond to Prozac at all, but will improve dramatically on Elavil. For Patient B, on the other hand, Prozac may seem a miracle while Elavil is utterly useless.

Painkillers are psychoactive drugs. I do not mean there are no guidelines. Demerol is *generally* a more potent pain reliever than codeine. It so happens, however, that I personally tend to obtain more pain relief from a standard oral dose of codeine than I do from one of Demerol.

Patients have not only different brains but also different metabolic rates. Demerol on the *average* will provide three hours of pain relief. A slow metabolizer will get three and a half hours. The nurses will consider her a "good patient." They will frequently judge a fast metabolizer who gets only two and a half hours of relief to be a "bad patient."

Furthermore, the duration of pain relief will vary with the intensity of the patient's pain. When I am in moderate pain a large dose of codeine will give me at least four hours of relief. In more severe pain the same dose may allow me to function for no more than two hours.

Most physicians are aware of all these things but are under great pressure not to think much about them. They cannot sit all day long at their patients' bedsides. They are trained to make their orders precise, not vague. Consequently, even when conscious that they are operating by formula, they will still make their orders formulistic:

"Demerol, 50 mgm IM q3h prn." Of course they know that if this is not enough the nurse can call them. Whether the nurse *will* call is another matter. Generally she will but only after the patient has been moaning in agony for a substantial period of time. And then the doctor may not be available for another substantial period of time.

Of course, the nurse may not be available either. As I indicated, the doctor's order "prn" ("as needed") means that the patient must ask for his pain medication. If he has not yet learned how to clock-watch, this means that when he begins to experience pain again he will press his buzzer. The buzzer will be answered, on the average, in ten minutes by an aide. The patient will say, "I'm in pain again. In fact, it's starting to get serious. Can I have my shot?"

The aide says, "I'll tell the nurse."

Ten minutes later the nurse shows up. "Do you need a shot?"

"Yes. It's really bad now."

Ten minutes later still the nurse will return with his shot—a half hour after he pressed his buzzer . . . if he's lucky.

Often he's not so lucky. Sometimes the nurse doesn't return. In absolute agony the patient presses his buzzer again. Once more, after yet another ten minutes, the aide reappears. "Yes?" she asks.

"I'm in agony," the patient pleads. "The nurse said she'd be here with my shot."

"Well, she's tied up with an emergency admission," the aide explains. "I told her you're in pain. I'm sure she'll be here as soon as she can."

What I've just recounted sounds like a caricature. It is not, however, a rare scenario. Who's to blame? The fact is that the nurse is busy with a perhaps even more desperate emergency. The fact is that aides and nurses, as well as physicians, are frequently overworked, if not burned out. Nonetheless, the fact also is that the patient has not received his "as needed" medicine for at least an hour after he expressed his need and has suffered an hour of needless torture because his need, even when it coincided with the scheduled orders, didn't coincide with the ward schedule. It is standard for hospital patients in pain to be reduced to helpless beggars.

That scenario is not the worst. The schedule is not always dictated by an emergency. Sometimes it is dictated by pure carelessness. A decade or so ago I awoke in the recovery room following lower back surgery. I urinated copiously, conversed, and otherwise demonstrated my alertness, although in between I drifted off from the aftereffects of anesthesia. After a while I no longer drifted off, and I began to hurt. Experienced with surgery and knowing the degree of pain to come, I called the nurse and told her I would soon need a shot.

"We're going to take you up to the ward in just a couple of minutes," she answered, "and they'll give you a shot as soon as you arrive."

That seemed reasonable. So I waited. And I waited. And I waited. Approximately half an hour later my pain had graduated from mild through moderate to severe. I called the nurse again. "You said I could have a shot as soon as I got to the ward, and they were going to take me right there. That was half an hour ago. When the hell are they going to take me?"

"The aide who takes the patients up has just gone to lunch," the nurse calmly explained.

I was not so calm. "You either fucking give me a shot right now," I shouted, "or you get an aide to take me up to the ward right now, or else I'll sue your ass off!"

Somehow she managed immediately to find an aide to get me to the ward, where I did indeed finally get my shot. Probably I was able to engage effectively in such combat only because I was a physician of considerable maturity. I hate to think of others without such authority who are the victims not only of rigid orders but also of lunch schedules that prohibit the fulfillment of the orders. I don't mean to imply adherence to lunch schedules is unreal, but it may be callous and careless. Schedules are bendable; pain is not. To attempt to make pain conform to routine organizational schedules borders on the sadistic.

I'm not saying that the nurse in this instance was actually sadistic; she was just *care*less. But, sadly, reality now compels me to deal with actual sadism in medical practice.

Sadism is an extremely complicated psychiatric disorder of

essentially unknown origin. Part of its complexity is that it varies greatly in its intensity. The sadism of some people is so mild, subtle, and sporadic that it is barely diagnosable as such. Such people may constitute 10 percent of the population. The sadism of others—less than 1 percent—may consistently be almost murderous. Whatever the percentage, approximately as many sadists enter the medical profession as any other profession. What I am saying is that roughly 1 to 10 percent of doctors, nurses, and medical aides are sadists to a greater or lesser degree. They are extremely difficult to weed out because they can so facilely exercise their sadism under the guise of practicing "good medicine."

Most people think of sadism solely as the enjoyment of inflicting pain upon others, without realizing that such enjoyment is, as often as not, unconscious. They also don't realize it's only half the problem. Sadists *love* to exercise control—domination—over others. What better way to dominate someone than to have almost total control over whether to give a patient pain relief or withhold it! In these days of modern medicine, nurses with reason tend to feel more or less powerless. Their control over pain medication may be just about the only power they have left. In no way do I wish to suggest that the average nurse is in the least bit sadistic. But I do wish to acknowledge the sad reality that pain medication schedules are, on rare occasions, ruthlessly adhered to, without calling the doctor, or ruthlessly extended for pathological motives.

In summary, formulas and schedules are inextricably interwoven. Yet pain frequently doesn't follow the formula or obey the schedule. One of the major reasons for inadequate pain relief in hospitals is that hospitals *work* on schedules and formulas. Furthermore, to the patient's detriment, the schedules may not even be followed because the medical personnel are often overworked, occasionally careless, and, in a few instances, downright sadistic.

Malingering

My tenth year was not a happy one for me at the private grammar school I attended. It didn't take me long to make an interesting discovery. I found that sticking a small wad of cotton up each nostril would make me sound very stuffy. If I did this before coming to breakfast and then greeted my mother, "Hunh, Muhmm," she would say, "You sound as if you've got a cold."

"Mmaybe," I'd respond, "yut ish nuthing baad."

"I think perhaps you ought to stay home from school."

"Nahh," I'd protest. "Uhm really oukay."

"Well, I'm going to keep you home anyway."

Perhaps by the time I was eleven my mother had caught on to me. In any case, one Saturday noon late in the autumn of that year, when school had turned much better for me, I was outside bouncing a ball against the wall of our apartment building. Suddenly I felt very tired. By the time I got upstairs to our apartment, I was feeling achy all over. I ran myself a hot bath. Within five minutes the ache seemed to ooze out of my limbs into my stomach. I told my mother I had a stomachache and was going to lie down. Ten minutes after that, I reported my stomachache was very bad. My mother took my temperature. I had no fever. Ten minutes later I started screaming. My mother said my pain couldn't be that bad. Shortly I was screaming very specifically for her to call the doctor. "I simply cannot believe your stomach is bad enough for that. No stomachache is as bad as you're making out."

I screamed continually for another hour, pleading every minute for her to call the doctor before she did. This was in the days of house calls. He came quite quickly. Within a few minutes he was phoning the surgeon. Sometime during the next hour before the surgeon arrived, my pain instantly stopped. No matter that my temperature began to soar; the cessation of pain felt like ecstasy. I had no idea, of course, that my appendix had just burst. But the surgeon did, and by five o'clock that evening I was on the operating table. Fortunately the era of antibiotics had also begun, and within a few days I was essentially well.

Moral number one: People do malinger.

Moral number two: It is easy, even for mothers, to think that people are malingering when they're not.

There are multiple reasons why people malinger, and it is difficult to estimate the frequency of malingering in outpatients complaining of mild to moderate pain, except that it is relatively low. If for no other reason than to avoid the hassle or expense of a hospital visit, the prevailing tendency is in the opposite direction. Most people will delay seeking medical treatment as long as they reasonably can—and frequently beyond reason.

Faking severe or excruciating pain occurs extremely rarely. Naturally, when it does occur the setting is usually a hospital, often in an emergency room or on the ward. The possible causes are multiple, but I would estimate the overall incidence to be less than 1 percent. In other words, I believe that no more than one out of a hundred patients complaining of intense pain are faking or exaggerating it. Yet I would also estimate that doctors and nurses rather casually suspect at least one out of four of them to be malingerers at one point or another.

How can this be? One reason I've already discussed is the medical profession's bugaboo about addiction. Medical personnel are continually worrying whether their patients in serious pain might not be addicts who are trying to put one over on them. A second reason is assumptions about "pain thresholds."

People seem to differ somewhat in their sensitivity to pain. This has given rise to the concept of the pain threshold: we say that some people have a high pain threshold—that is, they have a low sensitivity to pain—while others have a low threshold and are unusually quick to report pain. This is a difficult subject to research. Such studies as there are indicate that the difference between low and high thresholds is generally not all that great. As already indicated, frightened or anxious people are more sensitive.

Physicians or nurses who suspect that a patient is malingering will usually not actually speak the word. Instead they will use a euphemism: "Well, she certainly seems to have a very low pain threshold." This is also the euphemism for judging her to be a "bad patient." Good patients are those who are more compliant and less likely to protest the pain medication formulas and schedules.

Although there is no firm research to support it, I have another impression of pain sensitivity that almost seems obvious. I believe that the more conscious patients are—the more intelligent, alert, and self-aware—the more sensitive to pain they are. Conversely, the less conscious, alert, and self-aware patients are generally somewhat less sensitive and therefore, strangely, more likely to be thought of as good patients. Regardless of whether the threshold is low or high, the fact is that the patient is in pain—unless, of course, the patient is malingering. But that is rare. Nevertheless, the complaint of physical pain is one of those few conditions where a person is frequently assumed to be guilty until proven innocent.

My advice to physicians and nurses is to forget about pain thresholds and practice their humanity. Give the patient in pain the benefit of the doubt. If your doubt becomes truly serious—if you really do have reason to believe your patient is malingering—then call in a psychiatrist, and do so quickly. Remember that severe pain is a medical emergency. Do not withhold pain relievers on an assumption of malingering unless that assumption has become a psychiatrically supported diagnosis.

The Issue of Empathy

Although issues of malingering and addiction have been cited as the major contributors to inadequate medical treatment for physical pain, I believe an even greater contributing factor may be nothing more complicated than a deficiency of empathy.

Warren was a handsome thirty-two-year-old married man and highly effective air force sergeant who had begun to experience mild but chronic pain throughout his back and moderate pain in his lower back. He sought attention at the orthopedic clinic. When he failed to respond to aspirin or Tylenol and X rays of his spine looked perfectly normal, the doctors concluded that he was either malingering or "squirrelly" (vaguely unbalanced). So they referred him to Jesse, my predecessor as chief of psychiatry on Okinawa.

Jesse could not find the slightest hint of psychiatric disorder in Warren. He racked his brain for everything he had learned in medical school and remembered that a rare disease, brucellosis, could cause otherwise undefinable back pain. Jesse returned Warren to the orthopedic clinic with the recommendation that he be skin-tested for brucellosis. Lo and behold! The skin test was positive and Warren was started on the appropriate treatment.

Only a year later, by which time his treatment should have been effective, Warren still had back pain. If anything, it was worse. But X rays of his spine remained perfectly normal. Once again the orthopedists began to think he was malingering, and once again they referred him for psychiatric evaluation, this time to me.

I too could find nothing psychiatrically wrong with Warren. Only in this instance I had something more to go on than my psychiatric training. Although I was a year younger than Warren, I too had been suffering mildly for more than a decade from degenerative disk disease of the spine, and I personally knew something of the subject. I knew that the pain could start years before there was the slightest evidence of the disease on X ray. I knew that Warren sat down and later got up from his chair in the same stiff way that I did on my worst days—a way not easy to fake. Finally I knew that I had recently obtained considerable back relief from one of the early variants of NSAIDs (nonsteroidal anti-inflammatory drugs).

I gave Warren a prescription for this drug and an appointment to see me in five weeks. "Keep taking the pills," I told him. "Don't expect them to work right away. In fact, they often take at least three weeks to work. Of course, they may not work at all, but by five weeks we'll know whether they're helping you any."

Three weeks later the psychiatry clinic receptionist buzzed my office. Warren was in the waiting room. "He knows he doesn't have an appointment for two more weeks," she reported, "but he just wants to see you for a minute." I agreed.

Warren came into my office with the widest grin I've ever seen. "Doc, you're a miracle worker!" he exclaimed. "My pain stopped five days ago. At first I couldn't believe it. Five days now! Do you realize that these are the only days I've been free of pain for over two years? God bless you."

Were it possible (which it isn't), the ideal medical school would be one that afflicted each of its students with a brief personal taste of every disease in the book.

I have spoken of four categories of pain: mild, moderate, severe, and excruciating. Of course these categories are arbitrary, representing a continuum with degrees in between. I need to speak briefly about the extremes.

Some might look upon mild pain as "nothing." Warren had mild pain and continued to function with it in his job. Pain is almost "nothing" when it's brief, as with a minor cold. But when it is chronic—when it goes on week after week, month after month, year after year—it saps a person's energy in a way that someone who's never had chronic pain cannot understand. Yes, Warren was able to function in his job, but he felt more like a man in his mid-sixties than one in his mid-thirties, and he had no energy left over for his family. Later his wife was to thank me as well, but the pure joy on his face that afternoon was thanks enough.

We moan when we have moderate pain. We scream when we have severe pain, as I did for a few hours with the pain in my abdomen before my appendix burst. What, then, is excruciating pain?

I have experienced it only twice, thank God. Once in my arm and once in my leg, each time from the same cause: the sharp edge of a ruptured disk inexorably tearing into one of the major nerve roots as it exited from the spinal cord. I can describe it precisely. It was as if my limb, at a very exact level, had not only been dipped into but was being held in a vat of white-hot molten lead.

An external observer cannot tell the difference between severe and excruciating pain except by one measure. Screaming is screaming, and a patient with excruciating pain cannot scream any louder than one in severe pain. The only way to tell the difference is by the amount of morphine that must be added to the IV before the patient can blissfully slip into sleep for at least a minute or two.

Why is this important?

For two years before I retired from the lecture circuit I'd begun to think deeply about the issue of euthanasia. In doing so, I sometimes talked with my audience about physical pain. My audiences represented in many respects the spectrum of humanity: roughly 60 percent of the members, on the average, were female, and 40 percent were male; they ranged from lower middle to upper middle class and, in age, from fifteen to ninety, with the peak at around forty-eight. In these dialogues I discovered something that astonished me. I discovered that at least 70 percent of my audience had never personally experienced either severe or excruciating pain.

Some who reported they'd never experienced severe pain were women who had undergone labor while delivering babies. This would seem odd but for several factors. One is that they may have been well medicated for pain. Another is that the pain of labor is relatively brief and mostly intermittent with a generally positive outcome. In such circumstances there is a human tendency to forget how bad the pain was (and sometimes women in labor were specifically given drugs to enhance forgetfulness). Although there may be this tendency toward forgetfulness, we need to remember that there is also its opposite. A person who has experienced severe constant pain that goes untreated for a significant period of time will remember it not only with clarity but also, for the rest of his life, with terror that it will happen to him again.

If we can extrapolate from my informal data—and I believe we accurately can—this means that at least 70 percent of physicians and nurses have never themselves felt severe or excruciating pain. Or else they cannot remember it. They simply have no idea what it is like. When they care for patients in such pain they are witnessing something totally alien to their own personal experience.

Empathy, with the rarest of exceptions, is only a gift of personal experience. Unlike sympathy, which may be destructive, it is generally an individually learned phenomenon, forged out of the crucible of one's own real, real pain. It is therefore no wonder that the majority of medical professionals, when dealing with patients in severe or excruciating pain, are lacking in empathy. How could it be otherwise?

Forget about sadism. Forget about overconcern with addiction. Forget about formulas and schedules. The most common reason that medical professionals inadequately treat severe or excruciating pain is simple lack of empathy. They are dealing with something foreign. It is not unexplainable, then, that patients in genuine agony should hear so often from doctors and nurses, "You can't be in that much pain," or, worse, "You *shouldn't* have that much pain." The terrible problem is that those making such pronouncements usually don't have the foggiest idea of what they are talking about.

"Allergy" to Morphine

I have been speaking in some depth—and with passion—about the frequent failure of medical professionals to treat pain adequately. I do this for two reasons. One is the prevalent fear people have that they may die in great physical agony. This fear fuels the euthanasia movement. It only seems rational to kill oneself a bit early when a natural death holds out the prospect of dreadful, protracted, and useless suffering.

This fear is by no means totally unrealistic. Some do die in needless physical pain. Their friends and families may have watched them do so. Others, as recounted, have had hospital experiences of needless pain and have lived to tell the tale. Tell it they do, and their horror stories get heard by still others who may not have had such experiences themselves but nevertheless learn to dread them.

My other reason for focusing on the failure of medical professionals to treat physical pain adequately has been to point out clearly that this is a *failure*. These instances of suffering are not necessary. They are preventable. They are not inevitable. Hospitals need not be places of torture or protracted pain.

It has not been my intent to excoriate medical professionals and hospitals in general. As I indicated, the climate in regard to pain relief has improved dramatically in many medical communities over the past two decades. Sadism is rare. Carelessness, although more common, is hardly the norm. The fact of the matter is that the great majority of physicians and nurses are highly humane women and men who, given the pressure under which they must work, are remarkably caring and careful. I admire them greatly.*

---

* The freedom of medical professionals to relieve pain adequately may additionally be hampered by government regulations or policing that can range from appropriate to bureaucratically absurd.

Nonetheless, most are now agreed that the typical modern hospital is not the best place for those who are dying from a chronic disease. A Canadian sociologist has vividly drawn the distinction between treatment and care, pointing out that the primary focus of the modern hospital is treatment and that care, perhaps of necessity, has a lower priority. As a consequence, a new (for our culture) institution to serve the dying has sprung up throughout the land: the hospice. Here care is the priority, and rescuing treatment is secondary if not irrelevant. Adequate pain relief is considered an essential part of care. The purpose of hospice is not, through treatment, to rescue patients from death or prolong their lives; it is to ease their dying through care.

Initiated in London by Dr. (now Dame) Cicely Saunders in 1967 and brought to the United States the next year, Hospice is not so much a place as an approach. Its emphasis is on home care and on enabling patients to die at home with dignity whenever possible. When that is not possible, hospice will provide a place, a gentle habitation, for their final days. It offers emotional, psychological, and spiritual as well as physical care. In this chapter our subject is physical pain, and among the things that physical care means at hospice is the prompt provision to patients of all the morphine they need. Ideally, the problem of the so-called double effect is considered to be of no consequence. I shall speak more of this—and of hospice in general—in the final chapters.

But for this chapter on the complexities of physical pain treatment we must look at one final complication: a small minority of patients are "allergic" to God's gift of morphine.

I have used the word "allergic" in quotes because I would estimate that over half of such cases do not represent a true physical allergy but indicate a problem that is purely psychological. When I have been called in on a case of so-called allergy to morphine or to some other opiate, most of the patients have reported, "I feel like I'm losing control. My whole body feels fuzzy. I keep falling asleep when I don't mean to. My thinking seems fuzzy also. My thoughts aren't frightening, exactly, but they're not clear. I want to be—I need to be alert. Can't you give me something for my pain that doesn't knock me out like this?"

Usually—not always—with a bit of patience I've been able to talk such patients out of their "allergy." I explain to them that the word "morphine" is derived from the name of Morpheus, the Greek god of dreams, son of the god of sleep. Their drowsiness is a perfectly natural effect of the drug. But it's only drowsiness. They can rouse themselves if they really need to. All the major painkillers have a similar sedating effect. That's a big part of why and how they relieve the pain. "It isn't that you're out of control," I tell them, "but that you're afraid you'll be. Let me teach you a little bit about just how to lie back and enjoy your fuzziness or drowsiness."

Sometimes I need to go deeper. I may need to elicit a history of how all their lives they've been control freaks; of how, even when they were well, they were afraid to go to sleep at night; of how they had a secret fear that they would die in their sleep. Such psychological counseling of course begins to merge into spiritual counseling. The patient and I may need to talk about the fear of death and the possibility of afterlife, about how learning to give up control is not only an essential part of a healthy dying process but also a proper component of the spiritual journey and the learning of wisdom (a subject to which this book will later return in great depth).

Such psychospiritual counseling need not be done only by psychiatrists or highly trained mental health professionals. It is routinely and adeptly performed by many nurses, aides, and lay volunteers in the context of hospice programs.

A friend who is a lay volunteer informs me that the so-called allergy to morphine may sometimes reside more in the families of the dying than in the dying themselves. Families have complained to her that their relative isn't alert after he receives his morphine. "Of course we don't want him to be in pain," they will say. "And of course we know he's dying. But can't you give him something for his pain that won't make him so drowsy? We not only want to be with him when he dies; we want him to be all there with us."

Oh, Lord, let my people go.

Nonetheless, although really quite rare, there is such a thing as genuine allergy to morphine. Here one does not find a patient afraid of losing control but one who, on the drug, is out of control. Rather than making him drowsy, morphine has the opposite effect of stimulating him. His thoughts are not a bit fuzzy; he is actively hallucinating.

For such a rare patient, morphine is not the answer to physical pain. In my limited experience, with a modicum of patience, imagination, and care, there has always been an answer to even the very worst of physical pain.

First of all, a genuine allergy to morphine does not mean that the patient is allergic to all opiates, some of which, like heroin, may be even stronger pain relievers. In fact, more often than not, the adverse reaction will be to a particular variant of the opium derivatives. This I know most personally. I personally respond as well as anyone to morphine, which is considered a very powerful pain reliever. As I've recounted, I respond unusually well to codeine, which is considered a relatively mild painkiller. I respond in an average fashion to Percodan, a mid-level opiate. And to Demerol. Yet there is another mid-level opiate in common use that will predictably drive me right out of my mind with each and every pill. I am not at all allergic to opiates in general but only—as far as I know—very specifically to this particular one, which, among other things, renders me totally unable to sleep as well as distinctly confused.

Since severe unrelieved physical pain (after the diagnosis of its cause) represents a medical emergency, a genuine allergy to morphine is also an emergency. A treatable emergency. Substitution of a different opiate will generally take care of the problem.

Such allergies are, to some extent, dose-related. As indicated, the potency of small doses of opiates can be dramatically enhanced by the addition of a whole armamentarium of sedative or tranquilizing drugs, ranging from the benzodiazepines (like Valium) through the phenothiazines to the barbiturates.

No, the problem of morphine allergy cannot be solved by some immediate substitute formula that fits every patient. With a little care, patience, and trial and error, however, an individualized formula or concoction of opiates and sedatives—a cocktail, so to speak—can almost always be designed to serve adequately the pain-relieving needs of each and every patient.

Most pain is related to inflammation or nerve irritation of one kind or another. There are anti-inflammatory drugs (from aspirin and Tylenol to the NSAIDs) that can be used on a long-term basis to further enhance the potency of such cocktails. In the short term, artificial steroids, such as prednisone, can be as dramatically effective as opiates when used alone, and doubly or triply effective when used in combination. Then there are nondrug remedies for pain ranging from the noninvasive (hypnosis) to the mildly invasive (acupuncture) all the way to individually designed neurosurgery that can sever the nerves carrying pain sensation from a particular organ to the brain. And there are X-ray treatments that may not stop the spread of a cancer but can stop dead its effect in a pain-sensitive area.

I have known of a few patients who have died in severe chronic physical pain. I have never personally, in my limited experience, known of one who *had* to die that way.

How does all of this relate to the euthanasia issue?

I have gone on at length about physical pain for two reasons. One is that if I ever encountered a patient suffering serious chronic pain for which there was no hope of relief, I would consider euthanasia—physician-assisted suicide—a valid option. In this consideration, the patient would probably beat me to the punch. He would probably be begging me to help him die as quickly as possible. Unlike certain varieties of long-term emotional pain soon to be discussed, once the cause has been diagnosed there is absolutely nothing redemptive about intractable physical pain. It is only torture. Anyone and everyone will soon break under torture.

But this justification of euthanasia is purely theoretical for me since, as I have said, I've never encountered such a patient. Nonetheless, the nature of physical pain compels me to offer this theoretical caveat before proceeding to the real issue.

The other reason I have spoken in depth about physical pain is to make the point that the preceding caveat *is* theoretical. People have, in terror, sought euthanasia in order to avoid the physical suffering they assume will be involved in dying a natural death. Their terror is unnecessary. Given the medical armamentarium available to adequately relieve physical pain, the improving climate in regard to the full use of that armamentarium, and the option for those with terminal diseases to switch from hospital to hospice care, there is no reason for anyone to die with intractable suffering.

Yet some still do. The answer to the problem, however, is not euthanasia; it is continued improvement in the medical practice of physical pain relief using methods that are already available. Until such improvement occurs, the issue of physical suffering will remain a factor in the euthanasia debate. As we shall see, even now it is a peripheral factor. But I eagerly look forward to the day—it could, and I hope it will, come very soon—when it too is a mere red herring. For physical pain is not the central issue; the real issue is emotional suffering.

Chapter 3

EMOTIONAL PAIN

The subject of emotional pain is far more complicated than that of physical pain.

Like physical pain, emotional pain is a signal that something is wrong. When we are feeling sad it is usually because there is something in our lives to feel sad about. When we're depressed, there is something depressing us. If we are feeling angry it is a sign that we are out of sync—in conflict—with somebody or something.

As with physical pain, if we fail to receive such signals the effects can be disastrous. A person who is manic, for instance, may feel on top of the world while he is blowing away his family's entire savings on a dozen utterly harebrained schemes within the space of a week or two. Happy though he may be, he is mentally ill; of this there is no doubt in his family's or the psychiatrist's mind. Indeed, as we shall see, mental illness is as often characterized by its painlessness as by its painfulness. In this respect, a painless psyche has a variety of emotional analogues to leprosy. But while physical leprosy is a rare disorder, psychological leprosy is endemic—as common as dirt, unfortunately.

When we do receive painful emotional signals—sadness or grief, depression or anger, anxiety or terror—we are usually most unclear about what to do to reduce them. One does not simply rush off to a physician, as one would with severe physical pain—although these emotional pains, in their own way, may be just as severe. Usually they are part of the normal ups and downs of life. Usually they will pass with time, and usually we can do a few things on our own to facilitate their passing. If we are furious over a dispute with our neighbors, for instance, we can go to them to try to talk it out. Or we can sleep on it for a night or a week or a month. Or we can determine it was their fault but forgive them nonetheless. Or we can threaten to sue them.

Generally speaking—there are always exceptions—it is the chronicity of emotional pain that properly determines when and whether we seek medical attention for it. Grief immediately following the death of someone deeply beloved to us may be excruciating, but it is healthy, not sick. If the grief is unabated after three months, something may be wrong. After six months, probably wrong. After a year or two, undoubtedly wrong. A psychiatrist is definitely called for.

But the psychiatrist may well be as much at sea as the patient. First of all, the psychiatric diagnosis of emotional pain is seldom as clear-cut a process as that of physical pain. There are no blood tests or X rays for psychiatric illness, except to rule out nonpsychiatric causes. Psychiatric diagnoses are primarily made on the basis of history, observation, and the psychiatrist's intuition. In a minority of cases, an accurate diagnosis can be made in seconds. For the majority, however, it may take weeks, months, and occasionally even years of working with the patient.

Complicating the process, the diagnosis must be made on at least two levels. The question is not merely "What is the name of the disease" but whether the disorder is a purely biological or purely psychological one or a mixture of the two. If it's a mixture, which is the case as often as not, what are its proportions: 50-50? 90-10? 10-90? Social and spiritual factors also must be considered. I could argue that almost all diseases, psychiatric or not, are biopsychosociospiritual disorders. The adequate treatment of physical pain usually requires concern with only the somatic or biological component, but the adequate treatment of emotional pain usually requires concern with all four.

Consequently, not only the diagnosis but also the treatment of emotional pain is a more complicated process than that for physical pain. "Do I use just drugs," the psychiatrist must ask herself, "or just psychotherapy or some combination? What drugs? What kind of psychotherapy? What kind of combination and when?" Moreover, the answers to these questions are much less predictable than those involved in the treatment of physical pain, and sometimes they can be arrived at only through lengthy trial and error.

If all this were not enough, the treating psychiatrist must usually do battle with the patient's will. The many who are mentally ill, but who are not in pain, come to psychiatry most commonly only because they are brought there by relatives or by the police, if they come at all. Then their presence is just the beginning of the battle. People in physical pain, with very few exceptions, wholeheartedly want relief. With equally few exceptions, those in emotional pain are to a greater or lesser degree quite halfhearted in their desire for relief. Some are strangely attached to their pain, as if it were an old friend. Most are not. Most want relief but are almost desperately attached to the cause of their distress. Yes, they want to feel better, but only without changing in any way, and many will leave psychiatry, preferring their pain to its necessary treatment.

To do justice to the issue of euthanasia, we must wade deeper into this complexity. Such wading will inevitably be superficial, for I cannot write a textbook on psychiatry in a chapter. Nonetheless, the issue at stake in euthanasia primarily is one of emotional pain, and we must examine a few real-life cases and ground ourselves at least a little bit in the complexity of psychiatry before we can look at the issue with any clarity . . . indeed, before we can even arrive at a definition of euthanasia.

Biological Psychiatric Disorders

The distinction between psychiatric disorders and medical diseases is frequently arbitrary. Remember that Tony, the patient described in Chapter 1 with a highly malignant brain tumor, first came to the attention of psychiatrists, not internists or general practitioners, because his mind was obviously not functioning well. Yet one would not generally think of a malignant tumor as a psychiatric disease.

Alzheimer's is another case in point. Its first symptoms are usually both mental and subtle. Eventually, however, it becomes apparent that the patient's difficulties are more than just mental. Many Alzheimer's patients, for example, will expire by choking because they have lost the ability to swallow—hardly a psychiatric problem. So while psychiatrists are often the first to diagnose it, we no longer generally consider Alzheimer's a traditional psychiatric disease. This doesn't mean there are no ambiguities left. In fact, huge psychological factors may be involved in the causation of Alzheimer's—and even of malignant tumors—but we now think of these diseases as primarily physical.*

Two common and often devastating diseases that are mostly physical thus far remain firmly in the psychiatric domain: schizophrenia and manic-depressive disease (now fashionably referred to as bipolar disorder). In the interest of both brevity and simplicity I am going to speak about only a few aspects of schizophrenia—an extraordinarily complex disease—and give but glimpses of a few cases.

Perhaps five million people in the United States suffer from schizophrenia—five million *different* people. A psychiatric disease is not all there is to a person, and schizophrenia, like other disorders, is superimposed upon a unique personality (and soul). An accurate psychiatric diagnosis can occasionally be made in a matter of seconds of patients with severe and chronic schizophrenia; they are instantly recognizable by the common ravages of the disease they share. For most, however, the disease is not so severe and its signs may be subtle indeed. Yet the symptoms may be devastating, as they were for Roger.

In my capacity as director of a mental health clinic, I first saw Roger when he came to the clinic at age twenty-eight complaining, "I feel like shit." A skilled carpenter by trade, he lived in a shack in

---

* See again my novel *A Bed by the Window* for examples of the ambiguities of senility.

the woods on the edge of poverty because he could never hold a job for long. On the one hand, he always had an external reason for quitting a job: the boss was too demanding, or the customer too picky. On the other hand, I suspect he was closer to the mark when I asked him one day if he felt so bad because he couldn't hold a job, and he answered, "No, it's the other way around; I can't hold a job because I feel so bad."

There is no way I could convince another psychiatrist that Roger was, in fact, suffering from schizophrenia. The signs were too soft. Although handsome and dramatically attractive to women, he seldom dated. Although intelligent and witty, he was for the most part a social isolate. It seemed he couldn't handle relationships any better than he handled his jobs. Such friends as he had belonged to a pot-smoking culture, but Roger himself disliked marijuana because it made him distinctly paranoid. Alcohol gave him temporary relief. "It numbs me out," he explained, "but I can't stand hangovers, and I'm goddamned if I'm going to let myself become an alcoholic." He slept poorly and erratically and had bad dreams. Sleep gave him no pleasure. Nothing gave him pleasure.

I referred Roger to another psychiatrist on the staff for treatment with medications and to a variety of skilled social workers for psychotherapy. The other psychiatrist happened to agree with my presumptive diagnosis of a subtle schizo-affective disorder, a variety of schizophrenia where emotional distress of one kind or another is the predominant disability. As I've suggested, many psychiatrists would question this diagnosis, but they would be hard put to come up with a better one. Over the next four years he treated Roger with virtually every drug then in use for this type of schizophrenia: antipsychotic agents, antidepressants, and all manner of combinations thereof. None of them helped. Of some Roger admitted, "They do seem to clear up my thinking a bit," invariably adding, "but they make me *feel* even worse."

Attempts at psychotherapy were equally fruitless. No matter what the approach, Roger never became engaged in therapy. He was as erratic in keeping his appointments as he was in taking his medicines. Frequently he would drop out of the clinic for several months at a time, only to return eventually with the same complaint. We all felt we might have been able to do better by him had he been more regular, or more committed, in his attendance, but at the same time we recognized that his irregularity and lack of commitment were probably manifestations of his disease.

In my role as supervising psychiatrist of the clinic over those four years, I intermittently and briefly met with Roger. Because he did not look or otherwise seem depressed, my curiosity compelled me each time to push him to be more specific than simply saying, "I feel like shit." Condensing his many responses into one, it came out no more clear than "You know the expression to have a bug up your ass, Dr. Peck? Well, it's like I've got a bug up my ass. I *am* irritable, but that's only part of it. It goes deeper than that. It's like this bug is secreting a poison throughout my system. I'm not saying it's a literal bug. But it's as if the poison is everywhere. Not just my brain. My blood cells. Even my blood cells feel like shit."

After four years, when Roger failed to keep his appointments once more, we were not alarmed. We imagined he would eventually return as he had so many times in the past. But we were wrong. Six weeks after his last broken appointment a hiker in the woods discovered Roger's thirty-two-year-old body hanging by a rope around his neck from the limb of a tree next to his shack. The body was extremely bloated. The coroner judged he had been dead somewhere between ten and fourteen days.

———

Roger's consistent chief complaint was that of dysphoria.

Dysphoria is the opposite of euphoria. Although the literal translation of "euphoria" from the Greek is "feeling well," we use the word in English to denote an emotional state that feels better than well. Usually a state of euphoria is clearly psychological in origin and a response to a more or less external event such as falling in love or winning the finals at Wimbledon. But it may be clearly biological when it's a response to certain drugs that stimulate a euphoria center in the brain—drugs such as morphine and heroin, Dexedrine and speed and cocaine. The state of euphoria also seems to be at least partly biological when one is in the manic phase of a manic-depressive illness, or bipolar disease.

So it is with dysphoria, or "feeling bad." Whenever we experience any painful emotion—grief, sadness, depression, or anger, for instance—we are dysphoric, but the cause is usually obviously at hand: the death of a loved one, betrayal by a business partner, the loss of a job. Psychiatry, however, usually reserves the term "dysphoria" for cases when the bad feeling is not explainable in terms of either a psychological response to an external event or the distress of a physical disease diagnosable by tests.

I have stated that schizophrenia is primarily a biological disease, although not one currently diagnosable by materialistic testing. In attributing Roger's dysphoria to schizophrenia, I am positing that his pervasive bad feeling was primarily physical in origin. Schizophrenia is largely a hereditary and therefore genetic disorder. I do not believe his distress was just in his mind. I believe he was quite accurate when he described his pain as locatable in his blood cells as well as in his brain. His dysphoria was quite analogous, I believe, to chronic and severe physical pain, except that we had no acceptable physical means to relieve it.

In the end I shall argue that for both psychological and theological reasons suicide is *generally* unjustifiable. Yet, as I said at the beginning, it is not my purpose to condemn. And, as I am saying throughout, there is always an exception to everything. I believe that Roger was such an exception. I suspect that if I had been in his shoes—or, more specifically, his body—I too would have hanged myself. I believe it proper that his body was buried in hallowed ground. And I further have no reason to believe that his soul this day resides anywhere other than heaven.

———

One of the problems of suicide (which, of course, is the most central issue of euthanasia) is the guilt that it leaves in its wake.*

———

* I feel fortunate that during my career as a psychiatrist only two of my patients committed suicide. Roger was one. The other will be described shortly.

Usually this guilt is uncalled for. A suicide, however, should stimulate mental health professionals to review the case stringently to see where we might have failed the patient. At the time of Roger's death, those of us involved in his care experienced relatively little guilt. We had provided him with every acceptable form of psychiatric treatment and done so humanely. No one could have faulted us. But I have had a lot of time to think about Roger, and, oddly enough, I feel guiltier about him today than I did twenty years ago when we first learned he had killed himself.

In Chapter 1, on pulling the plug, I spoke of how we tend to write off the mentally ill. I spoke from personal experience. There is no doubt in my mind today that I wrote Roger off on a certain level while he was still under my care.

I have asked myself why Roger kept coming back to the clinic, even sporadically, when we seemed not to be helping him in any way. I have come up with only one answer: he was desperate. I've accused some other medical professionals of a lack of empathy in undermedicating certain patients for physical pain. I believe I was inadequately empathetic with Roger's desperation. Yes, we gave him every acceptable form of psychiatric treatment. But had I been truly empathetic with his desperation, I would at least have seriously considered *unacceptable* forms of treatment.

Today we refer to herbs and acupuncture as "alternative" methods of healing. We mean that they are an alternative to traditional Western scientific medical treatment. We M.D.'s are taught nothing about such alternatives in medical school, and we generally continue to know nothing about them. Today many of us have learned not to discourage our patients who are interested in exploring alternative methods, but back when I worked with Roger we considered them unacceptable. This is not where my guilt lies, however. Roger already knew more about alternative therapies than I ever would, and in his desperation he had tried most of them. They were no more helpful to him than our traditional remedies.

Two radical types of Western psychiatric treatment for schizophrenia—and also for depression—were widely used during the first half of the twentieth century: shock treatment and prefrontal lobotomy. With the discovery of antipsychotic and antidepressant drugs in the 1950s, these treatments largely fell out of use and came to be considered generally unacceptable. The pendulum has come very slightly back. Although insulin shock is no longer used, modernized electroshock therapy is an accepted treatment for selected patients, usually with depression, who do not respond adequately to other measures. I further hear through the grapevine that a rare prefrontal lobotomy is occasionally still performed, almost secretly, in otherwise hopeless cases.

Actually I did gently suggest to Roger the possibility of electroshock therapy. He was tart in rejecting it: "No way am I going to let them mess with my fucking brain with electricity." In retrospect I wish I'd been more persistent. Naturally, I never mentioned lobotomy, a damaging procedure that I wouldn't even have considered until we had tried electroshock, an undamaging procedure.

Only once did I ever hint at a lobotomy to a patient, a woman I saw for only twenty minutes and who was years later to remind me of Roger. We met when I was chief of psychiatry on Okinawa. She was a physically attractive, highly competent forty-five-year-old top career government executive in the foreign aid department. While en route from Vietnam back to the United States she asked to see me on an emergency basis. Nothing about her but her own story suggested a diagnosis of schizophrenia. I will let her tell that story in her own fiercely intelligent words.

"For over twenty years," she told me, "I have had the feeling that my intestines have become twisted and gangrenous. The pain is unbearable. Almost as bad is the stench of the gangrene. I cannot stand the smell of myself. Intellectually I know that my intestines are not twisted. Otherwise, I would have long been dead—and most of the time wish I were. But the knowledge doesn't take away the feeling. Of course other doctors always refer me to psychiatry. I have seen well over a hundred psychiatrists. They call what I have a 'somatic delusion' and think it is a symptom of schizophrenia. I have taken every drug in the book to treat schizophrenia for at least the prescribed period of time. Not one has given me a moment's relief. I've undergone two lengthy series of shock treatments. They did help, but as soon as my memory returned, so did the feeling. I've begged for more shock treatments, but they tell me it would be unsafe to keep me in the hospital for the rest of my life, buzzing my brain every other day. What else can I do?"

"You've had psychotherapy?" I asked.

"I'm sorry," she said. "I should have told you. I took it for granted that you'd know. Of course. I've been in psychotherapy all these years. I went through a dozen therapists in the first ten years. During the last ten I've been seeing the same man weekly whenever I'm in Washington, which is most of the time. It doesn't really help, but he's extremely patient and kind."

"I'm puzzled," I commented, "as to why you wanted to see me when you're only here for a couple of days."

She smiled. Yes, she could smile. "I don't blame you for being puzzled," she responded. "I am being ridiculous. I have no reason to believe there is any way you could be of assistance to me. But I'm desperate, and desperate people will do anything, even if it seems ridiculous. Here, this may help you to understand."

At that moment she reached up and removed her wig. No longer was she physically attractive. Save for an occasional black tuft she was bald. "You see," she said, "I pull my hair out. I don't only feel like pulling it out; I do it."*

To my relief, she replaced her wig.

"It must be awful for you," I said. "I wish to God there was something I could do, but there isn't. The only thing I can suggest is that when you get back to the States you might ask the psychiatrists whether they think neurosurgery has anything to offer."

---

* Today psychiatrists would be far less likely to diagnose this patient as schizophrenic, although they would probably see her disorder as a biological one. Also, over the past thirty years pharmacological treatment has been developed that is effective in some cases of trichotilomania, the psychiatric term for the compulsion to tear one's hair out. This impulse is sometimes seen in cases of mental retardation. In this unusual case, however, it was a symptom not of retardation but of the patient's agony.

She was very quick on the uptake. "A lobotomy? I didn't think they did those anymore."

"I'm not sure they do," I replied. "Nor am I suggesting it's something I'd recommend. Even if it worked, it would be a dreadful trade-off."

"I think I understand," she said, and then added, to my surprise, "Thank you. You *have* done something for me. I doubt I'd consider it seriously, but you've at least given me something new to think about. Thank you."

A prefrontal lobotomy is a relatively simple neurosurgical procedure that severs the connections between the prefrontal lobes and the rest of the brain. In other words, it renders useless the most evolved—the most human—portion of the mind. I wouldn't even have gently hinted at such a drastic treatment had I not during my training seen two patients who years before had undergone this procedure because of somatic delusions. Both patients clearly suffered from a loss of fine judgment as a result. They had been diminished. They had, I felt, lost a subtle but essential part of their humanity. Both patients also told me, however, that the lobotomy was the best thing that had happened in their lives.

I suspect that there was something very similar between the woman I saw so briefly on Okinawa, with the terrible somatic delusion that her intestines were twisted and gangrenous, and Roger, whom I first saw five years later, with his persistent dysphoria. What I am wondering about here is the distinct possibility that Roger's dysphoria was simply a vague form of a somatic delusion.

When we label something a delusion, we imply that it isn't *real*. Certainly, as she was so well aware, the woman's intestines were not *really* twisted and gangrenous. She did not have that sort of physical disease. Yet we have come to realize that schizophrenia is primarily a biological, physical disorder. So why shouldn't the pain of Roger's dysphoria—of having an unreal bug up his ass secreting an unreal poison, "all in his mind"—have been just as real a physical pain as if his intestines were actually twisted?

What I am asking is this: since we routinely treat physical pain with morphine, why did I not even once vaguely consider treating Roger with morphine? Or heroin, for that matter? Particularly since these drugs produce euphoria and he was suffering from dysphoria? The answer is clear: such treatment would have been—and still is—considered *unacceptable*. To understand why it is considered unacceptable, we return to the old bugaboo about addiction.

Roger was a strong-willed man, self-disciplined in some ways. Alcohol gave him some relief, but he would not allow himself to become alcoholic. Who is to say that he could not have used morphine in a similar manner for occasional dramatic surcease of dysphoria without becoming addicted? And so what if he had become addicted? Would he have had to keep increasing his dose to keep his dysphoria at bay? Possibly. But possibly not. We simply do not know. To my knowledge, the treatment of emotional pain of physical origin with opiate painkillers has not even been studied scientifically. Why not? Simply because these drugs are addictive they are considered unacceptable treatment for supposedly unreal pain. Yet, in retrospect, it seems to me that addiction would have been preferable to suicide.

Actually, were I working with Roger today, I would try a different kind of controlled substance before suggesting morphine. Dexedrine and its stronger variant, methedrine (speed), are non-opiate stimulant drugs that also can produce euphoria of a sort. Because they do so, they are definitely habituating and therefore under the control of the Drug Enforcement Administration (DEA). To illustrate the potential utility of Dexedrine, I will cite a clinical vignette of a patient who did not have schizophrenia.

Toward the end of my practice, when I was seeing patients only for consultation, Fred consulted me for a self-diagnosis of depression. The diagnosis was correct. Although he was in no way crazy or psychotic, he was quite seriously depressed. I would immediately have referred him to another psychiatrist had he not presented me with an emergency of sorts. At age forty-five, Fred was the vice president of sales for a major national corporation. He was flying the very next morning to Chicago for the corporation's annual sales conference, a complex and important event for which he was totally responsible. "I can't handle it feeling this way," he moaned. "You've got to help me get through the meeting somehow."

We explored all the alternatives. Traditional antidepressant drugs commonly took up to three weeks to work and often caused debilitating side effects at first. He was not quite depressed enough to require hospitalization. There was no question of canceling the meeting or of calling in sick. Although I agreed with Fred that he was depressed, I kept encouraging him by saying that he was definitely in shape to run the meeting. "I know you feel terrible," I told him, "but I see no evidence that you're not thinking quickly and clearly and speaking with total coherence."

The more I tried to encourage him in this way, the more agitated Fred became. "I can't make it. I'm not just dreading it. I really can't make it." Although I was almost certain that he could tough it out, he was even more certain that he couldn't. Finally I bowed to his certainty and prescribed for him a six-day supply of Dexedrine at a modest dosage. I told him that what I was doing would not be considered acceptable psychiatry because of the problem of habituation, but I thought the drug would probably help him over the hump, and I explained very clearly that it was a temporary one-shot deal. We made an appointment for follow-up six days hence, and I made sure he knew I would then refer him to another psychiatrist for purely traditional treatment.

Fred was ebullient when he came back six days later. "You're a miracle worker, Doc!" he exclaimed. "That stuff works like magic. I was on top of everything. The meeting went off smoothly. I spoke brilliantly. Thank you. Took my last pill this morning. God, I feel great!"

"Well, you're probably not going to feel that way tomorrow," I said. "Even though you're not aware of it, you look just as depressed as you did last week. Your mouth is pulled down, and your eyes are dull. You're speaking and behaving no differently."

"But I've never been more competent in my life."

"No," I said, "you just *feel* more competent. But that feeling is only a result of the drug."

As I'd expected, he pleaded for me to keep seeing him and

prescribing Dexedrine, but now I had reason to be adamant in referring him on. A year later the psychiatrist to whom I referred him told me that Fred had actually done very well with a combination of standard antidepressant medication and psychotherapy.

Back to Roger. As I indicated, were I still in practice working with him today, I think I would *experiment* with Dexedrine or morphine. But I would prefer not to. I would far prefer to see such an experiment performed aboveboard on appropriate selected patients in sufficient numbers and with sufficient controls to give psychiatry a clear scientific assessment of the potential efficacy of these kinds of drugs in treating cases of biogenic dysphoria or somatic delusion that not infrequently end in suicide.

As I've said, however, to my knowledge such an experiment has not been done. The reason it hasn't been done is that we underestimate the intensity of certain kinds of emotional pain even more frequently than we underestimate the intensity of physical pain. We do so simply because we assume emotional pain to be somehow unreal, since we cannot attribute it to a specific life event or a specific physical cause. In doing so, we write off many patients.

———

This business of writing a person off is critical to the understanding of euthanasia. Those who help someone commit suicide, for instance, have in some dimension written the person off. And of course those who opt for euthanasia, as it shall eventually be defined, have on some level written themselves off.

We psychiatrists write off many of our patients in a more common way that has nothing to do with pain. I alluded to it when I recounted how chronic schizophrenics were among those upon whom the Nazis practiced "mercy killing" in preparing for the Holocaust. Today in our culture the write-off is more subtle. Today we do not kill our chronic schizophrenics—except indirectly, when we turn them out onto the streets. But when we cannot make them dramatically better with our drugs, we generally do not consider them worth further attention. We assign them to a kind of psychological dustbin in our minds, as if they were the living dead. All we can see of them is their schizophrenia. We seldom have or take the time to see their souls.

By grace or good fortune, however, I have had the almost unique opportunity of seeing one chronic schizophrenic patient roughly twice a year over the course of the past twenty years. When I first saw Dolores in consultation at a local clinic, she was thirty years old and there was no question about her diagnosis. Dolores suffered from almost constant suspiciousness and "ideas of reference"—feelings that people were talking about her when they were not and that meaningless events had somehow been designed to give her messages. She was frequently depressed and apathetic. She had fleeting delusions and grave difficulty sustaining either employment or social relations. Additionally, she demonstrated profound ambivalence, a flatness of emotional expression, and extreme social maladeptness. Shortly after I first saw her, she was placed on Social Security disability, and she has remained on it ever since.

When I left my consulting position at the clinic, Dolores started dropping by my home approximately twice a year for a free visit of fifteen minutes. A longer visit she could not tolerate. Today, at age fifty, she demonstrates all the signs of moderate, well-entrenched chronic schizophrenia. Despite continuing clinic treatment with the most advanced appropriate psychoactive drugs, she has every symptom today that she had when I first saw her. The course of her disease over twenty years has been consistent and stable. From a traditional psychiatric point of view, she has neither deteriorated nor made any progress whatsoever. It would be easy to regard her as a chronic lost cause. Yet over the course of these years, she has moved from skepticism to a tentative interest in religion to a deep faith. Dolores now attends mass at least weekly. Her theology is not in the least bizarre; it is, as best as I can ascertain, not only traditional and sound but quite sophisticated. In return for my extremely minor ministrations, she regularly prays for me. I think I have by far the better part of the bargain. Many would regard hers as a wasted sort of life. From my point of view, while there has been no improvement in her schizophrenia or growth in her social skills, there has been immense growth in her soul. Something very profound has slowly been happening within her.*

When I speculate about this case where I had no medical help to offer, I wonder if Dolores wasn't sent here to teach me something.

Psychosomatic Psychiatric Disorders

Dolores is a case of obvious schizophrenia, one that is diagnosable within seconds. Roger was a more subtle yet fatal case. Although we have not, to date, been able to develop a biochemical test for its diagnosis or located a neuroanatomic defect to account for it, psychiatrists have gradually come to believe that schizophrenia is *primarily* a biological disease. By "primarily" I imply that exceptional cases of schizophrenia are more related to psychodynamics or social stresses than to biochemistry. But they are the exception.

Most emotional pain that humans experience, however, is primarily psychological. This doesn't mean biology is uninvolved (as we shall almost immediately see). It means that, assuming the normal functioning of our brains, the emotional distress can wholly be explained either by clear life stresses or by clearly entrenched psychodynamic patterns of responding to such stresses.

But there is a rather large area in between where emotional pain seems to be the result of impaired psychological *and* biological functioning. The suffering then is clearly a psychosomatic phenomenon. The patient should ideally be treated, as in Fred's case, with a combination of medication and psychotherapy. The ideal, however, is frequently not possible. The patient may be unwilling or unable to participate in psychotherapy, he may be unwilling to take medica-

---

* I recounted the story of Dolores in an address entitled "Psychiatry's Predicament" to the American Psychiatric Association on May 4, 1992, in Washington, D.C. An adaptation of that address can be found in the epilogue to *Further Along the Road Less Traveled: The Unending Journey Toward Spiritual Growth* (New York: Simon & Schuster, 1993), pp. 232–55.

tions, or the medicine may not be effective. Treatment can sometimes get rather complicated.

To illustrate the complexity of emotional pain let us consider the most common of all psychiatric complaints: depression. Knowing something of the complexities of depression in particular is central to our understanding of euthanasia.

In the middle part of our brain there is probably a collection of nerve cells—a center—that when stimulated produces the painful emotion of depression. There are also centers in the midbrain that produce other specific emotions such as anger and euphoria. Like these other centers, our depression center has been bred into us through many thousands of years of human evolution precisely because it serves a purpose. What purpose?

An interrelated complex of life events and other emotional responses is virtually guaranteed to stimulate our depression center to fire off. The most common is helpless anger, helpless rage. When life angers us and we can do something about it—chastise a perpetrator or write an angry letter, for instance—we do not usually get depressed. But when the anger is at all persistent and we seem helpless to do anything about it, we almost always become depressed. If a man is laid off from a job that he needs or enjoys, he is likely to feel angry yet helpless to rectify the situation. As a result, he becomes depressed. A modicum of depression of limited duration is a perfectly normal response to being laid off.

People feel depressed when they think they are in a trap, a cage from which they can see no way out. Frequently, however, at least some of the bars of the cage are of their own making. Usually such bars represent something to which they are excessively attached: a role, a person, often a dream or fantasy. Depression is useful because its pain is a signal to us that we need to give something up; the depression provides a motive for us to do the psychological work of relinquishing that person or that role. Consequently, I have written of "the healthiness of depression."* It frequently inspires people to

---

* *The Road Less Traveled* (New York: Simon & Schuster, 1978), pp. 69–72.

psychospiritual growth and the creation of positive changes in their lives.

At times the depression may be unusually prolonged, severe, or both, and then psychiatric treatment is called for. On the one hand, the depression center may be hyperactive, so to speak, and may need to be calmed down by medication before the patient can get on with making the necessary life changes. On the other hand, certain deep-seated psychodynamic factors, such as pathological guilt or shame related to childhood issues, may prevent the patient from changing—factors that can only be treated with psychotherapy. Psychiatrists often have to make subtle judgments about when or whether to treat a depressed patient with psychotherapy, with medications, or with both in combination.

Finally, the depression center in certain people will sometimes fire off for no apparent reason whatsoever. Such people may become severely depressed when there is absolutely no discernible precipitating life event or situation. We usually consider such depressions to be not a psychosomatic but purely a biological phenomenon related to a chemical imbalance, often hereditary, even though we do not understand the exact nature of the imbalance.

———

Like Fred, Howard was a forty-five-year-old vice president of a major national corporation when I saw him for depression. But there the similarity ended.

Unlike Fred, Howard did not seek my attention. Instead he walked into his local police station at 2:00 A.M. one cold January night to confess that he had murdered someone. Under interrogation he would not say whom he had murdered or when or how or what he had done with the body. He just kept insisting, "I need to be in jail. A person like me needs to be in jail." Finally he did reluctantly give the police his address, his phone number, and the name of his wife. The police called his wife, who had been unaware that Howard was even out of the house. When she arrived at the police station she acknowledged that Howard had seemed to be having some difficulty sleeping for the past week. Shortly after dawn the police escorted her and her husband to the emergency room of the hospital. That was when I was called.

In a suit and tie, Howard looked far more like the business executive he was than like a murderer . . . an extremely depressed-looking executive. By the time I saw him he had changed his tune. "Maybe I didn't murder anyone," he told me. "I guess I just felt like I had. I don't know why. Yes, I've been feeling depressed lately. A week, maybe two. I don't know why. I guess I'm just a nut. I guess I don't belong in jail; I belong in a nuthouse."

At least I would not have to commit him to the state hospital. He was quite willing—almost eager—to sign himself into the voluntary psychiatry ward of the general hospital of which I was then a staff member.

On one level the diagnosis was obvious: Howard had a psychotic depression. By "psychotic" we mean merely that the depression is so severe that it causes the patient to lose touch with reality. But there were other implications. Psychotic depressions tend to be unusually difficult to treat with either psychotherapy or medications. Not infrequently they will go away by themselves after six to twelve months without any treatment whatsoever . . . if the patient doesn't kill himself first. The danger of suicide in such cases is extremely high.

We think that most psychotic depressions represent a purely biological disease. In support of this presumption neither Howard nor his wife was able to tell me of any life change, event, or factor that might have kicked off his depression. I immediately started him on antidepressant medicines.

Yet I wondered. I could not elicit any history of previous depression or mood swings that might suggest a biological bipolar disease, nor was there any family history of depression. Why the bizarre act of confessing to a murder he didn't commit? Howard seemed to desire to be punished, and that smacked of guilt about something. Or possibly pathologic shame. I was soon to learn that he came from a poor family and had one sibling, a brother two years younger who was an only occasionally employed construction worker. Had Howard harbored murderous thoughts toward his brother? Howard could not have become a vice president without considerable ambition and competitiveness. Did his economic success relative to that of his brother somehow represent fratricide in his mind?

But all this was almost idle speculation. The reality was that, like many extremely depressed people, he was, to put it mildly, guarded. He volunteered nothing. No matter how hard I tried, I could elicit virtually nothing by way of feeling or psychodynamic information from Howard. He answered my questions in monosyllables. It was like attempting psychotherapy with a stone.

There was, however, another reason I suspected a psychological element in Howard's depression. Since I could get virtually nothing out of him, I tried to get a decent emotional history from his wife. Although not the least depressed, she was, if anything, more guarded than he. Their marriage was "fine," she reported. She portrayed herself, as well as Howard, as an emotional automaton. Indeed, she did not even seem particularly concerned about him. A more bland person I have never met. I have no doubt she would have scored well above average on an intelligence test, but emotionally she seemed to be strangely retarded. What would it be like to be married to such an obtuse woman? I wondered. Perhaps she was just the kind of wife that Howard needed, but I knew if I had been married to her I would have felt myself to be in a horrendous trap. Did Howard harbor murderous fantasies toward her? Was that it? I didn't know. I only knew that if I couldn't get out of such a trap I too would have gone psychotic. Nonetheless, Howard also insisted that their marriage was "fine."

After three weeks of intense inpatient treatment with such ineffective psychological probing, milieu therapy, and hefty doses of the most advanced antidepressant medications then available, Howard's depression remained unabated. He was convinced his corporation was going to fire him. Its officials assured me otherwise. But there was an equally compelling economic force lurking in the wings. Howard's health insurance program covered no more than six weeks of psychiatric hospitalization within any one given year. I referred Howard to another psychiatrist on the staff who was expert in the administration of electroshock therapy. (He was the only patient for whom I ever recommended such treatment over the course of ten years of practice as a general psychiatrist.)

My motive in doing so was not primarily economic. As I explained to him, no one knows how or why shock treatment works, but it was *dramatically* effective in approximately half of the cases such as his. I told him that, contrary to the fantasies of some of the lay public in this modern age, it was a humane procedure performed under brief general anesthesia. He passively agreed to it. Of course he was feeling so terrible that he would have agreed to almost anything.

The shock treatment was administered every other morning. When Howard awoke from his third treatment his depression was gone. He was smiling for the first time in the month I'd been seeing him, and he thanked me vigorously. We gave him three more treatments over the next week to cement his recovery.

It had been my hope that if he were to improve as well as he had he would be able to participate in meaningful psychotherapy. This was not to be. Although now smiling and eager to return to work, he was just as guarded as before and as bland, or as facilely evasive, as his wife.

So I was able to use his inpatient recovery period only for discharge planning. He had no discernible memory loss, as occasionally may occur temporarily after shock treatments, and he fully comprehended me. I explained that depressions such as his might well recur, so it would be necessary for me to keep close tabs on him for at least a few months after he left the hospital. Should his depression recur, I reassured him that it would likely be no major problem. "Usually just another shock treatment takes care of it," I said. "It can be done on an outpatient basis. Occasionally we even treat patients once a month that way." He understood and gave no hint that such a prospect daunted him in the least.

Two issues concerned me. One was that Howard had seemed to be seeking punishment the night he went to the police station confessing an imaginary or delusional murder. Although I'd never seen any evidence to suggest it, I still wondered whether shock treatment worked in certain cases because it represented a punishment to the patient. I gently explored this possibility with Howard, but it seemed to be my issue, not his. "Punishment, hell!" he exclaimed. "It's salvation."

The other issue that made me uneasy was Howard's unwillingness or inability to engage in even superficial psychotherapy. Without being sure why, I somehow felt less than optimistic about his prognosis. But there was nothing I could do about it. I discharged him from the hospital with an appointment to see me in my office in a week. Although I had no reason to believe they were doing him any good, I kept him on his antidepressant medications as a possible kind of insurance.

When I saw Howard the next week he seemed fine. Saying "I'm glad to be back at work," as I anticipated, was as close as he got to psychotherapy. We haggled over his next appointment. I wanted to see him again in a week, but he insisted he had a business meeting in Phoenix that he couldn't get out of. I capitulated, and we set up an appointment in two weeks.

The day before that appointment Howard called me to say he was being called out of town again. He told me he was still feeling fine, and sounded so. We rescheduled for the next week. I phoned in a prescription to his pharmacy for a refill of his antidepressants.

Howard did not show up for that new appointment. I used the time to call him. He was at home. He said he'd simply forgotten about it. He denied feeling depressed, but something in his voice worried me. I made an appointment for three days later. He promised me he would keep it. I asked to speak to his wife. She said she didn't *think* Howard was depressed. She agreed to make sure he kept the new appointment and said she would accompany him.

But they didn't show up. I gave them fifteen minutes. I was about to call them to say I'd make a house call that evening when my phone rang. It was Howard's wife. "I wanted to let you know that Howard will be unable to keep today's appointment," she said.

"Why not?"

"Because he's just shot himself in the head."

"Oh, my God!" I blurted. "Is he all right?"

"No," she replied matter-of-factly. "The medics are here. He's dead."

When I phoned a week later to offer my condolences, she was equally matter-of-fact. The police, she informed me, had discovered that Howard had purchased the pistol and ammunition at a local gun shop the afternoon I'd last talked to him on the phone. Twenty minutes before the appointment she'd promised to accompany him to, she'd announced, "Honey, we've got to leave now to see Dr. Peck."

Howard had responded that he just had to go quickly to the bathroom first. "He did it in the bathroom," she explained. "It was no more than a minute later that I heard the shot."

————

These days, when concepts of brain chemistry so dominate their profession, perhaps the majority of psychiatrists would think of Howard's depression in purely biological terms. While I too suspect that biology was involved, I continue to think it was not the whole story. For this conclusion I've already offered reasons. The most powerful reason, however, had to await the end of the story. It is, to my mind, the timing of Howard's death.

That timing was hardly an accident. It was not a matter of an involuntary shift of the chemicals of his brain. It was a conscious choice. His depression undoubtedly underlay his choice. But depression was not the reason he chose that particular moment to kill himself. The obvious reason he chose that moment was to escape from having to see me again.

Yet why? On one level, I do not know. Because of his unwillingness to open up to me and my inability to penetrate his psyche, I never knew what was going on in Howard's mind. I could only tentatively infer. As to the timing of his death, on one level, I have only speculations, ranging from my possible ineptitude as a psychiatrist to positing deep and irrational feelings of terror and shame on Howard's part, which can be involved in cases of serious depression.

On another level, I think I do know one tiny factor involved. I have been focusing in this chapter thus far on my limited direct experience with suicide because of the relevance of suicide to the issue of euthanasia. I have said that it is not my purpose to condemn. Nonetheless, as I have thought about Roger and Howard over the years, I keep bumping up against a certain difference in feeling that I have about the death of these two men. It is unfashionable these days for anyone, particularly a psychiatrist, to make any moral judgment about another person. Yet no matter how much I believe Howard's brain was indeed overwhelmed by a chemical imbalance, as I keep butting up against the reality of the timing of his suicide, I persist in wondering if there wasn't a tiny element of cowardice involved.

Forgive me such judgmentalism, with which I myself am uncomfortable. And let me turn, with brevity far greater than it deserves, to a very different kind of case of clearly psychosomatic depression in a very different kind of person.

———

Anna is a dear and close friend of mine, five years my junior. As she looks back on it now—and she can clearly recall much of her early childhood—she can see that she has suffered from some sort of depression for as long as she can remember. This is not to say that she never felt happy. But by the time she reached her mid-twenties, she realized that her outlook upon life was gloomier than most, that thoughts of suicide were persistently in the background, and that she was experiencing feelings of rage, guilt, and despair with a frequency and an intensity that were abnormal if not unnecessary. She was vaguely aware that effective antidepressant medicines had begun to become available. But her first, and not totally blind, choice was a psychiatrist who was distinctly a psychoanalyst. Her instinct was to conquer her psyche on her own.

Soon she was to learn that conquering her psyche was no easy matter. By herself and with the help of her first analyst—as well as other psychotherapists in two decades to come—she discovered many things she initially would have preferred not to look at: violence in her parents, competitiveness with her siblings, a streak of arrogance in herself, an immensely strong will that sometimes caused her to attempt unreasonably to bend reality to it, victimization by sexism, collusion with sexism, and on and on.

During these years she grew immensely in awareness and power. Like Fred and Howard, she became a major corporate executive, albeit one with a sophistication and consciousness of what she was doing that they both lacked. Still, she was often unhappy, even suicidal. Eventually she tried several of the first-generation antidepressant medicines then available. They did not help.

After twenty years of this, Anna had become a wise woman and a teacher to many. She was enormously successful in all the world's terms. There were no more psychiatrists or gurus to whom she could turn. She could run circles around the best of them. She had learned to analyze almost instantly the cause of each one of her feelings. Yet from time to time she still felt suicidal without any reason she could discern.

By this point a new-generation antidepressant medicine was on the market: Prozac. Forgoing her desire to conquer totally her own psyche, Anna requested, with humility, that her internist prescribe it. He did, and the suicidal feelings vanished, although almost intuitively she adjusts her dosage now and then.

The moral of the story can be quickly summed up in Anna's own words. "Thank God for Prozac," she tells me. "But I doubly thank God it wasn't available when I started out."

———

Anna's gratitude that Prozac wasn't around earlier points to a problem that the treatment of physical pain and the treatment of emotional pain have in common: the problem of masking. The premature use of physical painkillers may hide, or mask, the symptoms of an undiagnosed disorder urgently in need of treatment. Anna's depressive condition was clearly a psychosomatic one. But the psychological portion of it was more radically and fundamentally basic than the biological portion. Had she been treated with Prozac at the beginning, it is possible she would very quickly have felt much better. It is also likely, however, that as a result she would not have been willing to go on to do the vitally important psycho-spiritual work that she needed to do for real emotional health.

Busy physicians in all specialties have tended to hand out pills to their patients as a substitute for their time . . . and for caring. Over the past two decades, unfortunately, this tendency—and the tendency to masking—has become a far greater problem in psychiatry than in the rest of medicine. The reasons are complex. Ever more effective psychoactive medicines have been discovered. Studies have shown that many disorders, once thought to be primarily psychological, are at least partially biological. Organized psychiatry—blindly, I believe—has increasingly run with what's called the medical model: a vision of psychiatric disease as biological, whereby social, psychological, and spiritual factors are downplayed. Finally, the insurance industry, on the basis of questionable economics, has chosen to underwrite rapid biological treatments and has done its best to resist the underwriting of psychotherapy.

An entire book could be written about the above issues. Suffice it to say, the result is a society where the treatment of emotional pain with pills is being increasingly encouraged and psychological self-examination with professional assistance is being economically discouraged. Among the reasons this is disturbing is that the vast majority of emotional suffering continues to be, mostly or entirely, a psychological phenomenon. This kind of pain is the primary motivator of euthanasia.

Psychological Disorders

Most psychological pain is not a disorder at all; it is an inherent part of the human condition.

What is the human condition? A full answer needs a discussion of the soul, which I elect to defer until Chapter 6. But for our purposes now, it is really quite simple. The human condition is that we are conscious beings with a will of our own living in a world that often doesn't behave the way we would like it to.

Whenever our will is in conflict with the reality of the external world, we experience that conflict as conscious psychological pain. The flavor of that pain varies according to the nature of the conflict. If a stranger comes onto our property and starts picking our flowers against our will, we will experience that conflict primarily as the pain of anger. If that stranger threatens us with a knife, it will be more the pain of fear. When someone we deeply want to hold on to leaves us, the pain will likely be that of grief. And so on. Frequently these painful feelings will be mixed. Grief, as often as not, for instance, will be tinged with sadness, depression, and anger.

There is nothing disordered about this suffering. These painful feelings are normal and necessary to a degree. It is an inherent part of our human existence that the will is frequently in conflict with reality. We refer to such conflicts as problems precisely because they are painful. And life, as we know, is full of problems, including the problems of chronic illness, aging, and death. The pain of dealing with life's problems, therefore, is what I have come to call *existential suffering*.

We do not like emotional pain any more than physical pain, and our natural instinct is to avoid it or get rid of it as quickly as possible. We are pain-avoiding creatures. Since it is a conflict between our will and reality that causes our pain, our first and natural response to the problem is to deal with it by imposing our will to make reality conform to what we want of it.

Sometimes this response is quite appropriate. When that stranger comes onto our property uninvited and starts to pick our flowers, it is probably appropriate to order him away and, if he won't budge, to go into our house and call the police to do our ordering for us. Dominance comes naturally to us, and like its sister, competitiveness, it is not inherently wrong.

But life is not so simple that it's inherently right either. It is right for an infant to dominate its parents by crying to get not only its physical but also its emotional needs met. Yet when that infant becomes a toddler capable of picking up and throwing a glass, its dominance can become dangerous and destructive. So the terrible twos have begun. "No," Mommy and Daddy say. "No, don't do that. No, you can't do that either. No. No, you're not the boss.

You're very important, and we love you very much, but you can't do that. No, we're the boss. No . . . No . . . No."

This is humiliating for the child. Essentially what happens in the normal, healthy life of a two-year-old is that it is psychologically demoted from four-star general to private within the course of a year. No wonder the terrible twos are a time of depression and temper tantrums! But it is a necessary time. It is a time of socialization. The great psychologist Erich Fromm defined socialization as a process of "learning to like to do what we have to do." The essence of the two-year-old's pain is humiliation—yes, another variety of psychological pain—but God forbid we should not suffer it. Without it the human race would aeons ago have killed itself off. Most of us cannot remember how excruciatingly frustrating our terrible twos were, but we can recognize that the immense pain involved in absorbing the basic lesson of humility was a necessary portion of our existential suffering.

But what happens when we cannot impose our will upon reality *and* we are unwilling or unable to just grin and bear it? The answer is that we try somehow to avoid the pain. We have at our disposal a number of styles of pain avoidance.

One is to seek the attention of a psychiatrist. Most people who come to psychiatry do so seeking a magical solution. As soon as they realize the psychiatrist doesn't have one, they usually—and quickly—drop out of treatment.

A more common means of avoiding pain is to use illicit drugs such as speed or heroin or legal ones, like alcohol, to deaden the pain—to drink their problems down, so to speak. This seldom works for long and usually leaves the person worse off than before.

More common yet is the decision simply to run away from the problem. Wife difficult? Leave her. Children a drag? Abandon them. Job stressful? Quit. Not enough money? Steal. Such resolutions not only tend toward the criminal but are likely to leave the perpetrator in an even deeper mess.

The most common way to avoid the existential pain of problems is to practice some form of self-deceit that may be termed a neurosis. This never works for long either, but we have a capacity to build layer upon layer of self-deceit. Neuroses can become very convoluted and eventually cause us far more pain than the original pain we were trying to avoid. This convoluted pain I call *neurotic suffering*.

As Carl Jung succinctly put it, "Neurosis is always a substitute for legitimate suffering." By legitimate suffering he meant what I call existential suffering—the pain that is inherent in existence and that cannot be legitimately avoided. He was implying that there is always something illegitimate about neuroses. They are illegitimate not just because of the self-deceit involved but also because we have a great deal to learn from and through existential suffering. Neurotic suffering, on the other hand, never teaches us anything; it only impedes our learning.

Every individual's particular convolution of self-deceit is unique, but neuroses can be divided into categories that help to make sense of them. To illustrate the dynamics of neurosis I would like to begin with the category of neurotic phobias.

Freud was the first, among his manifold other contributions, to discern the central dynamic of these phobias: what he called *displacement*. The phobic displaces his existential fear, which he is unwilling to face, onto a seemingly more manageable object. Never was this more clear than when, early in my practice, I was visited by a man who arrived in a state of panic some three days after his brother-in-law had committed suicide by shooting himself in the head with a pistol. This man was so terrified he couldn't even come to my office alone. He had to come with his wife holding his hand. He sat down and began rambling: "You know, my brother-in-law, he shot himself in the head. I mean, he had this pistol, and I mean, all it took was just this, I mean, just an ounce of pressure and he's dead now. I mean, that was all it took. And if I had a gun—I mean, I don't have a gun, but if I had a gun and I wanted to kill myself, I mean, all it would take would just be—I mean, I don't want to kill myself, but I mean—all it—just this much."

As I listened to him, it became clear to me that his panic had not been precipitated by grief over his brother-in-law's death but that this event had put him in touch with his own mortality, and I told him so.

He instantly contradicted me. "Oh, I'm not afraid of dying!"

That's when his wife broke in and said, "Well, dear, maybe you ought to tell the doctor about the hearses and the funeral parlors."

He then proceeded to explain to me that he had a phobia about hearses and funeral parlors—indeed, to such a degree that every day walking to and from work, he would go three blocks out of his way—six blocks each day—just to avoid passing a funeral parlor. Also, whenever a hearse drove by, he had to turn away or, better yet, duck into a doorway or, even better, into a store.

"You really do have quite a fear of death," I said.

But he continued to insist, "No, no, no, I'm not afraid of death. It's just those damn hearses and funeral parlors that bother me."*

The case is particularly relevant to this book not only because of its simplicity (and almost simplemindedness) but also because of the essence of the painful emotion of fear. That essence is the fear of death and dying. Look at virtually any fear you might have and you will probably quickly be able to trace it to your fear of death and dying. Are you afraid of losing your job or of the stock market crashing? Is not your basic fear that you or your family will starve . . . and die? Most phobias are traceable to this basic existential fear. It is natural—human—that we should be afraid of death. This fear is an inherent pain of our conscious existence. But how we deal with this fear is a choice—a choice that will become increasingly meaningful in our consideration of the euthanasia issue. We can face our fear directly, existentially, legitimately, by staring it in the face and learning from it. Or we can cop out through an avoidance of one sort or another, like a phobia, that is neurotic. The neurotic solution, as in the case of the man I just described, is ultimately the more inefficient and painful.

Fifty years ago psychiatrists—with a wisdom many have since lost—were accustomed to discriminating between what they called ego alien and ego syntonic neuroses. By "ego alien" they meant a neurosis that the patient recognized as stupid and inefficient, some-

---

* This case was described in *Further Along the Road Less Traveled*, pp. 50–51.

thing he or she wanted to be free from. By "ego syntonic" they meant a neurosis that the ego—or "I" of the patient—regarded as natural, healthy, even friendly. Let me use phobias again as an example, specifically a phobia of snakes.*

Please realize it is normal to be afraid of snakes. Indeed, there is some evidence that this fear is built into our genes. What makes a fear a true phobia, however, is its intensity and, even more so, the degree of incapacitation it causes. During my three years on Okinawa I saw two women who were significantly incapacitated by their fear of snakes. This was not surprising, since Okinawa was inhabited by the poisonous habu, a large snake somewhere between the size of a rattler and that of a python. It is a nocturnal snake that sleeps during the day and is most likely to be found in the wilder parts of the island. Americans were warned not to go into the jungles at night, but officials considered the problem insignificant in the populous, manicured housing areas. Of the more than 100,000 Americans then living on the island, only one every two and a half years or so was actually bitten by a habu. Antitoxin was readily available, and as a result I never heard of an American fatality.

Janice, a top sergeant's wife, sought my psychiatric attention because of her phobia. "I can't go out on the streets at night," she told me. "I'm terrified of the habu. It's ridiculous. I know the likelihood of my being bitten in the housing areas is infinitesimal, but my fear is ruining my life. I can't go with my husband to the club at night. I can't take the children to the movies in the evening. As soon as it starts to become dark I'm totally housebound, huddling in the living room with all the lights on. It's silly—*stupid*—and *sick*. I'm such a coward. Can you help me somehow?"

Janice's phobia was clearly ego alien. She saw the fear as something alien to her, as sick, as something she did not want. She saw the limitations it placed upon her as "ridiculous." She berated herself for being "silly" and wanted to behave differently.

Although Hilda, a civilian executive's wife, was housebound at

---

* The two examples that follow are also related in *The Road Less Traveled and Beyond* (New York: Simon & Schuster, 1997), pp. 145–47.

night for the same reason, she was quite complacent about her neurosis, even proud of it. She did not come to see me in my office; I met her just once in her own home when I attended a party she and her husband were hosting. After dinner, we fell into conversation, and she told me how much she hated Okinawa because the habu *made* her housebound. "I know that other people go out at night," she said, "but if they want to be so stupid, it's *their* problem. Don't they know that the snake hangs from the limbs of trees and could drop on them anytime? Ugh! I don't understand why the government can't catch all the horrible things. God, I'll be glad when we go back to the United States."

Hilda's phobia was obviously ego syntonic. She didn't see it as abnormal. To the contrary, she thought of other people as the stupid ones. *They* had a problem. Indeed, she did not even see her limitations as her problem. It was all the fault of the habu, of Okinawa, of the government. Although Hilda seemed remarkably comfortable with her phobia, I was later given to understand that the limitations it put on their social life caused her husband considerable anguish, including the worry that it would adversely affect his career.

Since the victims of ego syntonic phobias do not see their neuroses as something unwanted, they are virtually impossible to help. Janice, because she wanted help, was another matter. While working with me she was gradually able to recognize that she had displaced onto the snakes her fear of death and evil, of the venomous, of the things she couldn't control—the bad things that might happen to good people. Slowly, for the first time in her life, she became able to speak directly about the existential issues of death and evil. By the time she returned to the States nine months later, Janice was able, albeit with considerable anxiety, to go out at night with her husband or children. While I would not exactly have called her healed, she was well on her way to healing.

After World War II, psychiatrists began increasingly to refer to ego syntonic neuroses as "character disorders." As I have previously written, it can be helpful to look at neuroses and character disorders as disorders of responsibility. As such, they are opposite styles of relating to the world. Whenever she is in conflict with the world, the neurotic tends automatically to think it is her fault. Whenever he is in conflict with the world, the character-disordered person tends to assume immediately it is the world's fault.

A significant portion of our lot of existential pain throughout life is the anguish of continually and accurately discerning what we are responsible for and what we are not responsible for. It can be seen that both neurotics and those with character disorders avoid this existential anguish. Granted that the neurotic may experience much more pain—unnecessary neurotic suffering—than a more well balanced person, nonetheless, she is relieved of the agony of discernment when she simply assumes she is responsible for everything.

Because they suffer pain and hold themselves accountable—even if for too much—neurotics, like Janice with her ego alien phobia, often seek psychotherapy on their own and often do find healing. Because they do not hold themselves accountable and suffer little, those with character disorders are much less likely to seek therapy. And when they do, they find it very tough sledding. In a sense, the point of psychotherapy with a character-disordered person is to help him suffer more rather than less. Naturally, this therapy is quite often too difficult to sustain.

Those with character disorders—and they are legion—are among the psychological lepers of whom I spoke earlier. But this does not mean that no suffering results from their emotional disorder. Although they themselves may experience little pain, those with character disorders usually cause *others* a great deal of pain. They are constantly blaming, shifting their proper share of responsibility onto others. In a myriad of ways, ranging from the careless to the criminal, they can be a real pain in the ass.

I have spoken of these psychological disorders—character disorders and neuroses—as if they were a choice. So they are. But it is important to point out that these choices of style are usually made in childhood, and often under overwhelming pressure.

It is not our task as parents to relieve our children of their own proper share of existential suffering. But it is our task not to augment it unnecessarily. Granted, no parent can do it perfectly, but at this task many fail grossly. All families are dysfunctional to some extent, but some are so dysfunctional that they produce more existential pain than children can bear. Then these children have little choice but to adopt pain-avoiding strategies—of which the defense of displacement is one among many—that inevitably evolve into neuroses and character disorders. Most patients who come to psychotherapy cannot remember their critical choice, because they made it so long ago.

Still, it was a choice and it can always be undone. I have seen patients with few apparent assets and from the most abusive of homes in the course of psychotherapy overcome severe neuroses and even character disorders against seemingly overwhelming odds. I have seen others, where the odds seemed infinitely more favorable for healing, refuse to budge and become even more entrenched in their disorder. Why some have such a strong will to grow and others seem utterly to lack it, I do not know. It is perhaps the greatest mystery of humanity.

———

Since neurosis, or character disorder, is always a substitute for legitimate suffering, the ultimate task of deep psychotherapy is obvious: it is for patients to move from their pain-avoiding substitutes to face directly the real issues of their existence. In terms of the phobia examples I have used, it is to move from the inefficient fear of snakes or funeral parlors to face the reality of death and evil. Such movement is great growth. Death and evil are fearful realities, but if we can live with our existential terror we have much to learn from them. We have nothing to learn from walking out of our way to avoid funeral parlors or staying home every night lest by some off chance we might encounter a snake in the garden.

Learning to live with reality should be easy, but it isn't. Given the fact that their existential pain-avoiding styles are usually unconscious, in some distorted way effective, and of such long standing

that they fit like old shoes, *all* patients resist the growth psychotherapy requires of them. The intensity of their resistance, however,
varies. This intensity in most cases is the primary determinant of
whether psychotherapy is a success or a failure. And it is the patient's
will that primarily determines this intensity. Strong-willed patients
do the best or the worst. As I have indicated, although it is infinitely
mysterious, some patients have an immense will to grow and others
have an equally immense will *not* to grow.

Very early on in *The Road Less Traveled* (p. 16), I made this seemingly outrageous statement: "With total discipline we can solve all
problems." It seemed outrageous only because I failed to add that
the solutions to certain problems require that we accept the reality
that there is no solution. Patients with the most severe resistance are
characterized, in my experience, by their absolute refusal to accept
this reality on some essential level.

Never was this refusal clearer than in the case of Janet, a thirty-
eight-year-old woman whom I attempted to treat for four months
without success. Her chief complaint was that of serious depression,
which had begun the day her husband of twelve years, Ralph, sep-
arated from her. When I first saw her, their divorce was imminent.
What was so dramatic about Janet was her overt unwillingness even
to begin to come to terms with it.

Three months after the divorce became final I said to her, "You're
speaking of the divorce in the present tense, as if Ralph was divorc-
ing you now. But the reality is that the divorce is past. He did it to
you. It's over. It's done. Yet you feel as if it's still happening. I can
understand that. It's hard to shift gears. But that's also why you're still
depressed. And I don't see how you can stop being depressed until
we can help you put the divorce in the past."

"I don't want to put it in the past," Janet stated without the slightest hesitation.

I was startled by her honesty, being accustomed to more
labyrinthine neuroses. It was a long moment before I could respond,
"Yes, I can understand that also. But it places us in a predicament,
doesn't it? There is a conflict between what you want and what is

possible. Between your will and the reality of the situation. That conflict is the 'why' of your depression. And obviously you're going to stay depressed until you can accept reality, even to the point of forgiving Ralph."

"I would rather stay depressed than forgive him," she responded bluntly.

This time I replied instinctively, "Somewhere in the Bible—I don't know where—it says, 'Vengeance is mine, saith the Lord.' What do you think that means?"

"I'm not going to listen to that religious horseshit," Janet proclaimed.

Three sessions later Janet terminated therapy because it "wasn't working."*

It is no accident that the topic of what Janet called "religious horseshit" surfaced toward the end. It is my impression that whenever resistance is markedly severe, it is at least as much a spiritual as a psychological problem. The person is unwilling to suffer the slightest dethronement of his or her ego in submission to any higher power, even when that power is merely labeled "life" or "reality." Something is seriously out of whack at a radical level in such a person's relationship to the world.

———

As noted at the beginning, this chapter is not intended to be a textbook on psychiatry. Given the fact that most emotional suffering is purely psychological, my coverage of psychological pain thus far has been particularly brief and shallow. This is pardonable, I believe, only because we shall return to the concept of psychological pain when we consider one kind in great depth: the psychological pain of dying. For the existential suffering involved in dying is the central issue of the euthanasia debate.

Before moving on, however, I feel it necessary to note briefly a type of emotional pain that may be existential and relevant to the

---

* This case was described in much greater depth in my book *A World Waiting to Be Born* (New York: Bantam, 1993), pp. 96–105.

discussion of euthanasia but is not mentioned in psychiatric text-books and deserves a name of its own: *redemptive suffering*. Redemptive suffering might be said to occur when a person bears the emotional pain of others in such a manner that others are in some way healed or redeemed as a result.

On one level redemptive suffering can be quite simple. Let's say that you are a good friend of mine and you're currently in emotional pain because your mother is dying. Since you're my friend, your pain causes me pain. But I don't like to feel pain. So to heal you of your pain in order that I might feel better, I throw you some sop like "Oh, don't feel bad about your mother. You know she'll go to heaven."

How does that make you feel?

Chances are it makes you feel even worse—isolated, misunderstood, and discounted. And well it should. Because my real motivation has been to care not for you but for myself.

The only truly loving thing I can do in this situation is to be willing to share your pain, to take upon myself the suffering of your existence, and to say with genuine feeling, "God, I'm sorry. It must be awful for you. Can I sit here with you for a while, or would you rather be alone?"

This response might not help you at all. But there is a significant chance it will at least leave you feeling respected and less alone.

There's nothing mysterious about redemptive suffering. I hesitate to talk about it, however, because I have reason to suspect there are other levels at which it can get quite mystical. Is it possible for certain people sometimes to share the pain of others unconsciously—without even being aware of what they are doing or why they are suffering? To bear the pain of others not only with them but *for* them? I suspect so, but I cannot prove it. I know it is possible for someone, at least to some small extent, to feel the world's pain, but I don't know whether there's anything effectively redemptive about doing so.

Many people have reported to me, however, that they have actually felt strangely uplifted—redeemed, in a sense—by their intimate involvement in the dying of a close friend or relative. They invariably refer to it as "a good death." By this they do not mean a death from euthanasia. To the contrary, as we shall see, euthanasia seems always to leave at least profound ambivalence in its wake. What they mean is a death that somehow manages to meet six criteria:

1. It is a natural death, not a result of suicide or homicide.
2. It is physically painless, whether the painlessness is natural or effected by adequate medicinal relief of pain.
3. The person dies in relationship, which is to say that he or she has achieved forgiveness and reconciliation with those who will live on.
4. The person consciously is ready to die—in other words, he is not in denial, pretending that his death still isn't happening.
5. In some fashion or another the person has expressed that readiness and has said her good-byes.
6. The person is able to do so because he or she has worked through the existential suffering required to meet death with full acceptance. (This type of work will be described in depth in Chapter 7.)

It strikes me as almost amazing that any death can simultaneously fulfill all those criteria. Nevertheless, a remarkable number of deaths do, and they seem thereby to serve a redemptive function. It is not necessary to linger further in this potentially murky area. Yet this I can say for certain: when human beings do the work of their own existential suffering, while they may not be redeeming others, they are at the very least redeeming themselves.

Chapter 4

MURDER, SUICIDE, AND NATURAL DEATH

One of my intentions has been to demonstrate that emotional pain, physical pain, and pulling the plug are often complex issues. I do this because I am against approaching any subject so important as euthanasia simplistically. In this chapter I will finish covering the complexities involved by looking at the distinctions between murder, suicide, and natural death. Many at first glance might not think of these distinctions as complex, but we shall see that they too have their share of ambiguity. This ambiguity we must wrestle with before we can finally arrive, by the end of this chapter, at a definition of euthanasia.

Murder

Murder and suicide are both forms of killing. But our attitudes about them are remarkably different. Toward the murderer we usually feel rage and a desire to see him punished. Toward the suicide we more likely feel pity. Suicide, per se, is no longer illegal in the United States, and I cannot recall anyone attempting it who was ever formally brought to justice. Hospitalized, perhaps involuntarily, but never jailed.

Why the difference? It is obviously a matter of will. He who murders deprives another of life against the other's will. Suicide may be self-violation, but it is a violation in accord with the victim's will. Murder is not.

So the definition of murder would seem simple: depriving another of life against the other's will. Yet it is not so simple at all.

Consider first the matter of bringing a murderer to justice through the legal process. It is not a simplistic matter of guilty or not guilty. There is a whole range of possible verdicts: guilty of murder in the first degree or in the second degree, guilty not of murder but of manslaughter, not guilty by reason of insanity.*

Of course, many who kill do so accidentally. The sober driver whose car hits a dark-clothed biker on the road at night has deprived the biker of life against the biker's will. But the driver had no intent to kill. He wasn't even careless. So murder seems to have a great deal to do not only with the victim's will but also with the perpetrator's will. The driver is unlikely to even be prosecuted.

Neither will the soldier be prosecuted if, in his nation's service, he deliberately kills an enemy on the battlefield. The soldier very much had the intent to kill, yet his reward will be a medal, not punishment. The concept of murder seems to go by the wayside in time of war.

Not entirely, however. In modern times we try to draw a distinction between combatants and noncombatants. The soldier who kills an unarmed civilian might actually be tried for a war crime. But these distinctions too tend to go by the wayside as a war heats up. It is not always clear how to distinguish combatants from noncombatants. Eventually, as occurred with the atomic bombing of Hiroshima and Nagasaki and the firebombing of Dresden and Tokyo, even the good guys may decide to exterminate whole centers of civilian population.

———

* I have considerable difficulty with the wording of this last verdict, rare though it actually is. The insane person who kills is, to my mind, still guilty of murder. What is at issue, I believe, is not responsibility but how the murderer should be treated.

Long overdue, perhaps, is a discussion of the difference between code ethics and situational ethics.

It is the thesis of situational ethics that no moral judgment can be made about any act without considering the entire situation or context within which it occurs. It is one situation, for instance, when the licensed driver who kills the biker at night is completely sober. It is quite another if the driver is intoxicated and has no license because it was taken away from him for drunk driving.

Code ethics is the opposite of situational ethics. The Code of Hammurabi and the Ten Commandments are examples of ancient ethical codes that declare certain acts to be wrong in and of themselves, regardless of the situation. The Sixth Commandment, for instance, states flatly: "Thou shalt not kill." It doesn't say, "Thou shalt not kill except Philistines," or "Thou shalt not kill except in time of war," or "Thou shalt not kill except in self-defense." It says, "Thou shalt not kill," period!

For hundreds of years the evolution of society has been in the direction away from code ethics and toward situational ethics. Visit your lawyer's office and you're likely to see a wall lined with large leather-bound books. Many of those books will contain precedent-setting judicial opinions such as "Thou shalt not break a contract . . . except as in the case of *Jones v. Smith* . . . or as in the case of *Liebowitz v. O'Reilly* . . . or as in the case of *Hosaka v. Ciu*." These opinions set precedent precisely because they describe situations where the code is judged not to apply.

By and large, I am very much in favor of this societal movement. It is generally a civilized evolution out of simplism and toward complexity. Yet, like some of the more thoughtful members of the so-called religious right, I also have a concern. My concern is that situational ethics may actually encourage the creation of certain situations in which anything goes. Warfare is such a situation. Granted that war is filled with ambiguity, situational ethics in time of war can almost propel us to the proposition that the end justifies the means. But this is a most shaky proposition. On the one hand, someone once asked, "If the end doesn't justify the means, then what does?" On the other hand, a real contamination is involved when people become war criminals in order to combat other war criminals. I am not saying there is no such thing as a just war. But I do believe that only the primitive, absolutist code ethic "Thou shalt not kill" may give us pause before we engage in war so that we can at least think about whether it would be a just or unjust endeavor.

———

In addition to self-defense and war, the state legitimizes "murder," with greater or lesser degrees of ambivalence, in two other situations: abortion and capital punishment.

I put the word "murder" in quotes here because it implies a code ethic judgment that is most questionable. Indeed, the state generally legitimizes abortion and capital punishment because it considers situational ethics to apply to both decisions. It holds that pregnancy can be such a burdensome situation that the sanctity of life need not apply. Similarly, it holds that certain crimes are so heinous as to constitute a situation wherein fatal vengeance is justified.

The application of either code or situational ethics in these matters has not been noted for its consistency, however. Many who are pro-choice (situationalist) in regard to abortion are the most vigorous opponents of capital punishment. Conversely, many who would outlaw abortion on the basis of an absolutist code ethic about the sanctity of life are those most in favor of easing restrictions on the execution of criminals.

Striving for consistency, a number of commentators and some jurists have already linked the euthanasia debate to the abortion debate. If a woman has the right to terminate a pregnancy with professional medical assistance, it is argued, why shouldn't people have a similar right to medical assistance in terminating their own lives? But I am reminded of Emerson, who said, "A foolish consistency is the hobgoblin of little minds." I think he put it a bit strongly. Much of the time I do believe it valid to strive for consistency. I think it is foolish, however, when we make of consistency an idol. Specifically, in this instance, I believe we'll be in trouble if we try to link the issues of abortion, capital punishment, and euthanasia too tightly.

As we shall see, some of the theological concerns about euthanasia overlap with the other two. But that does not mean they need to be debated in the same breath. To do so will only muddy the waters and detract from each debate. I am not advocating a lack of integrity. Of course the issue of the sanctity of life is central to all three debates and should be considered in each. But it is also rather central to questions of animal rights, plant rights, and environmental conservation. At the same time, there are profound issues that abortion, euthanasia, and capital punishment do *not* have in common. The subject of this book is euthanasia. I cannot do justice to all three debates. Abortion and capital punishment are, I believe, receiving adequate public attention. Euthanasia is not, in my opinion. So, arbitrary as it may seem, I am not herein going to delve into the intense ambiguities of either abortion or capital punishment.*

But I will say this: I am glad for the intense public debate over capital punishment and abortion. Were one extreme side or the other triumphant in either debate, I would shudder. I have a modest tendency to be a gloom- and doomsayer who often sees society going to the dogs. Yet in regard to capital punishment and abortion, I think at the moment we are just about where we ought to be. Unpleasant and difficult though this debate is, I am proud of our society for engaging in it. We are not avoiding its complexities. At least in these two instances, as a nation, I believe we are doing the proper "corporate" existential work of legitimate suffering.

———

Where does so-called mercy killing fit in?

I have defined murder as the taking of another's life against his or her will with deliberate intent. Although it may seem tedious, we need to look at some of these words more closely.

First, "life" and "taking." If "life" is defined as the presence of a heartbeat and a brain wave or two in an unconscious and undoubtedly terminal patient who's on massive multiple life-support systems, and if "taking life" is defined as partially eliminating one of

———

* I briefly dipped into the ambiguity of abortion in *Further Along the Road Less Traveled,* pp. 181–82.

those supports, then I was guilty of murder that morning in the neurology ward more than thirty years ago when I twisted the clamp on Tony's IV tube. But I do not think I "killed" that patient. I think there is a crucial distinction between taking life and allowing death. Terminating heroic measures under such clear circumstances is not, I believe, murder. It is not killing. Hence, it is not mercy killing. Nor is it what I will eventually define as euthanasia. It is simply pulling the plug or allowing the natural death of someone already dying.

I have already mentioned that between late September 1939 and early August 1941, the Nazi government in Germany put to death by gas or lethal injection 70,000 assorted people who were mentally retarded, schizophrenic, or senile. They referred to this well-organized project as the Euthanasia Program. Here the taking of life was not in question. These people were not allowed to die. They were killed, and the Nazis themselves called it mercy killing. They regarded it as merciful on the assumption that the quality of life of their victims was so poor that they would be better off dead.

But assumptions are always questionable, and the obvious question is this: what was the *will* of the victims? The Nazi officials might have claimed that the victims were so far gone that they couldn't even express their will. Yet until they were killed, the victims hungrily ate and thirstily drank the food and beverages provided them. They were not on life-support systems. There is no evidence that they were the least depressed or suicidal. We can justifiably assume that the victims were killed against their will, just as we can also assume that the Nazis were far more motivated by economics than by a desire to be merciful.

But what motivates a husband today, as occasionally occurs, to kill his chronically crippled wife who still hungers and thirsts? Without even asking for her consent? The husband will say, "I had to put her out of her misery. It was a mercy." But without evidence to the contrary, the presumption is that the misery he wanted to relieve was his own, and that his mercifulness was the self-justification of a killer.

Then what about assisted suicide? Is that murder? Here things become murkier. When the person clearly wants to die, the assistants—if they are guilty at all—are guilty of a victimless crime. Can a victimless crime ever be called murder? Even if it's declared a crime in some states, is it *truly* a crime?

These questions are too complicated for me to answer for the moment. I will eventually offer opinions, but before I can decently do so, we need to look at a number of other issues. For instance, we have not yet even looked at suicide and how it is to be distinguished from natural death. Other issues will follow as well, of which a definition of euthanasia is but one. In fact, the question of assisted suicide will be the very last issue to be addressed in this book.

Suicide

Having discovered that the definition of murder is not nearly so clear a matter as it might seem, we shall now make the same discovery about suicide.

Sometimes it is actually impossible to separate suicide (self-murder) from murder (the killing of another person). Consider the soldier or terrorist who deliberately volunteers for a suicide mission.

The permutations of human behavior are almost infinite. I remember several decades ago reading in the newspapers about a man who hired one criminal after another to murder him out in the desert. (The criminals were not dumb; they kept absconding with their fee, leaving the deed undone.) That was an extreme case. Thousands of people each year, however, set themselves up to be murdered in more subtle ways. Usually they deny being suicidal, but the psychiatrists who see them know differently. An intense desire to die may be quite unconscious.*

Suicide and murder also seem to be culturally related. Those

---

* Those who are more deeply interested in the ambiguities of suicide might want to read John Donnelly, ed., *Suicide: Right or Wrong*, Contemporary Issues in Philosophy Series (Buffalo, N.Y.: Prometheus Books, 1990).

cultures that have a high homicide rate tend to have a low suicide rate, and vice versa: those nations with an unusually high suicide rate tend, with exceptions, to have an unusually low incidence of homicide. I am not saying that suicide and murder are two sides of the same coin, but they are relatives of a sort.

Are there different degrees of justification or nonjustification for suicide as there are of murder? This is not a legal matter, since suicide is not against the law, but, yes, I do believe some suicides are more or less justified than others. I mentioned my very different feelings about Roger's suicide and that of Howard and suggested that had I been in Roger's body with his intractable dysphoria I too would very possibly have hanged myself. On the other hand, I also suggested that Howard shot himself, at least in part, to avoid seeing me and that his action contained an element of cowardice. Although many psychiatrists would have considered Howard the more mentally ill of the two, I believe his avoidance, not only of me but of so many other things as well, was something of a cop-out. And issues of avoidance and cop-out will come to be of increasing concern to us in understanding the phenomenon of euthanasia.

The suicides of Roger and Howard were not cases of euthanasia, however, and euthanasia—not suicide in general—is our subject. So let us consider a case of suicide that, if not euthanasia, was very close to it.

———

The tale of Victoria was told to me by my friend Jason, a family practitioner. Jason tells me that in the realm of family practice similar tales are not at all unheard of.

In many ways, Victoria was a most successful woman. During his earlier days, her husband, Arthur, four years her junior, had made an enormous amount of money. She had borne and raised three daughters, each of whom also did well in her own right. By the end of her life, Victoria had seven healthy young adult grandchildren who would soon be giving her great-grandchildren. She was, without question, a family matriarch.

But her life was not simple. Although she hadn't sought psychiatric treatment, she'd suffered a two-year period of significant depression in her thirties and another in her fifties. These depressions were possibly related to a rather distant relationship with Arthur. In their later years, after his retirement at sixty-five, Arthur maintained the distance with alcohol. Mentally, much of the time, he was not there. His absenting himself in this way may have been partly the result of the fact that Victoria was, to put it mildly, a bit domineering.

The relationship between her daughters and her was ambivalent. On the one hand, they admired Victoria's great dignity and appreciated her matriarchal skills, including her obvious loving dedication to them. On the other hand, they often resented her subtle or not-so-subtle efforts to control them. Within reason, and occasionally beyond, Victoria very much liked to be in control.

It was therefore particularly distressing for her when, at age seventy-nine, she suffered a stroke that left her right arm totally paralyzed. For a year, Victoria seemed to do quite well, but then she became significantly depressed once again. It takes two hands to clothe oneself, so she now had to rely on either the maid or Arthur to help her dress and undress. This fact of life caused her daily helpless outrage.

Feeling terrible, Victoria sought out my friend Jason for medical attention. He recognized her depression and referred her to a psychiatrist. The psychiatrist was no match for her. She kept returning to Jason as her anchor, but during her eighty-first year she also went to a number of other physicians looking for a magical solution. In the process, she accumulated a vast number of different medications, many of them sedatives.

At age eighty-two, she began to overdose on these medications. In the morning she would occasionally be found in her bed by Arthur or, more likely, the maid comatose or semicomatose. One or more of her daughters—and usually Jason—would be called. Sometimes, in explaining these events, Victoria seemed to be senile. How could she possibly remember what pill she had taken, or how many, or why? At other times her daughters sensed that Victoria was only pretending to be forgetful to cover up her experiments with suicide.

As she turned eighty-three, Victoria's overdoses became almost weekly in frequency. The lives of her daughters were being seriously disrupted. They convened for an "intervention" with their mostly beloved mother. They told her it was clear that she was no longer capable of managing her own medications. To manage them and to help her bathe and dress, she obviously needed the care of around-the-clock practical nurses, who were easily affordable. Victoria objected. In doing so, the issue of suicide surfaced. So what if she fatally overdosed? she asked. Unlike Victoria, who was a most secular lady, her daughters were somewhat religiously oriented. They did not want to see her die before her time, they told her, and they offered certain theological reasons why suicide was anathema. Their mother seemed to understand.

Within two days of their appearance, Victoria fired each of the first three practical nurses her daughters hired to care for her. Another intervention was called. Although they would pay attention to her complaints, her daughters informed her, they were rescinding her right to fire the nurses. Victoria was furious. "You might as well stick me away in a nursing home," she argued. Her daughters countered that they were taking over control precisely so they wouldn't have to put her away.

After that there were no more overdoses or firings. Victoria looked defeated and almost in a daze. Three weeks later she seemed to perk up slightly. At the same time, however, she gradually stopped eating. Thin as a rail and a picky eater since her stroke, she claimed she had no appetite. She became weaker and weaker. Her daughters suspected she was deliberately starving herself to death, but she refused to talk about it.

When Victoria was near death from starvation, they called Jason. He went into her room alone. Victoria was alert. Their conversation was very brief. "You're going to kill yourself if you don't eat," he told her.

She looked at him quite keenly. "You've got the point," she said. "And it's my choice."

Back in the living room with her daughters, Jason described the interaction. They decided to give her her choice. Forty-eight hours later, after some semicomatose restlessness, as if she were having bad dreams, Victoria died. Her daughters could not bear to watch it. When it was over, they toasted her as a fine lady who had died largely as she had lived: in control.

———

Victoria's death cannot be classified as a case of euthanasia for several reasons. She did not have a fatal illness. She was not trying to circumvent the actual physical process of dying. She had a clear-cut psychiatric disorder: depression. Indeed, one of the common symptoms of depression is a profound loss of appetite, and this may have had something to do with her choice of the means to kill herself. It would be reasonable simply to call her death a suicide and leave it at that.

This was also not a case of assisted suicide. But here things begin to get cloudy. Except when suicide is assisted, as in certain cases of euthanasia, the customary response of both relatives and health workers is to do their damnedest to prevent it. Yet here Jason, a physician, and Victoria's daughters together decided not to prevent it. Why such neglect? Although suicide is not defined as a crime, assisting one is usually so defined. What about neglecting one? Were Jason and Victoria's daughters guilty of criminal neglect?

I do not believe they were. I do not think there was anything criminal about their deliberate passivity. They were in a bind. To my mind, it might have been far more criminal to exercise the heroic measure of force-feeding a chronically depressed, crippled eighty-three-year-old person who was clearly determined to die as soon as she could. In one sense, they allowed Victoria to pull her own plug.

In any case, life's categories—as in the distinction between murder and suicide—are not always as clear as we might like them to be. Here we are in a never-never land between classical euthanasia and classical suicide. Indeed, it is precisely because Victoria's case demonstrates several classical features of euthanasia that we shall be discussing it further.

———

One thing the case illustrates is the depth of determination some people have to kill themselves. Although not the worst way to die by any means and, as Jason suggested, not at all unheard of, self-starvation is slow. It took Victoria more than three weeks. Throughout that time her intent never wavered.

This determination should not be underestimated. At the risk of being gruesome in order to make the point, I have heard from colleagues of two people who, because they were suicidal, were in the locked ward of a psychiatric hospital and yet still managed to kill themselves with brutal suddenness. One, a young man, simply lowered his head, ran the length of the ward, and bashed his skull against the wall at the far end. The other, a middle-aged woman, was playing bridge one afternoon with two other patients and a nurse. When it came time for her to be the dummy she calmly excused herself, saying she needed to go to the bathroom. When she did not return, the nurse went into the bathroom to check on her. She found the patient dead in a toilet stall. On autopsy it was discovered that the woman had asphyxiated herself by jamming a wad of toilet paper down her own windpipe.

The moral is that not all suicides can be prevented. Euthanasia occurred long before there was any Hemlock Society to encourage it and will continue to occur long after the Hemlock Society is extinct. It would not be a realistic motive of this book to prevent all euthanasia.

Although we are both pro-choice, my wife and I do a little bit to help an organization called Birthright. The purpose of Birthright is not to condemn anyone who has an abortion but to support women who choose not to have an abortion. We have allied ourselves with the organization because we believe in options. So it is with the purpose of this book. It is not to condemn those who opt for euthanasia or even most who assist in it but to encourage the option of a natural death.

Natural Death

Like "murder" and "suicide," "natural death" is not always easy to define. I mentioned people who repeatedly put themselves in danger of being murdered. The fact is, there's an almost infinite variety of self-destructive lifestyles. Let me use my own as an example.

I was taught how to inhale a cigarette at the age of thirteen, and I have been smoking a pack a day ever since—forty-seven years now. Having attempted to quit several times unsuccessfully, I have no intention of trying again. I hope to God I'll never have to. I enjoy smoking enormously.

Although not addicted to alcohol as I am to nicotine, I am strongly habituated to it. With rare exceptions I drink quite heavily every evening. I enjoy this enormously too.

The ill effects of the chronic use of these drugs upon my body are quite obvious. I am an old sixty. In fairness I might add that I have several other chronic diseases, among them glaucoma and severe degenerative disk disease in my spine, that are likely not related to my bad habits.*

In any case, if I die before my time from something directly or indirectly related to my drug use, will it be a so-called natural death? Or might it be thought of as suicide? Since I am likely hastening my death through the use of alcohol and cigarettes, am I practicing euthanasia upon myself?

Before I can answer these questions we need to look at some facts of life. In doing so I may seem to be self-justifying, which is part of the risk of using myself as an example. But it is necessary for me to be up front about my biases.

---

* Anyone with a prurient interest in delving deeper into my bad habits is welcome to read my somewhat autobiographical book *In Search of Stones* and its chapter on addiction in particular.

First, life is not only difficult; it is stressful. Alcohol and cigarettes, in addition to sleep, have been my primary means of coping with stress. They are crutches for me. In reference to my smoking, frequently someone in a lecture audience used to ask me, "How can you, as a psychiatrist, use a crutch?"

I would usually look the questioner in the eye and respond, "Sometimes it is better to walk with crutches than not to walk at all."

We are all of us walking wounded.

Sometimes I would go into greater depth about the nature of addiction and talk about nondrug addictions. Some of these are relatively benign, like the addiction to hand washing or computer games. Others are far more destructive than drug addictions—the addiction to money, for example, or to power, to control, to complacency and self-righteousness. When I was done I would ask of my audience, "Would everyone here who does not have an addiction please raise your hand?" No one ever did.

Life is stressful, and it wears us down, each in our own different way. Although it is impossible for anyone ever to totally put himself in another's shoes, we become more civil and more understanding when we at least try. And there are some things we can all eventually understand.

Occasionally someone in my audience would request, "Dr. Peck, will you give us yet another example of grace?"

"Yes," I responded, "we get to die. I don't know about you, but I'm getting a bit tired. Not so tired that I'm ready to call it quits, but if I thought I'd have to wade through this crap for another three or four hundred years, I would probably cash in my chips sooner rather than later."

Everyone seemed to understand.

———

In the latter years of his life, Freud came to believe that almost everything about human behavior could ultimately be reduced to two opposing forces: Eros and Thanatos.

By Eros, named for the Greek god of erotic love, Freud did not mean just sex, nor did he mean just love. He meant everything involved in the urge to live and grow: what the philosopher Henri Bergson called the élan vital, or life force. This force is not merely psychological; it is embedded in every cell of our bodies. That is why it is not easy to die; each of our cells shrieks out against the necessity. Nor is Eros limited to humans or even to the animal kingdom. It is what the great Welsh poet Dylan Thomas referred to as "The force that through the green fuse drives the flower."

And by Thanatos, named for the Greek personification of death, from which the word "euthanasia" is also derived, Freud meant much more than an overt desire to die, such as that which motivates obvious suicides. He included my addictions and his own. And still more. He meant every neurosis and character disorder. Indeed, he came to the concept through his study of neuroses as he pondered most radically why neurotics would choose to live such narrow, self-defeating lives. Ultimately he meant all that is in us that seeks to avoid life, to avoid reality and the existential suffering inherent in life.

Dylan Thomas gave us not only that beautiful description of the life force but also perhaps the most eloquent exhortation against dying and death ever written. Watching his father's fatal illness, he wrote, "Do not go gentle into that good night; . . . Rage, rage against the dying of the light." Yet the same man who penned those immortal lines was himself dead from alcoholism but a few years later, at the age of thirty-nine. What's going on here? Was Dylan Thomas just an enormous hypocrite?

I do not think so. I have no reason to believe he was any more prone to hypocrisy than the rest of us. What I do know of Dylan Thomas, however, is that he was one of those rare people we sometimes refer to as "larger than life." He was a giant. Within him Eros was gigantic. And so was Thanatos. If it seems he spoke out of both sides of his mouth, it was not hypocrisy in the ordinary sense but the reality of a man in whose breast a titanic death wish continually struggled with an equally titanic life wish. Or we might look at him as a man possessed by Eros. A man who was worn out by Eros. Perhaps not so much a man who died before his time as one who simply lived more in his years than most of us.

My point is that an early death caused by a certain lifestyle—a lifestyle that conceivably may be dictated more by the result of biology and other factors than by psychological choice—should not necessarily be considered an unnatural death. Yet it usually is. And this brings me to a personal pet peeve: the worship of longevity.

The idolatry of longevity in our culture is another element that needs to be factored into the complex equation of the euthanasia debate. It places a dreadful burden upon a great many people, causing them to feel unnecessarily immoral, as if any death before the age of eighty is a betrayal on their part. The message is: "You *should* not die." Naturally, I suppose, the burden of this idolatry is greatest for our cultural idols and those who are famous one way or another. This was dramatized for me with the death in August 1995 of Jerry Garcia, the longtime lead guitarist in the famous rock band ironically called the Grateful Dead, at age fifty-three in a drug treatment center.

Perhaps the media's treatment of his death seemed particularly dramatic to me because I was not a fan. I hardly knew who Jerry Garcia was. But his renown was such that I could not escape reading seemingly innumerable newspaper articles about him at the time. Every one of them mourned his passing. Every one of them also made a point—without great evidence—that he had died solely as a result of his drug-using lifestyle. Nowhere was it so boldly stated, but the message I kept receiving was "You shouldn't have let yourself (and us) down that way, Jerry."

The idolatry of longevity, however, can be just as much of a burden for the not-so-famous, and it is perpetrated not only by the media and the public but equally by private physicians, families, and friends.

————

Simone was a grande dame. Her husband had been a famous man of letters, and she had spent most of her life amid the highest intellectual circles of New York City. By the time I knew her, however, she'd long been widowed and lived quietly in the country. She was a brilliant iconoclastic woman whose company my wife and I very much enjoyed. Although our relationship was primarily social, from time to time Simone referred young people in distress to me for my psychiatric attentions. Usually these patients were poor, and she paid their way. But she was not above haggling over my fees or somewhat haughtily instructing me how she thought the patient should be treated.

I was surprised one day when she phoned to seek an appointment for herself. When she arrived at my office she got right to the point. "My doctor tells me I've got emphysema," she said. "He tells me I have to stop smoking. I don't want to stop. But he's making me feel so *guilty* about it. So I wanted to find out what you think."

"Simone, I'm not sure I'm the most objective person you could talk to about this," I responded. "You know I'm a smoker. That may make me understanding, but it also gives me a big bias."

"You can set aside your bias," Simone snapped. "That's what you've been trained for. And, no, I didn't come to see you because you smoke. I came to you because you're not just a technician like my internist and because you're one of those rare psychiatrists who can talk about God."

"Tell me about your emphysema," I said.

"There's not much to tell. He says my chest X ray shows my lungs are hyperinflated, and my chest sounds hollow when he taps on it. He says smoking is the worst thing I can do to myself, that I'm going to kill myself, and that emphysema's a terrible way to die."

"I don't know whether smoking is the worst thing you could do to yourself," I commented, "but he's right, it's the worst thing for emphysema and emphysema's a tough way to die. How short of breath are you?"

"I'm not," Simone answered. "I've got a chronic cough, but I'm not short of breath at all. Hell, three times a week I take the dog and we climb up the mountain behind my house."

It was, I knew, a substantial mountain. "Does your doctor know how long it will be before you do become short of breath?"

"No. I asked, and he said he couldn't predict that sort of thing."

"If you were to have some real trouble breathing," I inquired, "do you think you'd want to stop smoking then?"

Simone looked at me acutely. "I'm not sure."

"You said something about God?" I hinted.

"I don't give a hoot what that young twerp of a doctor thinks about my smoking, but I do worry what God thinks."

"Go on," I urged.

"I'm sixty-seven years old," Simone said. "I've had a very full and generally fortunate life. I have no desire to remarry. My children are grown and doing quite well by themselves. We're not all that close, but I've become used to that. I'm not depressed. You can see that for yourself, but there's not much that interests me anymore. Frankly, if I died tomorrow I wouldn't mind. But I want it to be up to God when I die. That's why I'm feeling guilty. If I keep on smoking, am I really leaving it up to God? I don't care about the 'defiling the temple of your body' business. That's not what worries me. You know I've never been one of those kind of Christians. But I feel guilty that maybe God wants me to have a long life, and by continuing to smoke I'd be cheating Him. Yet I love my cigarettes. Am I betraying God by not really caring how long I live? There, that's it. What do you think?"

"I don't know the mind of God, Simone."

"Of course you don't. But what do you think?"

"I *think* that God is glad when anyone has had a full life," I said. "Beyond that I don't think He cares much how long the life is. And I think He's going to welcome you royally whenever you happen to die."

"Thank you," Simone said. "That's what I think, too. But it's nice to hear it from someone else."

We chatted for a few minutes more about several mutual friends, and then she left.

Simone continued to smoke and climb the mountain behind her house. Almost two years later to the day of our talk, at the age of sixty-nine, she suddenly collapsed while talking with her occasional housekeeper. She had suffered a massive stroke and was dead within minutes. There is no evidence that her stroke had anything to do with her emphysema and, given the fact that her blood pressure was normal, no great reason to believe it was caused by her smoking.

———

Eros and Thanatos . . . coexisting.

Like Simone, I continue to smoke because I'm addicted, because I enjoy it, because I've had a full life, and—here's the death wish—because I have no ambition to live a long life. Yet just as she regularly climbed the mountain behind her house, so every morning I do twenty minutes of vigorous back exercises. I *hate* these exercises. They are somewhat painful and excruciatingly boring. Nonetheless, I do them faithfully because I know that if I don't, my spine will be frozen solid within a year and shortly thereafter I'll be dead. So I also have a life wish. I must admit, however, that on some mornings it is unclear to me how much my faithfulness represents a burning desire to live and how much it reflects a deep terror of dying. But maybe they're the same thing. And while sometimes I hope I can go like Simone, on other days, for reasons I'll soon be discussing, I hope for a much more lingering death.

One final comment about the way the idolatry of longevity can be a burden is related to aging but not necessarily to death.

The most exciting, playful, pleasant, and creative aspect of my life over the past four years has been the adventure of moving as rapidly as possible into at least semiretirement. This has involved, among other things, leaving the lecture circuit. Although I am not nearly as much of a public figure as Jerry Garcia, thank God, dozens of people these past years have exclaimed to me, "But you *can't* retire!"

Lord, let your people go.

Finally, a Definition

The Euthanasia Society of America, founded in 1938, defined euthanasia as the "termination of human life by painless means for the purpose of ending severe physical suffering."

This is a totally inadequate definition. The society's definition does not distinguish between the will of the person whose life is terminated and the will of the terminator. It says nothing about whether the severe physical suffering is temporary or chronic, treatable or untreatable. It does not posit whether the "dis-ease" is terminal or not. It ignores the issue of pulling the plug in cases where the patient is unconscious and therefore presumably not in physical pain. It does not distinguish clearly between emotional distress and physical distress. It certainly doesn't cover the cases handled by Dr. Kevorkian and others who also operate under the banner of euthanasia, cases where the ending of severe physical suffering is not the real issue at all.

I make no pretense of being a rigorous scholar. I have made no effort to read all of the literature on the subject. What I have read, however, also fails to make such critical distinctions. One book, *Euthanasia: The Moral Issues,** for instance, although published in 1989, does not even attempt a definition. It merely includes divergent opinions of lawyers, physicians, and others attempting to be ethicists on a wide variety of subjects ranging all the way from abortion to pulling the plug, from suicide to murder, with little specification. It is very confusing.

I do not mean to impugn the intellectual rigor of any scholar. But society—its mores and its technology—is changing rapidly. Matters that were of grave concern a decade or two ago have been largely resolved, and new concerns have arisen. Relatively recent scholarly articles are already and inevitably out of date. Meanwhile the issue of euthanasia is becoming one of ever more heated debate. At the same time the debate is virtually incoherent. It has no way of being coherent without an adequate definition. And the more specific the definition, the more coherent the debate will be. The moment has come for the most specific definition possible if we are to have any sense of perspective whatsoever. I therefore propose the following, deliberately narrow definition:

---

* Robert M. Baird and Stuart E. Rosenbaum, eds., Contemporary Issues in Philosophy Series (Buffalo, N.Y.: Prometheus Books, 1989).

> True euthanasia is the act of suicide, assisted or unassisted, with
> the predominant motive to avoid the existential emotional suf-
> fering inherent in physical dying from a currently existing fatal
> disease in its relatively terminal stages.

Typically, however, nothing is quite as clear as I might like it to
be. Earlier in this chapter I recounted the story of Victoria, who
starved herself to death in her old age, as an example of a case that
fell into a never-never land between euthanasia and other types of
suicide. With the increasing age of our population I suspect this
never-never land will be receiving increasing attention. Consequently I believe it deserves a category of its own that I would call
quasi-euthanasia—"quasi" means "resembling"—to distinguish it
from true euthanasia, despite the multiple similarities of the two. Here
is my definition of this second category:

> Quasi-euthanasia is the act of suicide, assisted or unassisted, with
> the predominant motive to avoid the existential emotional
> suffering inherent in a debilitating old age or a chronically
> debilitating physical disorder for which there is no hope of cure.

I suspect the euthanasia debate will continue to generate more heat
than light until society learns to limit the use of the word
"euthanasia" to the two narrowly defined categories above—and to
exclude all other issues, not because they are unimportant but
because they deserve to be discussed as essentially separate issues in
their own right.

———

That means excluding a lot.

Abortion and capital punishment would be excluded. As indicated, they need to be the subject of separate debates in their own
right.

Questions about the employment or nonemployment of heroic
medical measures to prolong life would also be excluded. I have
pointed out that these questions are no longer a matter for national

debate. Twenty to thirty years ago they very much were. That was when the issue of pulling the plug was unmentionable and hence not subject to appropriate local decision making. But, as I indicated, the climate has changed. Indeed, I am most grateful to the euthanasia movement for the role it played in helping to change the climate. Due to its success, however, the matter is no longer an issue of euthanasia; pulling the plug and the timing in doing so is merely a question of good medical practice.

The subject of physical pain would also be excluded. Here again I would not have so argued a decade or two ago, and again I wish to express my gratitude to the euthanasia movement for whatever role it played in encouraging the development of hospice care and the beginning of a changing climate elsewhere in regard to the relief of physical pain. I do not mean to imply that the work is finished. National attention is still needed to combat the lingering prevalence of inadequate medical treatment for pain. But the answer to physical pain is not euthanasia; it is physician, nurse, and patient education to the point where adequate physical pain relief is an acknowledged patient right.

So-called mercy killing would be excluded for all of the reasons already discussed.

Finally, all manner of suicide would be excluded except those cases where chronically debilitating or terminal physical illness is not only present but is the primary motivating circumstance. As we shall see, on one level suicide is suicide, and the act of euthanasia as defined shares at least one dynamic with most other forms of suicide. But euthanasia also has its own dynamics, and to lump it together with the other varieties of suicide can again only obscure the issues.*

Assuming the reader can accept my rather precise definitions of

---

* For instance, although the public generally associates the agenda of the Hemlock Society with euthanasia, it has been unclear at times whether its unstated agenda may be to encourage suicide of some other types as well. It seems telling that two of its four founding members have killed themselves. Of those two, one had no physical illness and the other had an early-stage cancer that was not demonstrably terminal or debilitating.

true euthanasia and quasi-euthanasia, along with all that they exclude, I believe we are now at a point where we can view the euthanasia debate in its proper updated (1997) perspective. That doesn't mean that the debate will be eliminated. What it does mean, however, is that the issues of debate are few and clear, even stark. We shall see that, in essence, there are but two issues: the *meaning* of life and death. We shall see that these two issues are inextricably interwoven. Moreover, we shall see that each is subject to two fields of inquiry which for several centuries have been held to be separate: theology and psychology. That separation, however, is specious. I have already spoken of existential, emotional suffering as being psychospiritual. I do not hope to end all debate. I do not expect the reader to accept my opinions blandly, but I do ask her or him to strive to think on both the level of theology and the level of psychology and make an effort to integrate the two.

Part II

AN UNDERLYING SIMPLICITY

SPIRITUAL PERSPECTIVES

Chapter 5

SECULARISM

In the Introduction I dated the beginning of my unease about euthanasia to the suicide pact of Dr. and Mrs. Van Dusen in 1975. The case was one of those I have defined as quasi-euthanasia. Neither of the Van Dusens was in the terminal stage of a specific fatal illness. They were, however, chronically debilitated in their old age. Dr. Van Dusen, who was sixty-nine, had suffered a stroke that had severely impaired his ability to speak—a particularly great affliction for a renowned preacher who loved the pulpit. His wife, a woman in her eighties, had suffered for years from crippling and painful arthritis. Both had long been public members of the Euthanasia Society of America, and, as was clear in suicide letters to their friends and family, they intended their deaths to be a public statement as well as a relief from their personal suffering.

Had I known these facts at the time I might have been less surprised. But I didn't. All I knew was that Dr. Van Dusen was a famous liberal Christian theologian. My mild sense of shock at the event was entirely related to his religious identity. Without quite understanding why, I felt that something was deeply incompatible between the profession of religious belief and the advocacy of euthanasia.

I might also have been less surprised had I back then any understanding of the nature of secularism.

———

It so happened that the next decade was one of intense spiritual and religious development for me. By 1985 I had become quite sophisticated on the subject of spirituality . . . and on the nature of secularism.

Late in that decade I received the only request I ever had to assist with euthanasia. It was from an acquaintance of mine who was, believe it or not, a clergyman. Not yet elderly, he was in vigorous physical health. Nor was he the least depressed. He asked me to prescribe for him—and possibly for his spouse as well—a large supply of potent sleeping pills. He was quite frank about it. "I have no trouble sleeping," he told me. I want the pills in case I become physically ill, seriously ill. I believe in planning this sort of thing, and I want a supply on hand, for my sake and my family's, so I won't have a prolonged and messy death."

I rejected his request, simply stating in a single sentence that fulfilling it would be incompatible with my beliefs. I did not elaborate, nor did he ask me to do so, and that was that.

We had worked quite closely together in several medical areas, and I knew him well, but I would not have called us friends. Although he was a loving man whose pertinacity and fidelity to his parishioners I much admired, we were ideologically many, many miles apart. In particular, despite his professional identity as a minister, he was one of the most secular people I have ever known. I did not elaborate on my beliefs or attempt to change his mind about euthanasia because I knew he would only resent me for my sermonizing.

There are a remarkable number of morals to this brief story. The greatest moral is that euthanasia, as I have defined it, is a profoundly secular phenomenon. To this we shall return over and again.

One of the lesser morals is that there is not necessarily any concordance between secularism and religious identity. Religious professionals—like my acquaintance, some others I have known, and possibly the Van Dusens—may be secular to their core. Conversely, many who are not overtly religious in the least may be among the most deeply spiritual of people. Don't get me wrong. I'm not saying that the overtly religious are all hypocrites any more than all the seemingly secular are the religious in disguise. What I am saying is that a superficial religious or secular identity is simply that: superficial. The underlying reality of the person may or may not coincide with the superficial identity.

Secularism is a complex system of beliefs or assumptions, perhaps most simply defined by comparing it with its opposite. This is what the theologian Michael Novak did so clearly when he distinguished between what he called the sacred consciousness and the secular consciousness.*

The individual with a secular consciousness essentially thinks that he is the center of the universe. Such people tend to be quite intelligent. They know full well that they are but one of six billion human beings scratching out an existence on the surface of a medium-sized planet that is a small component of a tiny solar system within one galaxy among countless galaxies . . . and that every other human being thinks that *he* is the center of the universe. Consequently, intelligent though they may be, people with a secular consciousness are likely to feel a bit lost within this hugeness and, despite their imagined centrality, often to experience a sense of meaninglessness and insignificance.

The person with a sacred consciousness, on the other hand, does not think of himself as the center of the universe. For him the center resides elsewhere, specifically in God—in the sacred. Yet with his lack of centrality, he is actually less likely than the secularist to feel himself insignificant or meaningless. This is so because he sees himself existing in relationship with that Sacred Other, and he derives his meaning and importance from this relationship.

But let us beware of simplistic black-and-white thinking that can so often lead to condemnation. Both types of consciousness come

---

* *Ascent of the Mountain, Flight of the Dove,* rev. ed. (New York: Harper & Row, 1978). I have used his distinction in several of my books.

in hybrid varieties as often as they exist in thoroughbred forms. It is common for people to fall in between, with one foot in sacred consciousness and the other in secular consciousness. Moreover, there are different types of secularism and religiosity. Specifically, we need to comprehend secularism within the context of the stages of religious or spiritual development. I have written about four such stages.* Very briefly, they are as follows:

- Stage I, which I label Chaotic, Antisocial. In this most primitive stage people may appear either religious or secular, but either way, their belief system is profoundly superficial. It may be thought of as a stage of lawlessness.
- Stage II, which I label Formal, Institutional. This is a stage of the letter of the law in which religious fundamentalists (meaning most religious people) are to be found.
- Stage III I label Skeptic, Individual. Here is where the majority of secularists are situated. People in this stage are usually scientific-minded, rational, moral, and humane. Their outlook is predominantly materialistic. They tend to be not only skeptical of the spiritual but uninterested in anything that cannot be proven.
- Stage IV I have called Mystical, Communal. In this most mature stage of religious development, which may be thought of as one of the spirit of the law, women and men are rational but do not make a fetish of rationalism. They have begun to doubt their own doubts. They feel deeply connected to an unseen order of things, although they cannot fully define it. They are comfortable with the mystery of the sacred.†

---

* The person best known for writing on this subject is Professor James W. Fowler of the Candler School of Theology at Emory University, the author of, among other works, *Stages of Faith: The Psychology of Human Development and the Quest for Meaning* (San Francisco: Harper, 1981). Jim speaks of six stages, which I condense into four in the interest of simplicity, but basically we are saying the same thing.

† I have described these stages in much greater depth in *The Different Drum* (New York: Simon & Schuster, 1987) and, to a lesser extent, in both *Further Along the Road Less Traveled* and *The Road Less Traveled and Beyond*.

Again I must caution that these stages should not be taken simplistically. Superficially, many people might appear to be in a more advanced stage than they truly are. A considerable number of New Agers and scientists, for instance, are basically fundamentalists, while some evangelicals are Stage IV mystics. Furthermore, there are not only gradations within each stage but also people who are in transition from one stage to the next. And while some are developing, others, for various reasons, are deeply stuck, or fixated, in a particular stage.

Nonetheless, the stages are essentially developmental. One of the things this means is that the secularists of Stage III are actually more spiritually developed than the majority of religious people. Many in Stage II are highly critical of the secular humanists but would be well advised to become more humanist themselves.

Still, the criticism of secular humanism is not entirely off base. Humanism—the belief that humans are precious—is noble, but secular humanism is often like a house built on sand. Having no roots in theology, the humanism of Stage III people may be blown away quite easily in times of stress and temptation. Journalism, for instance, is a disproportionately secular Stage III occupation. Its practitioners regard themselves as deeply humanistic. Yet it is not uncommon for their humanism to fly out the window in their eagerness to get a story.

I do not mean to imply that secularists are any more prone to hypocrisy than others. Perhaps the greatest sin of all is one of which only the overtly religious can be guilty: the sin of blasphemy. Blasphemy is not the use of dirty, bawdy language or of saying "God damn," as so many think. Rather it is the use of sweet religious language to cloak irreligious behavior. "Using the name of the Lord in vain" means espousing God in words while denying God in action. It is the failure even to attempt to integrate one's way of life with one's proclaimed theology.

I also don't want to imply that the two clergy I have mentioned— Dr. Van Dusen and my acquaintance who was so secular-minded— were guilty of blasphemy. Remember that the stages are developmental. It is not uncommon for a young man in Stage II to enter the ministry only to soon evolve into Stage III, where he begins to doubt the very existence of God. It is not my intent to cover all the many problems—as well as the blessings—that these developmental stages can produce. Just one such predicament is that of the minister whose job it is every Sunday morning to preach about a divinity in which he's no longer sure he believes.

The greatest problem produced by the stages of spiritual development is that persons in each stage believe their particular outlook is superior. This is mitigated somewhat in Stage IV, where people have begun to envision their entire life as a pilgrimage, where they see themselves as being on a spiritual journey with a long way to go. People in Stages II and III, however, believe that they have *arrived*. This is most blatant in the case of Stage II religious fundamentalists who feel that they've got God all sewn up in their back pocket, that they have the whole truth and nothing but the truth, and that those poor slobs who think differently are heathens, beyond the pale and unsaved.

The secularists of Stage III are more discreet, but they too feel they have arrived. They look down upon the religious as essentially irrational, if not primitive. In regard to the euthanasia debate, such disparagement of others is not the most problematic issue. The core problem is that they think they have no further distance to evolve. They have no sense of the soul's journey and, unlike the religious, often no sense of the soul at all.

———

Although the man gives me the shivers, I suppose I must credit Dr. Kevorkian more than any other individual for the genesis of this book. Almost single-handedly over the past five years he has turned the debate over euthanasia—euthanasia as I have defined it—into a national issue within the United States.

He did not, however, inspire me to write this book. What has inspired me is the public response to his behavior. I have been surprised by the number of people who admire him. I have been even more surprised by the larger number who feel no affection for him but deeply approve of what he has been doing in assisting the suicides of those who are ill. Most of all, I have been surprised by the huge number of Americans who do not find Dr. Kevorkian's work particularly objectionable. As I commented in the Introduction, the euthanasia debate in many quarters has seemed to me strangely passionless. It is this passionlessness—this vast, tacit approval of euthanasia—that has alarmed me.

The extent of the active or passive support for euthanasia in America bespeaks the depth of secularism in our society. As I have taken pains to point out, secularism is a most understandable phenomenon and not alarming per se. Yet when it comes to the issue of euthanasia, I feel deeply disquieted. Why? What is going on, I believe, is the widespread denial of the human soul. And it is this pervasive lack of acknowledgment of the soul that seems to me to bode so ill for our future . . . unless we can awaken.

I am implying, of course, that I myself am awakened. If this is the case, it is not a fact in which I take any particular pride. I did not *earn* my soul or my awareness of it. It is, in a sense, something that just happened to me.

I have chosen to write from both a subjective and an objective point of view. In the pages to come I shall often write about the human soul as if I were an utterly detached theologian. Yet I do not know how to do justice to the subject without also writing personally. Besides, there is a minor tradition within science—to which I subscribe—that the scientist should lay out any bias he might have before proceeding to the facts. So let me begin with a bit of the personal, with the understanding that I shall also be returning from time to time to the subjective and personal in the midst of my seemingly more objective discussion of the soul and of its implications for the meaning of human existence.

As far back as I can remember, I always felt connected to something larger than myself. Throughout my childhood that something was primarily the beauty—and power—of nature. I loved the wind and all manner of storms. I loved to watch the snow fall and to smell the first scent of spring in the air. I thrilled to waves crashing on the beach, to salt marshes and to mountains, to forests and glens on cool September days. I assumed that God was somehow behind all this, lurking in the background of my life. But I took Her or Him pretty much for granted and paid little or no attention to this matter of the soul.

Because my parents were relatively wealthy I had far more exposure to the beauty of nature than most, and I have wondered whether my sense of connectedness might not be accounted for by this good fortune. Yet over the years I have met many from backgrounds of unrelieved squalor who early on had this sense at least as strongly as I. Conversely, I have also met many raised in luxury who lacked the sense.

Be that as it may, at age thirteen I went off to Exeter, a prestigious boys' boarding school. My older brother, whom I very much looked up to, also was at Exeter, happy and successful. It was not just that my parents very much wanted me to go there; I myself wanted to go there and succeed like my brother.

Only I was miserable there from the start. After two and a half years of toughing it out, I quit. My parents were so disappointed—even horrified—that they sent me to a psychiatrist. This seemed quite appropriate to me. I was depressed. I felt like a quitter and a total failure. Within a year, however, I was thriving and knew that changing schools had been a good move for me.

I recount this story, as I often have elsewhere, because it marked the beginning of my encounter with my soul. Metaphorically, it also seemed to mark the beginning of my life. Everyone has a sense of his own *I,* a sense of *I*-dentity. This *I* is sometimes referred to as the ego, sometimes the self. But now it gradually dawned on me that there had to be more to it than that. You see, *I* wanted to go to Exeter. I wanted my *self* to succeed there. I most definitely didn't want to disappoint my parents or to quit. Yet I did. But if I didn't want to quit, then *who* was doing it?

Most psychiatrists would simply say that my ego was conflicted. Some would say more specifically that my ego was in conflict with my true self, implying that the self is somehow larger and deeper than the ego. The latter explanation I can live with, but it seems to me to beg the question. What is this true self? Why doesn't it get defined? Could it be the soul, and if it is, then why isn't it so named? And what might be the definition of the soul?

Secular psychiatrists would say that the true self—the whole self—is a conglomerate of multiple psychic components: the id, the ego, and the superego; the conscious and the unconscious; the genetically determined temperament; and possibly more. No wonder I might have been in conflict! So many different parts. These parts are real, and they can indeed be in conflict. Moreover, effective psychotherapy can be accomplished using this conglomerate model.

The problem was, I didn't feel like a walking conglomerate back then. And, strangely, the older I grew and the more I recognized the reality of these different parts of me, the less I felt like a conglomerate. I felt that something deeper yet was going on, something very important that somehow made me larger than myself. I had come to recognize that I had a soul.

The word "soul" is probably in the vocabulary of every second-grader. We hear of "soul food" and "soul music." We speak of particular people as "having soul." While these uses of the word may be more popular than accurate, the fact is that almost everyone understands the real concept. Then why is it that the word "soul" is not in the professional lexicon of psychiatrists, other mental health workers, students of the mind, and physicians in general?

There are two reasons. One is that the concept of God is inherent in the concept of the soul, and "God talk" is virtually off-limits within these relatively secular professions. Religious though individuals in these professions might be personally, they would not want to offend their secular colleagues. Nor, for that matter, would they care to lose their jobs. The fact is that to speak of God or the soul in their professional gatherings would be politically incorrect.

The other reason is that these professionals properly have a taste for intellectual rigor, and the soul is something that cannot be completely defined. We can only fully define those things that are smaller than we are. I have in my office, for instance, an electric space heater. Were I an electrical engineer, I could take that heater apart and explain to you exactly how it works. I could precisely define it, so to speak. Except for one matter. The heater is connected by a plug to something called electricity, and there are aspects of electricity, or energy, that even the most advanced nuclear physicists cannot explain or define. This is so because when we get into electricity we have gotten into something that is bigger than we are.

Many things are too large to submit to any single adequate definition: love, death, prayer, consciousness, light, and so on. I do not believe it an accident that all such things have some connection to God, the largest, most indefinable and mysterious thing of all.* Yet this impossibility of adequate definition is not the primary stumbling block. Psychiatrists have no difficulty including "light," "love," and "consciousness" in their professional vocabulary. Their primary problem with the "soul word" is the blatancy of its connection to God.

———

Polls indicate that the vast majority of Americans believe in God. The concept of the soul is embodied in our everyday vocabulary. Yet these words—"God" and "soul"—cannot be mentioned in medical professional meetings, and scholars frequently refer to our society as secular. Why?

There are significant numbers of Stage III secularists in positions of power in our society. As noted, they tend to dominate the media. They also dominate the field of psychiatry. They would not be so powerful, however, were it not for the fact that many of the supposedly religious are not particularly strong in their faith. Many do not apply their religious ethics to their practice of commerce. They are as obsessed with money and accumulating possessions as those who never attend church or synagogue. They may picket abortion clinics, but with hardly a peep they've allowed their public education system to become a void of values where the curriculum is dic-

———

* This is the reason for the Muslim prohibition of all images of God, since any such image would represent but a tiny piece of the whole reality and hence be a desecration of sorts.

tated by a soulless notion of knowledge. The proverbial observer from Mars would have great difficulty discerning a difference between those who are religious and those who are not. Most in both camps look more like materialists than anything else. Were it not a contradiction in terms, one might speak about "the secularization of religion."

Ours is definitely a secular society. The reason is not so much the strength of our secular minority, I believe, as the weakness of its religious majority. Our religion is watered down to the point where most of the religious are more passionate about their minor, divisive doctrinal disputes than about their spiritual effectiveness.

I have implied that it is not the secularists who worry me in relation to the widespread denial of the soul that empowers the euthanasia movement. It is the religious majority who do not take their religion seriously. It is not surprising that secularists should deny the soul. But there are two types of denial. One is to reject something outright. The other is to ignore it—to speak of it but fail to afford it significant credence or importance. What most alarms me about the secularism of our society is that because the religious do not take their religion seriously, they don't take the soul seriously. They simply don't give it much thought.

Let us now begin to give it the degree of thought it deserves.

Chapter 6

THE CREATURELINESS
OF HUMANS

The fact that many things can't be perfectly defined doesn't mean we shouldn't talk about them. Or that to talk about them well we shouldn't attempt the best definition possible.* Therefore, with full awareness of its inadequacy, let me be so bold as to offer the following definition of the soul:

> The soul is a God-created, God-nurtured, unique, developable, immortal human spirit.

I imagine this definition will strike most dyed-in-the-wool secularists as so much gibberish. My greater concern is that it may strike some religious people as so obvious that it does not merit further consideration. The definition does have a certain stark simplicity, but obvious it is not. Indeed, the entirety of this chapter will be

---

* For instance, in *The Road Less Traveled* I offered a definition of "love"—the will to extend one's self for the purpose of nurturing one's own or another's spiritual growth—that many seem to have found helpful even though I acknowledged its inadequacy from the start and concluded by speaking of the things the definition failed to explain.

devoted to explicating it—parsing each of its components in order, with particular reference to its relevance to the issue of euthanasia.

God-Created

We commonly refer to all members of the entire animal kingdom, including ourselves, as creatures. By this we imply that we are creations. We have been created.

By whom?

"By our parents," secularists would say right off the bat. How? By their mating, their rutting around in bed or in the backseat of a car or some other location, whether inside or outside the state of marriage, with or without the intent to produce a child. Specifically by the father in a moment of reflexive sexual arousal ejaculating millions of different sperm into the mother's vagina, one of which sperm, for reasons we do not understand in the least, manages to beat all the others to an egg that happens to be available on that day of the month, thereby establishing a genetic combination that has never before existed on the face of the earth and never will again.

As purely genetic creations (with the possible rare exception of identical twins) each of us human beings is unique. Each of us is also an accident. We are accustomed to referring to an unplanned pregnancy as "an accident." If the biology of reproduction is all that's involved, the best-planned pregnancy in the world is only a tiny bit less accidental than any other.

"But the biology of reproduction is not all that's involved," the secularists would immediately retort. "There's nurture as well as nature. Parents also create children by the way they raise their offspring." As someone who practiced psychotherapy for twenty years on the strength of that supposition, I have a certain investment in its truth. I do believe there is a tendency for good parenting to "create" children who are mentally healthier than they might otherwise have been. And that bad parenting has a tendency to diminish the mental health of progeny.

But only a tendency. There is no one-to-one correspondence. I've known saints who were raised in the most abusive of homes and thoroughbred criminals whose parents heroically and genuinely loved them. If both nature and nurture are involved in the creation of the human personality, obviously there'll be some conflict between the two—some infants with good genes born into bad homes and some with defective genes born into the best of homes. This might be called the "Bad Seed" theory, after a drama about a murderous little girl who wreaked fatal havoc with her most decent parents.

Yet here again we're involved primarily in the realm of meaningless accident. What might good parents have done to deserve a bad kid . . . or careless parents to earn a good one? Perhaps the answer to this question will become clearer someday if we can develop tests for psychological goodness and badness. For the moment, however, family dynamics remain relatively obscure and we've hardly begun to be able to read the genes much better than tea leaves. The fact is, we understand very little about either the biology or the psychology of character.

Or the sociology. Sociologists would say that our character is largely shaped by our culture and even point out that there can be such a thing as a national character. They are significantly on the money, yet they too fail to account for the frequent exceptions. Although I hardly understood my fifteen-year-old motives at the time, as I look back on my decision to quit Exeter it is clear to me that I was driven by an instinctive and profound dissatisfaction with the culture of that school and, indeed, most of the WASP culture it represented. Why? What caused me at such an early age to reject almost totally the entire culture in which I had been raised, to be a cultural misfit and a sociological accident?

I am not denying in the least the powerful influences of genes and child care and culture in creating the self. What I am saying is that there is a missing piece to the picture. A big missing piece.

I believe that huge missing piece is God. I believe that God subtly works through our genes, our childhood, our culture—and through other means—in our creation. How He or She does this, I have no idea. It is a behind-the-scenes operation.

Because it is such a hidden, mysterious, offstage operation, incapable of being proven, secularists discount it as, at best, a theory and, as such, not to be taken seriously. I believe the opposite. I believe its behind-the-scenes nature signifies its extreme importance. It is the primary source of our being, the source of creation, the Author who is not onstage but is more responsible than any other for bringing the drama to life.

There are three immediate implications of this "God theory."

One is that we are more than our genes, more than our childhood upbringing, more than our culture, more even than our self. Specifically, along with all these things, we have a soul. No, not just along, but at the very core of our being.

A second is that we are not mere accidents. I am not saying there is nothing accidental about life. Again, I'm saying that there is something more: namely, that in the most important of ways we—each of us—have been *designed*.

The third implication is that we have been created—designed— for a purpose. We may not know what that purpose is. We are actors in a cosmic drama, and the best we can hope for in this lifetime is to get little glimpses of what the drama is all about and little glimpses of how we might best play our roles. And there *are* glimpses. Indeed, quite a number of them, as we soon shall see.

But what does this have to do with euthanasia?

Euthanasia, as defined, is a form of suicide. I hope I have made it clear that the suffering of those who commit suicide may be dreadful, that suicides often deserve our sympathy, and that my motive is to condemn the sin, not the sinner. Nonetheless, I do regard most suicide as a sin. Specifically the sin of arrogance. Whether they are aware of it or not, what most people who commit suicide are saying to themselves is "It's my life to do with what I want. Since I am my own creator I have the right to be my own destroyer." This is arrogance in spades.

We are *not* our own creators. I can no more create myself than I can create a rose or an iris. I can nurture and steward flowers, but I cannot create them. Similarly, I can nurture and steward myself— indeed, I have an obligation to do so—but I am not my own creation or property. Along with my parents and my culture, God has created me. God has a stake in my existence. If anyone owns the "property" of me, it is not my agent or my publisher, not my family, not even myself; it is God. This is not solely my life to do with as I see fit. To kill myself is to deny God, to deny Her timing and right to my life.

More than anything else, to my mind, what is meant by God creating us in His own image is that He gave us free will. So of course we can commit suicide. He gave us the freedom to deny Him, to reject Him and sneer at Him. He also gave us the freedom to choose to cooperate with Him. Our relationship with God is not passive. We can ignore the relationship. We can run away from it. But if we choose to attend to it with some diligence and attempt to cooperate with God as best we can, while we cannot be our sole creators, we can become co-creators. Therein lies the essence of our potential glory.

I have suggested that the choice of euthanasia generally represents a denial of the soul, a rejection of its Creator and Her timing. The converse is also true. The choice of a natural death may represent an act of co-creation with God. This doesn't mean that secularists never accept natural death. What it does mean is that many actually and deliberately cooperate with God when they are dying and may thereby ease the process.

One of the motives of those who choose euthanasia is to avoid a prolonged or messy death. I suggest, however, that the choice to cooperate with God is not unlikely to result in a less prolonged and messy death. I took a relatively favorable stance for pulling the plug because physicians, with their use of technology, are not only trying to beat death but also in many instances trying to beat God. Similarly a significant number of patients unnecessarily prolong and mess up their dying because they too are trying to beat death and beat God.

Recall the case of Malcolm who was dying from cancer of the lung in the hospital while undergoing radiation treatment and trying to force himself to eat. He didn't want to be a quitter; he was a fighter. But when I pointed out to him that it was not necessarily bad to quit, he decided, with his wife, to go home, where he died peacefully within two days. We had not discussed theology, so for all I know, his choice was simply to quit. But in my imagination he also chose to cooperate—to give in to God.

God-Nurtured

My primary identity is that of a scientist before that of a religious person. I believe in—I require—evidence wherever possible. I am not sure how seriously I would take this God theory had my soul simply been created before my birth and memory and had God left it alone after that. But God has not left me alone. Ever since my early adolescence I have been aware from time to time that God has been speaking to me and gently interfering in my life.

I am saying here not only that God creates us but that She continues to attempt to nurture us throughout our lives.

The evidence? I could fill an entire book with it. Indeed I filled a significant portion of my first book, *The Road Less Traveled,* with examples of God's nurturance, which were subsumed under the title "Grace," and I have continued to write about other such examples in other books. But this book is about euthanasia, and I mention God's grace only as it relates to the subject. So here I shall restrict myself to two personal examples.

One of the ways God speaks to us—attempts to nurture us—is through some of our dreams—those that Carl Jung labeled "big dreams." Again I could give many examples, but because it so perfectly fits my purposes here, I am going to recount one that I have written about before in *Further Along the Road Less Traveled* and in *The Road Less Traveled and Beyond:*

> After *The Road Less Traveled* had been accepted for publication, I decided I deserved a vacation. I didn't want to do anything with the family, but I didn't want to travel alone and just sit on the beach someplace. Then I got this crazy idea to go on a retreat—that would be something different! So I went off for two weeks to a convent.
>
> I had a number of agendas for this retreat. One was to try to

stop smoking, which I succeeded in doing for that time alone. But my largest agenda item was to decide what to do if by some dim chance *The Road Less Traveled* made me famous. If that happened, should I give up my privacy and go out on the lecture circuit, or should I retire into the woods like J. D. Salinger and immediately get an unlisted phone number? I didn't know which way I wanted to go. And I didn't know which way God wanted me to go. So, at the top of my agenda was the hope that in the quietness of the retreat and the holiness of the atmosphere, I might get a revelation from God about how I should deal with this dilemma.

I thought I would do my best to help God out by paying attention to my dreams, since I believe that dreams can serve a certain revelatory function. So I started writing down my dreams, but they were mostly very simple images of bridges or gates, and they didn't tell me anything I didn't already know—namely, that I was at a point of transition in my life.

But I had one dream that was far more complex. In this dream, I was an onlooker in a middle-class home. In this two-car family there was a seventeen-year-old boy who was the kind of son that every mother and father would love to have. He was president of the senior class in high school; he was going to be valedictorian at graduation time; he was captain of the high school football team; he was good-looking; he worked hard after school at a part-time job; and if all that wasn't enough, he had a girlfriend who was sweet and demure. Moreover, the boy had his driver's license, and was an unusually responsible, mature driver for his age. Only his father wouldn't let him drive. Instead, the father insisted on driving this boy wherever he had to go—football practice, job, dates, proms. And to add insult to injury, the father insisted that the boy pay him five dollars a week out of his hard-earned after-school earnings for the privilege of being driven around, which he was quite capable of doing himself. I awoke from this dream with a sense of absolute fury and outrage at what an autocratic monster the father was.

I didn't know what to make of the dream. It didn't seem to make any sense at all. But three days after I had written it down, when I was rereading what I had written, I noticed that I had capitalized the *F* in "Father." So I said to myself, "You don't happen to suppose that the father in this dream is God the Father, do you? And if that's the case, you don't suppose that you might be that seventeen-year-old boy?" And then I finally realized that I had gotten a revelation. God was saying to me, "Hey, Scotty, you just pay your dues and leave the driving to me."

It is interesting that I had always thought of God as being the ultimate good guy. Yet in my dream I had cast Him in the role of autocratic, overcontrolling villain, or at least I was responding to Him as such, with fury and outrage and hatred. The problem, of course, was that this wasn't the revelation I had hoped for. It wasn't what I wanted to hear. I wanted some little bit of advice from God such as one might get from his agent or accountant, which I would be free to accept or reject. I didn't want a *big* revelation, particularly not one where God said, "I'm going to do the driving after this."

Twenty years later I'm still trying to live up to this revelation, to abandon myself to God by learning the surrender that welcomes His or Her being in the driver's seat of my still-adolescent life.

I have chosen to rerecount this dream because of its dramatic relationship to my ego or self. As I said, it was not a dream that *I* wanted. Its script was not one that I my*self* would have written. It clearly came from someplace else, some reality different from that of my ego or self. Indeed, it depicted me as a seventeen-year-old when I was actually a supposedly mature forty-one at the time. It was an insult to my ego and was calling me to ego-surrender.

Note that at the time I was attempting to cooperate with God. Yet it still took me three days to get the message, because I was so resistant. How long would it have taken me, I wonder, had I not been desirous of a cooperative relationship with the Creator of my soul? Probably forever.

———

Among the ways in which God speaks to us, the most common is through Her "still small voice." This is a strange phenomenon. It is not in the least a great booming masculine voice from heaven; as the Bible puts it, the voice is "still" and "small"—so still and small it is hardly a voice at all. It seems to originate inside us and for many may be indistinguishable from a thought. Only it is not our own thought.

The closeness between this voice and an ordinary thought calls for a note of caution. One would be ill-advised to go around regarding all or most of his thoughts as the word of God. That could quickly lead to insanity.

There are some guidelines for discernment. First, take time (unless you are in an emergency situation) to do a reality test to determine whether this voice might be that of the Holy Spirit or merely your own thought. And you will have that time. Indeed, if you disregard the voice at first, it will almost always repeat itself.

Second, this voice of the Holy Spirit—or Comforter, as Jesus called it—is always constructive, never destructive. It may call upon you to do something different, and that may feel slightly risky, but it won't be a major risk. If you hear a voice telling you to kill yourself, to cheat or steal, or to blow all your life savings on a yacht, get yourself off to a psychiatrist.

On the other hand, the voice will usually seem just a little bit crazy. This is what distinguishes it from your own thought. There is a faintly alien quality to it, as if it came from elsewhere, which it does. This is inevitable. God doesn't need to speak to us to tell us something we already know or to push us in ways we don't require pushing. Her voice always comes to us with something new and unexpected—to open us up and therefore to break gently through our existing boundaries and barriers. Consequently, one's usual reaction upon first hearing the voice of the Holy Spirit is to shake one's head.

I need to preface my second and very recent example of God's nurturance of me by acknowledging that I am not only a poor scholar in general but a particularly poor student of the Bible. As far as the New Testament is concerned, I've never been able to get through the Book of Revelation, and I've had hard sledding with the Letters. As for the Old Testament, I've simply never read much of it.*

Be that as it may, this incident occurred in early autumn 1995. I'd completed the first draft of a new novel, *In Heaven as on Earth,* and it had been accepted for publication. The moment for rewriting was upon me, and I had a problem. In the first draft I'd used myself as the main character, but I was certain this needed to be changed in the second draft. During the rewriting I needed to step outside myself and otherwise improve the development of the character. Yet I've never been very good at stepping outside myself. Moreover, the plot demanded that the main character be someone very much like me—specifically an intellectual with psychiatric training and an amateur theologian to boot. Minor though this problem might seem, solving it was important for the book, and I hadn't the faintest idea how to do that.

At this point one afternoon, when I was working on something else and my problem was on the back burner, I heard a still small voice say, "Read the Book of Daniel." Slightly, I shook my head. I knew what was meant was the Book of Daniel in the Old Testament. Like most schoolchildren, I knew that Daniel was a prophet who for some reason had been thrown into the lions' den and managed by God's grace to survive. Beyond that, however, I knew nothing. I had never read the Book of Daniel. I'd never had any intention to, and I had absolutely no idea why this voice should be telling me to read it. I shook my head again and returned to dictating letters.

The next afternoon, while I was searching for some papers in my wife's office, the voice returned. "Read the Book of Daniel," it repeated. This time I did not shake my head. Somewhat experienced with the Holy Spirit's capacity for persistence, I recognized that God might be nudging me toward something, although God only knew what or why. Still, I was in no hurry.

---

* The example that follows was recounted in *The Road Less Traveled and Beyond.*

At noon the following day, while I was taking my daily walk, the voice came back in the even more insistent form of a question. "Scotty, *when* are you going to read the Book of Daniel?" it asked. So, when I got home, having nothing more pressing to do, I pulled out one of our Bibles and read the Book of Daniel. It helped that the book is mercifully short. I learned many things. For the moment, however, the most useful thing I learned was that there were some rather remarkable parallels between Daniel and me. Although far the more courageous, faithful, and noble, he too was clearly an intellectual; as a dream interpreter he was something of a psychiatrist; and as a prophet he was a theologian. It quickly dawned on me that I had the solution to my problem: henceforth the central character of my novel would be a Daniel, not Scotty, and both the similarities and the differences between us allowed me to step outside myself in a myriad of little ways so as to make that character believable.

What are we to do with this sort of phenomenon? Many who write about creativity, without mentioning God, have offered examples of how the solution to a difficult problem can suddenly come to someone when she is not actively thinking about the problem. But in these examples the solution is immediately recognized and welcomed. It is not experienced as coming from outside oneself. Yet here I received not a solution but the gift of a path to the solution. The gift made no sense to me; I was unaware it had any relation to my problem. It was a path I would not ordinarily have followed. I did not welcome it. Indeed, my first reaction was to reject the gift because it seemed so alien to my ego.

As problems go, mine was not huge. Am I suggesting that God would go out of His way to help me with such a relatively small problem? Yes, that is exactly what I am suggesting. Why God should care so much about me I do not really know. What I do know is that I have been receiving such assists—both major and minor—from Him since I first became aware of them over four decades ago.

———

Am I weird? Undoubtedly so, although not in this respect. As we shall very soon see, each one of us is unique, and hence just a little bit weird. But millions have reported experiences such as I've described. I may not be part of the majority, but I do belong to a very large company.

I have spoken of these experiences of grace as evidence not only of the existence of God but also of the fact that She nurtures us on an ongoing basis. But what about the secularists who either do not believe in God or seriously discount His importance in their lives? They very much appreciate evidence. Does God somehow fail to nurture them?

I do not think so. I am certain that secularists have souls that operate according to the same dynamics as the souls of religious folk. Then what's the difference?

One possibility is that God nurtures secularists in a different way, a way more difficult to construe as evidence. I have no trouble believing this. I know that God very much needs different kinds of people, and different types of people need different kinds of nurturance. I even know for sure that God needs there to be some secularists in the world to help keep the rest of us sane, and it wouldn't be beneath Him—tricky as He is—actually to nurture their secularism.

On the other hand, I feel about secularists much as I do about lawyers (and investigative reporters). We will always need some good lawyers around. But in our extraordinarily adversarial society I believe we would be better off if there were far fewer of them to fan the flames of our adversarialism. There are secularists and then there are secularists. While I have no doubt that God nurtures some of them in their secularism, I also believe that God desperately wants others of them to recognize Her. But they don't.

Why don't they? Why are they immune to the evidence? Two reasons, I believe. One is that people are threatened by change, and those with a secular mind-set are simply not likely to be open to evidence that would call their mind-set into question. The other is that there is something particularly frightening about seriously acknowledging God for the first time. The dethronement of one's ego is involved in putting God in the driver's seat, and this results in a distinct loss of control. This issue of control is a big one and will very much be a focus in the chapters to come. In any case, as Saint

Paul put it, it can be "a terrifying thing to fall into the hands of the living God."

I have spoken of these secularists' rejection of the evidence for the God theory as if it were a neutral or passive sort of phenomenon. That is not the case in my experience. It is common these days to speak of addicts and others who reject massive evidence of their problem as being "in denial." Denial is an active psychological process. In this respect, I believe we can think of some secularists as being addicted to their secularism. No amount of challenging evidence is going to change their minds. It isn't so much that they don't have the same hot line to God as others as it is that they have deliberately left their receiver off the hook. This is one of the reasons for my choice of title for this book on the predominantly secular phenomenon of euthanasia: *Denial of the Soul.*

The Uniqueness of the Individual Soul

Although I formally retired from the practice of psychiatry over a dozen years ago, every three months or so I continue to see a single patient, Barbara, for a token fee. Barbara is now eighty. We have been working together for twenty years trying to help her with a number of issues, most of which relate to aging and death. I have never met anyone who so dramatically demonstrates the distinction between ego and soul.

Barbara has a monumental ego. By this I do not mean that she is either conceited or selfish; she is neither. What I mean is that, with the very best of intentions, she would like to run the world. She would like to control everything, including death and old age. Far beyond the average person, she continually suffers enormous anxiety and frustration over all the situations she cannot control. What I do with her might best be called ego therapy. She has made some progress. Secular at first, she has learned how to pray, how to surrender a little bit of her will to God, how to ask Him to take over now and then. She has become better able to distinguish between the important and unimportant. She worries less about the totally inconsequential. In other words, she has become less phobic and obsessive. And more humble. Nonetheless, despite her insight, her instinctual belief that she *ought* to be able to control everything for the good remains almost delusionally grandiose.

So far I have said nothing about Barbara that sounds unique. Call it obsessive-compulsiveness, call it perfectionism, call it what you will, her ego problem is not out of the realm of the relatively ordinary. The psychodynamics are quite common. Yet I have said something mildly unique about her: she is my sole remaining paying patient. Why? Why do I keep seeing her when I am retired, when her progress is painfully slow and her monumental ego is not particularly interesting?

The reason is that I love her soul.

Certainly Barbara is "a good soul." She is an unusually loving person (she'd be less of a worrier if she cared less about others). There is nothing deceitful about her. She has a good sense of humor when her worries don't get in the way. But so what? I have the opportunity to know other good souls who sparkle with love, honesty, and good humor. How are they different? How is Barbara different?

I can't tell you.

Although souls can be defined in general, almost banal terms, as I have done, their uniqueness is such that it places them beyond any adequate description. While I can describe egos quite fully, I can tell you very little about individual souls.

Secularists acknowledge the uniqueness of persons but see no need to make any mystical distinction between soul and ego. "Since everyone has a unique genetic complement as well as a unique set of life experiences," they would say, "naturally everybody's ego is different." Yet it is the relative sameness of egos that impresses me.

Richard Bolles, author of *What Color Is Your Parachute?*, in a sermon once referred to us humans as "the comparative creatures," suggesting that it is an inherent part of our nature to compare ourselves to one another continually, almost obsessively. This tendency is occasionally constructive but usually destructive. Although she can run circles around her friends (those who are still alive) intellectually, Barbara was recently complaining to me how she couldn't physically keep up with them. As usual, she construed this fact as a massive imperfection on her part. "I ought to be able to keep up," she said. "Compared to them I'm a miserable wreck."

"Barbara," I asked, "the part of you that's doing the comparing right now: is it your ego or is it your soul?"

"It's my ego, of course," she snapped back.

Her response was so rapid because she'd learned to find the distinction useful in our work together. She'd learned that there was nothing unique about her ego except for its being overblown in one dimension. She'd come to know we were doing ego therapy and leaving her soul alone, since there was nothing wrong with it. She even realized that insofar as she'd succeeded in whittling away at the overblown, neurotic part of her ego, her soul somehow had been freed to blossom—that she'd become an even more exceptional human being.

In this respect, Barbara is not unique. The liberation of the soul occurs whenever someone seriously elects a path of psychospiritual growth for the remainder of his or her lifetime. It is as if ego pathology is like mud, and the more it gets cleared away, the more the soul underneath will shine forth in glory—in a distinct pattern of glorious color that can be found nowhere else on earth.

It is no accident that the person I know best—Lily, my wife—strikes me as particularly unique. I would have told you that Lily was unique more than three decades ago when she first entered psychotherapy during the sixth year of our marriage. In the decades since, her uniqueness has seemed to magnify itself by leaps and bounds. But how to describe it? I can't.

I could tell you that she likes to find four-leaf clovers and is very good at doing so. She can amble through a meadow snatching them up by the dozens, as if they were as visible as violets. I can tell you that on a golf course she will sometimes deliberately hit into the rough for the pure pleasure of finding her ball, along with four or five additional balls that other golfers have lost. But what does this really tell you? That she has great eyesight? In fact, she doesn't. Despite her early cataracts, she manages to scavenge as well as ever. No, I am sorry, I cannot truly bring Lily's soul to life for you on the printed page.

A major part of the art of writing decent fiction is known as character development. Great novelists have a genius for bringing their characters to life so that the reader not only finds them believable but actually comes to care about them. Particularly memorable characters stand out in the history of literature. But no one, in my opinion—not Dickens, not Shakespeare, not Dostoyevsky—has ever succeeded in capturing a soul. Great caricatures, yes . . . so great they don't even seem like caricatures. But scratch the pages and you still don't come up with a real soul. The uniqueness of the soul transcends even art at its very best.

When God creates a human soul He does so differently each and every time. This doesn't mean there are no unanswerable questions about how He accomplishes the feat. Indeed, this chapter will conclude with a discussion of the mystery of the soul.

But however mysterious, the process of soul creation is *individualized*. The uniqueness of individual persons is undeniable (except at peril to one's own soul) and cannot be explained away by mere psychology or biology.

The Soul as Developable

There would be no point in my doing ego therapy with Barbara—or major psychotherapy with anyone—unless people could change. Egos can change. This doesn't mean that they will. But they can. Our egos can learn and develop.

I suggested that when egos change for the better—when they are refined, so to speak—the underlying soul invariably shines forth in its uniqueness with greater power. Put simply like this, it might suggest that the soul is just sitting there passively waiting to be exposed, as if the soul were inert. That's not the case. Souls, too, are capable of development.

But bear in mind that souls and egos, being different phenomena, operate on different levels. Take the matter of time perspective, for instance. The perspective of a three-year-old is dramatically different from that of a thirty-year-old, which, in turn, is dramatically different from that of a sixty-five-year-old. This is mostly a fact of chronology. It has primarily to do with how long your ego has lived and how long it's got left to live.

Theologians speak of two radically different types of time: chronos and kairos. By chronos they mean time as our egos know it, the world of the clock, of the predictable changing of seasons, of the very visible processes of *physical* birth, growth, aging, decay, and death. By kairos they mean God's time. They cannot define God's time except to suggest it is extremely different from chronos, that it has more to do with the eternal than the temporal and that the rules aren't the same. They would further suggest, as do I, that the ego dwells primarily in the realm of chronos and the soul primarily in the realm of kairos. In the realm of chronos, the fact that Barbara couldn't keep up with her friends—and her shame about it—seemed to her a matter of great significance. In the realm of kairos, however, she was able to recognize it to be utterly without consequence.

We know remarkably little about how human beings learn. Naturally, since the ego is closer to the surface, what we do know makes learning appear to be an ego phenomenon. The soul being deeper, we understand nothing of its learning. Nonetheless, we do at least get hints from time to time that this deeper learning does occur. The stages of spiritual development that I described in Chapter 5 are an example.

Many people are stuck for all their lives in one of these stages. Others, however, move forward from one to another and perhaps even another. When it occurs, the sequence of this progression or development is predictable. One does not jump from Stage II to Stage IV without going through the more or less secular skepticism of Stage III. But how and why a particular individual makes such progress we do not understand in the least. It does not appear to be an ego phenomenon. The shifts are hidden. Although the ego will definitely be affected as a result, the movement seems to originate in the soul.

The movement from one stage to another clearly deserves the term "conversion." (And, yes, there is such a thing as conversion to skepticism from a more primitive belief system!) But I do not know how to convert anyone. This doesn't mean I never try. Sometimes, as we shall very shortly see, conversion may be a legitimate goal of psychotherapy. Usually, however, the attempt is unsuccessful. But when a patient of mine has converted, it has seemed to me to be more the result of an interaction between the soul and God than of any interaction between me and the patient's ego.

Speaking of interactions, although I believe the distinction between the soul and the ego is both valid and important, this doesn't mean there is no interaction between the two. I've already indicated that a conversion in the soul will dramatically change certain ways in which the ego functions . . . for the better. When a secularist converts to Stage IV, for instance, he may gradually become eager for the very same information he used to reject vigorously. His ego will learn differently. Conversely, I also believe that ego learning will encourage soul development. But exactly how the soul and ego interact remains mysterious to me.

––––––

In the later days of my practice I was consulted by four remarkably similar women in their late sixties and early seventies who came to me with the same chief complaint: depression at growing old. Each was secular-minded. Each had either made money or married money. All their children had turned out golden. It was as if life had gone according to a script. But now they were getting cataracts, requiring hearing aids or dentures, and facing hip replacements. This wasn't the way they would have written the script, and they were pissed. I saw no way to assist them without *converting* them to a vision of old age as something more than a meaningless time of watching themselves simply rot away. I tried to help them buy this perception of aging as a spiritual period of their lives, a time of preparation. It was not an easy sell. In attempting it, I kept saying to each of them in every possible way, "Look, you're not the scriptwriter; this just isn't your show." Two of them shortly left my ministrations, preferring to be depressed rather than come to terms with the fact that life was not solely their own show.

Although she was the most depressed, I had a much easier time of it with another elderly woman who had a distinctly Christian mindset. In her mid-sixties she had suffered detached retinas in both eyes.

The ophthalmologist was unsuccessful in reattaching them using the most advanced laser treatment. She was furious at him. Although there was no evidence for it, she was convinced he had botched the job and was guilty of unprovable malpractice. Ninety percent blind, she was incensed at her fate. A theme emerged at the beginning of her second session with me. "I just hate it when they have to take hold of my arm to help me out of the pew or walk me down the steps at church," she ranted, and "I hate being stuck at home. Lots of people volunteer to take me places, but I can't ask my friends to drive me around all the time."

"It's clear to me," I told her, "that you've taken a lot of pride in your independence. You've been a very successful person, and I think you needed that pride for your many accomplishments. But, you know, life is a journey from here to heaven, and it's a good rule of journeying to travel light. I'm not sure how successful you're going to be in getting to heaven carrying around all this pride. You see your blindness as a curse, and I don't blame you. Conceivably, however, you might look at it as a blessing designed to relieve you of the no longer necessary burden of your pride. Except for your eyes, you're in pretty good health. Likely you've got at least a dozen more years to live. It's up to you whether you'd rather live those years with a curse or a blessing."

When she returned for her third session, her depression of four years' duration had lifted.

I wish that all cases were so easy. And I'm not sure that I could be as graceful as this woman.* It is not easy to *choose* to see one's own blindness—or any disease or aging or dying—as a blessing. It takes great will.

All five of the women I've just described were strong-willed, yet some of them chose to direct their will toward healing and others elected to resist healing. Why the difference? I don't know. What I do know is that we have the power of choice. It is said that God created us in His own image. What is meant by that, more than any-

---

* These cases were described almost exactly as here in *In Search of Stones*, pp. 134–35.

thing else, I believe, is that He gave us free will. We are free to choose, for good or for ill, according to our will, and not even God can heal someone against her will.

Where is the locus of the will? Does it reside in the soul or the ego? I suspect neither. My suspicion is that the will is biological, that it is built into our genes and exerts itself out of the very cells of our bodies. But how that will is directed—not that we choose but how we choose—is determined by those mysterious interactions between the ego and the soul.

———

Learning and developing during childhood does not seem to be much a matter of choice. It just happens. In adulthood, however, the paths that human beings take dramatically diverge. Many stop learning much of consequence and hence cease developing. Yet for others, their process of psychospiritual development, if anything, speeds up. Perhaps the most critical choice in people's lives is when and whether to discontinue their education.

We can rephrase this choice in a number of ways. One person might say it is the choice of whether or not to be a co-creator with God. Others could say it is the choice to love. Choose the path of genuine love and you will choose a lifetime of stretching yourself. Your soul will inevitably develop. But for the purpose of this book I will focus on the choice to learn. Specifically to learn wisdom. The essence of this choice is whether or not to approach life as a learning opportunity.

Herein lies, I believe, the meaning of life. Why would God not only create us but continue to nurture us unless we were developable? Unless She desired our development, our learning?

I defy you in your imagination to concoct a more ideal environment for human learning than this life on earth. It is a life filled with vicissitudes and existential suffering, but as Benjamin Franklin said, "Those things that hurt, instruct." Many have referred to earth as a vale of tears. Keats, however, went deeper when he called it "The vale of soul-making."

I have known some to make the choice to approach life as an

ongoing learning opportunity in adolescence or early adulthood. They may do so with an easy fluidity, as if their souls were somehow already prepared on a certain level. More commonly the choice is made as a result of a crisis—alcoholism, a failed marriage, the death of a beloved, anything that propels them into a twelve-step program or meaningful psychotherapy. Often it is a midlife crisis. For still others it is the final crisis of their own dying. But most never make the choice.

No work I ever did as a psychotherapist was as fulfilling to me as that with a number of dying patients. People tend to learn best when they have a deadline. (What a wonderful word!) Mind you, the majority seem to deny that they are dying up until their final breath. But those who are not in denial, who know they have little time left, tend to speed up their development. They may choose to face issues they have been avoiding for a lifetime. It is a pleasure and a privilege to work with them at such a moment. Deathbed confessions and conversions do happen, as do forgiveness and reconciliation and leaps of learning that never seemed possible. People who are dying can get very real and move very fast.

Because dying can be the opportunity of a lifetime for learning and soul development, dying as a learning process will be my primary focus in the next chapter. We shall see that it is not an easy process. While the physical pain of it can and should be alleviated, the existential suffering involved is enormous. It is quite understandable that some should opt for euthanasia to short-circuit that suffering. Nonetheless, euthanasia also short-circuits the opportunity for learning and soul development. By opting for euthanasia, one denies the very meaning of human existence. He or she tries to escape from the reason for our being. In a very real sense euthanasia is an attempt to short-circuit God. As such, however, it not only shortchanges God; even more important, it shortchanges ourselves. This is the stark simplicity of the matter.

The Immortality of the Soul

I have spoken of old age and dying as a potential time of preparation. It seems a bit strange to me that, when I was still on the lecture circuit, the question I was asked most frequently was not whether I believed in an afterlife but whether I believed in reincarnation. I'd answer that in regard to the matter of reincarnation I was an agnostic. I neither believe nor disbelieve in reincarnation. But sometimes I would say to the audience, "Whether we had a previous existence before our conception and birth seems to me an issue of relatively little consequence. On the other hand, the question of whether there is life after death—an afterlife—strikes me as absolutely crucial."

If there is no afterlife, much of what I have been saying is rot. Granted there would be a point to learning in our youth so that we could improve our parenting skills and thereby possibly contribute not only to the survival but even to the spiritual evolution of the species. But what would be the point of learning and developing once our children have left the nest? So that we might pass on further wisdom to them in our old age? I have not been impressed by the capacity of the elderly to pass on their wisdom—at least not in our society, at least not to our own children. No, we might just as well cash it in after age fifty. Or eat, drink, and be merry, because tomorrow we die. Although I am distinctly in favor of being merry in my old age these days, I'm not sure how well I could pull it off without a reason to learn, without seeing these days of physical degeneration as an opportunity for learning, for development, and for preparation. If there is no afterlife, there is nothing to prepare for. If our souls are not immortal, if we just die, there is no reason not to hasten our death. Cash it in a bit sooner rather than later. Euthanasia would then, in truth, be the sensible solution.

I am a believer in the afterlife. This is not a pure matter of wishful thinking—although one of the things I have learned is that just because thinking seems wishful doesn't mean it is false.* The secularists do not find the idea of an afterlife compelling, but there is some evidence. I could speak of near-death experiences,

---

* One of the better books of wisdom that I know is Frederick Buechner, *Wishful Thinking: A Theological ABC* (New York: Harper & Row, 1973).

apparitions, the existence of ghosts, and the resurrection. The strongest foundation of my belief, however, is that of reason.

One of Lily's and my greatest delights is the beautiful flower garden at our home in Connecticut. Flower gardens do not happen by accident. The beauty of ours is the result of consistent effort, thought, and physical labor over the course of twenty-five years. The idea of just bulldozing the whole thing is incomprehensible. It is conceivable that when we sell the home its buyers might choose to bulldoze the garden, but we shudder at the thought of such waste.

One of the few things I know about God is that She is efficient. She does not waste.* When I think of the energy that God pours into the nurturance and development of souls until the moment of their physical death, it is incomprehensible to me that She should just toss them away, waste them. No, She has something more in store for us, some kind of afterlife She has been trying to prepare us for.

What kind of afterlife I do not know. I can only speculate. Indeed, I've written a short novel on the subject.† But it is a novel. The details of the afterlife, since no one has returned to tell us about them, remain in the realm of speculative theology, and any book about them is inherently a work of fiction.

It is no accident that dying is both the greatest of life's learning opportunities and life's greatest adventure. An adventure is a journey into the unknown. If we know exactly where we're going, how we'll get there, what we'll see along the way, and what we will find when we arrive, it's not an adventure. There's also no learning involved. We learn only through adventures. It is human to be frightened of going into the unknown, and personally I am terrified of dying. I don't even have a map. "My God, my God, do not forsake me," I'll be praying. At the same time I'll be believing. There's something more ahead of us, but God knows what it

---

* See *Further Along the Road Less Traveled*, p. 172, for a compelling example of this in my life.
† *In Heaven as on Earth* (New York: Hyperion, 1996).

is. Still, there's something more. Only our bodies are mortal and temporal.

Souls, Human and Otherwise

In defining the soul as "a God-created, God-nurtured, unique, developable, immortal human spirit," I have begged many questions, but only one word in the definition is potentially misleading: "human." It implies that only humans have souls and that is something I do not wish to imply.

Nonetheless, I have kept the word in because I *know* that humans have souls. Since I am unable to communicate with other creatures, I do not know for certain whether they have souls.

Actually, I suspect they do. Some of them at least. Pets, of course, are the creatures we know best. I have mentioned uniqueness as a quality of the soul. While I can detect subtle differences between any two pets of the same species, I have not usually been tremendously impressed by them. But on occasion I have run across a cat or a dog whose "personality" so stood out from the crowd that I found myself thinking, "That animal has soul."

I used the word "personality" in quotes because we customarily reserve the word "person" for humans. Personality would then seem to be an attribute of humans. It did strike me that there was something distinctly human about these very special pets. But I was looking at them through my human eyes and with the narcissism that so disposes us humans to look down on creatures the more unlike us they are. How it would all look through the eyes of an average dog or cat I have no idea.

We have the same problem with consciousness. We humans narcissistically tend to assume ourselves to be the sole possessors of consciousness. It is a most questionable assumption. Although likely different in quality, there is much to suggest that the other creatures—even plants—have consciousness of a sort. Indeed, I have little difficulty thinking of the entire world as being alive with consciousness . . . and soul.

Spirit

Be that as it may, herein I am restricting myself to issues of the human soul. And I have specifically designated that soul to be a spirit.

Right away this creates difficulty not only for die-hard secularists but for most people in our culture. I have pointed out that despite church attendance statistics and polls professing the prevalence of religious belief, ours is an essentially materialistic culture. This does not simply mean that we are addicted to chasing after ever fancier automobiles and other material possessions or that, as Emerson put it, "things are in the saddle, and ride mankind." It means we are accustomed to thinking only about "things." Materialism is a basic attitude—a fundamental philosophy, if you will—that what you can see and touch is all you get. If it can't be measured, then it can't be studied, it can't be manipulated, and to all intents and purposes it doesn't exist; you might as well forget about it. Materialism either denies the spirit (and hence the soul) entirely or, at the very least, holds it to be airy-fairy and of little consequence in the affairs of men.

In speaking of the soul of a person, I've been talking of her or his essential *spirit*. It is the spirit of different people that is unique. In attempting to portray the uniqueness of the soul, I ultimately had to admit it was beyond description. Because it is spirit, we cannot measure it. We cannot get our hands on it, our fingers around it. We cannot capture it. We can ignore the spirit (and soul). We can resist it; we can even, upon occasion, drive it out; but we cannot codify it.

This makes a great many people profoundly uncomfortable.

Distressed by the materialism of our culture, some have taken solace from the fact that in the twentieth century subatomic physicists, the deepest students of basic matter, seem to have stumbled into the realm of spirit. A century ago they felt they could codify the atom. Today, having delved into the subatomic level, they recognize that on the deepest level they can't. Matter turns into energy, and energy into matter. Speeds, directions, and positions have become unpredictable. The basic building blocks of matter are now being described as "complex fields of statistical probabilities." Atoms have begun to look very much like spirits.

A strong note of caution is called for, however. Atoms may be spirits of a sort—and I have suggested that the whole world may be alive with spirit—but that doesn't necessarily mean that atoms have souls. Or personalities. Or that the laws of physics will ever be identical to the laws of theology. Indeed, once you get above the subatomic level, matter becomes ever more predictable and demonstrates little or nothing of the uniqueness that is characteristic of souls.

Matter is matter, not soul. No one is more aware of this than those who work with the dying. In old age we can watch the body decaying. If one's physical death is gradual, we can see that process of decay speed up as the moment of death approaches. But the *person* does not decay. Sometimes it is even the other way around. In people who have truly accepted their dying and death, we frequently get the opportunity to watch their spirit—their personhood, their soul—become ever more vibrant and alive as their material decay proceeds.

And then suddenly—instantly—the spirit is gone and only the corpse, the matter of the body, remains to continue its process of decay.

Although I consider myself a middle-of-the-road Christian, I do not believe in the doctrine of the resurrection of the body. It seems to me to confuse bodies and souls. They are not the same thing at all. Our bodies are matter . . . material. Our souls are spirit, and follow different laws entirely. We are so accustomed to our bodies that it may be difficult for materialists to imagine any existence without them. But I am quite certain that God's imagination exceeds our own.

The Mystery of the Soul

I've already stated that my definition of the soul begs many questions. This is not an apology. My limited vision is inherently human. And to our limited vision God is inevitably mysterious. Since our souls are ongoing creations of God, through them we partake in

God and thereby, whether we like it or not, we partake in His mystery.

Several of the questions I've begged I have already mentioned. Do plants and animals have souls? How do the soul and the ego interact, as separate as they are? I could go on at great and improper length listing questions about the soul to which I have no answer. One, however, is of such obvious significance that it deserves at least mention and some minor, ambiguous discussion: can people have evil souls?

That there are evil people I have no doubt. But I have never been able to get close enough to one of them—generally they wouldn't let me—to discern whether the evil resided in a deranged ego or a deranged soul.*

One evil man has been studied posthumously in the most extraordinary depth: Adolf Hitler. A huge variety of historical data and countless analyses, hypotheses, and theories have been offered to explain him. Yet even when all these are added up, one gets the distinct feeling that a very big and crucial piece is missing. After fifty years, scholars have failed to capture the man. If his malignancy originated from within his soul, this failure would actually be what one might expect. Souls, as I have said, cannot be captured and pinned down.

Again, therefore, unpalatable as the notion might be, I suspect that a very few humans *may* possibly be born with evil souls.

How could this be? If God creates souls, how could He create one that is evil from the start? I don't know. But I can offer a two-part hypothesis.

The first part requires our understanding that God is *not* omnipotent. Here I feel that I am on firm ground. I am aware that God is generally portrayed as omnipotent in the Bible and that for anyone raised in a monotheistic tradition it is almost instinctive to think of God as omnipotent. Yet there are all manner of reasons—including

---

* For more about evil people and the even greater ambiguities of disembodied evil spirits and demonic possession, please see my book *People of the Lie* (New York: Simon & Schuster, 1983).

the above questions and the freedom of the human will—seriously to doubt His omnipotence without having to discard a monotheistic belief in Him. This book is not meant to be a treatise on the fine points of theology. Suffice it to say that a large number of modern Judeo-Christian theologians have become quite comfortable with a more subtle notion of God, a God who is hardly impotent but whose enormous power is constrained by multiple factors—one of them being His own gentleness. Einstein, a theologian in his way, was not talking of the God of Sodom and Gomorrah when he said, toward the end of his life, "Subtle is the Lord."

The second part of my hypothesis is more speculative. Dealing with these issues in my novel of the afterlife, *In Heaven as on Earth,* I suggested that soul creation—indeed, all creation—is an *experiment.* Scientists have learned to expect that many of their experiments will fail to support the hunch they initially set out to prove. We sometimes refer to these endeavors as failed experiments, although we recognize we have just as much to learn from them as from successful ones. They send us back to the drawing board.

This is not meant to take away the mystery of it all. Indeed, if soul creation is, in fact, an experiment of God's in each and every instance, it then becomes mysterious why there are so very few such obviously failed experiments. Saint Paul spoke of the "mystery of iniquity," the mystery of human evil. Yet, if we are to be objective, we must admit that the even greater mystery is that of human goodness. From my point of view the average human being is far more decent and heroic than might be predicted by chance alone.

In any case, I have chosen to suggest this highly speculative hypothesis that our souls are experiments of God because it hints at the potential for a kind of glory. Already I've mentioned that it is within our power in this "vale of soul-making" to be co-creators with God. Now I am suggesting we may be co-experimenters. There can be a considerable drama to experiments that often smacks of glory. I suspect the experiment continues long afterward. But at no time is the experiment of soul-making likely to be more dramatic than when we are rapidly approaching the hour of our physical death.

Chapter 7

THE LEARNING
OF DYING

In the last chapter I put forth the two reasons I am critical of euthanasia. One is distinctly theological and relates to all suicide in general. It is that, as our Creator and Nurturer, God is as much a stakeholder in our lives as we ourselves are. As creatures with free will, we have the power to kill ourselves. Whether we have the ethical or moral right to do so is a different matter entirely. Through the act of suicide one sets the timing of one's death without reference to the Life-Giver. It is a denial of God and God's relationship with the soul.

The other reason I am critical is psychological as well as theological and pertains specifically to euthanasia as I have defined it. We have an enormous amount to learn from the process of dying a natural death. To kill oneself in order to avoid the existential suffering of aging and dying is to shortchange oneself of that learning. It is also, I believe, to shortchange the God who designed us for such learning. In the previous chapter my treatment of this subject was superficial. The purpose of this chapter will be to go deeper.

The Stages of Death and Dying

Elisabeth Kübler-Ross, M.D., was the first scientist who ever dared to sit down repeatedly with people who were dying and ask them what they were feeling about it. From this experience she wrote the classic work *On Death and Dying* (New York: Macmillan, 1969). In it she said that upon receiving the diagnosis of a terminal illness, patients tend to go through the following emotional stages in this order:

Denial
Anger
Bargaining
Depression
Acceptance

In the first stage, denial, they say, "The lab must have gotten my tests mixed up with somebody else's. It can't be me; it can't be happening to me." But that doesn't work for very long. So they get angry. They get angry at the doctors, angry at the nurses, angry at the hospital, angry at their relatives, angry at God. When anger doesn't get them anywhere, they start to bargain, saying, "Maybe if I go back to church and start praying again, my cancer will go away." Or "Maybe if I start being nicer to my children for a change, my kidneys will improve." When bargaining doesn't get results, they begin to realize they're really going to die. At that point they become depressed.

If the dying person can hang in there and do what some of us therapists refer to as "the work of depression," then he or she can emerge at the other end of that depression and enter the fifth stage—acceptance.

Like any book of extraordinary significance, Kübler-Ross's systematization of these stages has been criticized and in the process clarified. Critics have pointed out that stages may be skipped; the stages may be circular and repetitive rather than linear; patients may regress; a person may be in more than one stage at the same time;

the system is not a formula and should not be used formulistically. All these criticisms are valid. Nonetheless, the system is fundamentally sound and, when not applied formulistically, extremely useful.

––––

Kübler-Ross described the fifth stage, acceptance—if it is reached—as one of great philosophic calm and spiritual light. That is almost an understatement.

As a psychiatrist I have had the good fortune to see several patients in the stage of acceptance, a lovely experience. I have been with two different dying men, who were not my patients, at dinner parties in their homes, an even more dramatic experience.

One man, close to seventy, had cancer of the bladder for which he'd just undergone an unsuccessful course of chemotherapy. He was extremely cachectic, or wasted. He also happened to be completely deaf from a different disorder, but he was adept at lip-reading. Because of a fungal infection of his esophagus due to his severely compromised immune system, he was unable to eat solid food. While the rest of us ate, he had to drink a ghastly looking nutritional mixture. That dinner was his last social occasion beyond the family, and he died three weeks after that night.

The other man, in his early forties, had suffered for over a decade from ALS (amyotrophic lateral sclerosis, or Lou Gehrig's disease). By the time of our dinner he'd become completely paralyzed below the neck. He had to be fed with a spoon while seated in his wheelchair. He was, of course, incontinent and required total nursing care from the other members of his religious community. He was to die within six months.

Because I'd known beforehand how terribly ill these men were, I'd dreaded those two dinner parties. I had no reason. Although the men were very different in personality, my experiences with the two of them were extraordinarily similar. Each, early in the evening, volunteered succinct and realistic information about his illness and impending death. Their intent was clearly to put me at ease. They succeeded. I have never seen two people who were so alert, so conscious of what was happening, so totally with it and *present*. Both sparkled; they were filled with light, and their light seemed to embrace the entire company assembled. While the dates were not special, both dinners seemed like celebrations. The mood was one of serene hilarity. I have never enjoyed any social occasion more than those two evenings.

———

The final stage, acceptance, is very real and beautiful to behold, but most people do not die in that fifth stage. Most die still denying or angry or bargaining or depressed. The depression, when they hit it, is so painful that they do not know they can work through it, so they retreat back into the earlier stages, particularly denial. My distinct impression, although I have no scientific statistics to support it, is that the majority of people die even gradual deaths still denying the fact that they are dying.

How can this be? How can an intelligent adult be given a fatal diagnosis, watch himself deteriorate despite the best medical treatment, see the deterioration become ever more rapid, and still deny that he is dying? There is indeed something absurd, even deranged about this denial. Nonetheless, it is normative behavior. And if we are to understand why it is the norm rather than the exception we must not underestimate either the power of denial or the terror of death.

The power of denial is a direct reflection of the power of the human will. Given our freedom, we may choose to submit our will to a Higher Power—be it God, truth, love, or even reality. But if our will is not truly submitted, we are free to think and believe whatever we *want*. The facts be damned. It is actually easier to deny reality than submit to it. Not right, but easier.

For the most part, we do not want to die. As I've suggested, the will to live is built into every cell of our bodies. It is also built into our consciousness. Being alive is all that we know. Death is naturally terrifying. Despite any belief we may have in an afterlife, we still tend to worry that death may be nonexistence or worse.

Plumbing the depths of my own terror of dying I have discovered a strange fantasy that's even more terrifying than the prospect of my nonexistence. It is the prospect of existing amid nothingness, in the void. In this fantasy I continue to exist after death, in the sense of being conscious, only I don't exist anywhere. I am conscious of being nothing in the midst of nothing . . . in the midst of utter emptiness. The analogy is that of a space traveler who has accidentally become unhooked from his ship and is helplessly floating in dark outer space, utterly alone, yet somehow alive and aware that he is doomed to be that way for eternity. Rationally, it is a fantasy that begs many questions. But it is terrifying, and a number of perfectly rational people have confessed sharing it with me.

Our terror of nonexistence is so monumental that Ernest Becker, in *The Denial of Death* (New York: Free Press, 1973), ascribed most human evil to the attempt to avoid the full consciousness of our mortality. Becker was not concerning himself, as we are, with those suffering a diagnosed terminal illness; he was speaking of the physically healthy. If his thesis is correct—if the denial of death is the root psychological cause of human evil—then think of the pressure to deny a fatal illness upon someone who is actually in the final stages, who is in the very midst of dying!

No matter how great the pressure, no matter how understandable and normal the denial of death is, it is not healthy. Nowhere have I seen this point made more compellingly than in the book *Midstream: The Story of a Mother's Death and a Daughter's Renewal* by LeAnne Schreiber (New York: Viking Penguin, 1990). It can be used as a case study of denial. It is perhaps so compelling because the author did not intend it to be such. She was simply witnessing the facts of her mother's dying and her own involvement in the process.

Her mother, around the age of seventy, developed cancer of the pancreas. She survived slightly more than a year from the time of diagnosis, probably as a result of a positive effect of radiation treatment, and she died more as a result of metastases than of the primary tumor. In the early stages, the emotional and physical pain-relief treatment she received from the medical establishment was highly flawed. But what made the book's account so grim for me was the patient's persistent denial that she was dying up until the very moment she was dead.

Just one of the powerfully realistic details of this case study is the matter of religion. The mother was a lifelong Catholic, overtly religious and involved for many decades in the activities of the church. The daughter was, and has apparently remained, overtly secular. At one point the mother and daughter together attended a healing service at the church, where the mother was prayed over. At best, this seemed like bargaining behavior. Her Catholicism gave the patient no apparent solace whatsoever. I was left with the distinct impression that she was more a cultural Catholic than a real one and that, despite her superficial religiosity, she was, as is so often the case, fundamentally as secular-minded as her daughter. Any discussion of religion was apparently avoided between them, perhaps because it seemed irrelevant to the lives (and deaths) of mother and daughter.

Ms. Schreiber gently tried to penetrate her mother's denial, but her mother would have none of it. This is typical of many dying people. Efforts to pierce through denial are usually ineffective, and the more vigorously one pursues them, the more likely one is to fail. Persistence can even border on cruelty. The best approach is to give patients as many opportunities as possible to talk about dying—to welcome discussion of the subject without insisting upon it. Otherwise we should be respectful of the patient's need to deny.

Often, however, it is the family members and medical professionals who, because of their own denial, fail to welcome a discussion of dying. This is another way in which Ms. Schreiber's book is accurate. She demonstrates that her father was as much in denial as her mother. When those close to the patient are unwilling to discuss the subject of dying, they encourage rather than discourage the patient's denial, in this case placing her in a position of isolation where she can't talk about her deepest feelings even if she wants to.

Denial thus virtually ensures that no meaningful communication can take place. Ms. Schreiber's brother, a physician, was aware from the start that his mother was dying but, supposedly because of the demands of his practice in a different region of the country, kept his distance from her. He maintained his distance even during his many phone calls by hiding behind medical jargon and never expressing personal feelings. So the author, throughout the year, had no one to whom she could really talk—which is why, I suspect, she later wrote the book.

At the conclusion of Chapter 3 about emotional pain I commented briefly on the phenomenon of redemptive suffering. I noted there the many reports I have heard of "good deaths" and the characteristics such deaths had in common. Most notable was the lack of denial on the part of the dying person and the completeness of his or her communication with friends and family. Good-byes were said with love. Frequently children and parents reconciled. Often the whole family came together in a deeper way than ever before. My reporters consistently described it as a privilege to participate in these deaths. To their surprise the experience was not dreadful but redemptive and uplifting.

For Ms. Schreiber, however, watching her mother die was not uplifting because family members could not talk to each other about the most important things. Despite the upbeat subtitle about "renewal," I personally found *Midstream* to be a profoundly sad book. I could discern in it absolutely nothing redemptive about the mother's death or dying, no evidence that Ms. Schreiber's mother learned anything of significance during that last year of her life. I spotted no sign that her soul developed or grew.

Denial arrests the learning process. You cannot learn anything from your dying if you cannot even face the fact that you are dying. Hers was a natural death but not necessarily a good one.

The Kübler-Ross Stages and Learning

Although Dr. Kübler-Ross didn't quite realize it at the time she wrote *On Death and Dying,* she had outlined stages that we go through anytime we make a significant psychospiritual growth step at any point during our lives.

Let's imagine, for example, that there is a serious flaw in my personality and that my friends start criticizing me for the manifestations of this flaw. What's my first reaction? I say, "She must have just gotten out on the wrong side of the bed this morning." Or, "He must really be angry at his wife. Doesn't have anything to do with me." *Denial*.

If they keep on criticizing me, then I say: "What gives them the right to stick their noses in my business? They don't know what it's like to be in my shoes. Why don't they mind their own damn business!" I may even tell them that. *Anger.*

But if they love me enough to keep on criticizing me, then I begin to think: "Gee, I really haven't told them lately what a good job they're doing." And I go around giving them lots of pats on the back, smiling at them a lot, hoping this will shut them up. *Bargaining.*

But if they truly do love me enough to keep on criticizing, then maybe I get to the point where I think, "Could they be right? Could there possibly be something wrong with the great Scott Peck?" And if I answer yes, then that leads to *depression*. But if I can hang in there with that depressing notion that maybe there really is something wrong with me and start to wonder what it might be, if I contemplate it and analyze it and isolate it and identify it, then I can go about the process of killing it and purifying myself of it. Having fully completed the *work* of depression, I will then emerge at the other end as a new man, a resurrected human being, a better person. *Acceptance.*

None of this is really new. I am fond of quoting Seneca, who said almost two thousand years ago: "Throughout the whole of life one must continue to learn how to live and, what will amaze you even more, dear friends, throughout life one must continue to learn how to die." Of course, we have the choice not to learn anything about the art of living and dying. But if we choose to be deep learners and co-creators of our souls we will suffer little deaths all the time. In *The Road Less Traveled* (pp. 67–69) and other works I recounted how at the age of thirty-nine I went through all the stages of death and dying in the course of a single evening.

One night I decided to spend some free time building a happier and closer relationship with my daughter, who was fourteen at the time. For several weeks she had been urging me to play chess with her, so I suggested a game and she eagerly accepted. We settled down to an even, challenging match. It was a school night, however, and at nine o'clock my daughter asked if I could hurry my moves because she needed to get to bed; she had to get up at six in the morning. I knew her to be rigidly disciplined in her sleeping habits, and it seemed to me that she ought to be able to give up some of this rigidity. I told her, "Come on, you can go to bed a little later for once. You shouldn't start games that you can't finish. We're having fun."

We played for another fifteen minutes, during which time she became visibly discomfited. Finally she pleaded, "Please, Daddy, please hurry your moves."

"No, goddammit," I replied. "Chess is a serious game. If you're going to play it well, you're going to play it slowly. If you don't want to play it seriously, you might as well not play it at all."

And so, with her feeling miserable, we continued for another ten minutes, until suddenly my daughter burst into tears, yelled that she conceded the stupid game, and ran weeping up the stairs.

My first reaction was one of denial. Nothing was seriously wrong. My daughter was just in a fragile mood. Perhaps it was her period or something. Certainly it had nothing to do with me. But that attempt at denial didn't really work. The fact was that the evening had turned out exactly opposite from what I had intended. So my next reaction was to become angry. I became angry at my daughter for her rigidity and the fact that she couldn't give up a little sleep time to work on our relationship. It was her fault. But anger didn't work either. The fact is that I too was rigid in my sleeping habits. So I thought I might run upstairs, knock on her door, and say, "I'm sorry, honey. Please forgive me for being rigid. Have a good night's sleep." Yet I had some sense at this point that I was bargaining. That would be a cheap apology. Finally it began to dawn on me that I had seriously goofed. I had started the evening wanting to have a happy time with my daughter. Ninety minutes later she was in tears and so angry at me she could hardly speak. What had gone wrong? I became depressed.

Fortunately, albeit reluctantly, I was able to hang in there and do the work of depression. I began to face the fact that I had botched up the evening by allowing my desire to win a chess game to become more important than my desire to build a relationship with my daughter.

I was depressed in earnest then. How had I gotten so out of balance? Gradually I began to accept that my desire to win was too great and that I needed to give up some of this desire. Yet even this little giving up seemed impossible. All my life my desire to win had served me in good stead, for I had won many things. How was it possible to play chess without wanting to win? I had never been comfortable doing things unenthusiastically. How could I conceivably play chess enthusiastically but not seriously? Yet somehow I had to change, for I knew that my competitiveness and seriousness were part of a behavior pattern that was alienating my children from me and would continue to do so, causing other episodes of tears and bitterness, if I could not modify this pattern.

Since I have given up part of my desire to win at games, that little depression is long over. I used my desire to win at parenting to kill my desire to win at games. When I was a child my desire to win at games had served me well. As a parent I recognized that it got in my way. I had to give it up. I do not miss it, even though I thought I would.

———

I have told the story of that chess game often because it is the clearest example I know of how an individual can move rapidly through the stages of death and dying in dealing with a situation not of physical dying but of everyday life—and do so in the precise order that Kübler-Ross first outlined for those stages. But, as I mentioned, that is not always their order. In fact, more often than not, a minor depression will descend on me suddenly, without warning and without my having discernibly experienced the preliminary stages of denial, anger, or bargaining. So let me tell a story of such a depression of mine, a story I have not told before.

Twenty years ago I was co-leading a weekly evening therapy group of some ten patients. Only fifteen minutes into the session I was clobbered by a feeling of depression so severe that I could neither think nor talk. It went on and on. Finally one of the patients asked, "What's wrong with you, Scotty? You haven't said a word. It's like you're not here."

"I'm not," I somehow managed to stammer. "I've suddenly become depressed. I have no idea why. I'm totally out of it. I can't even listen. I'm sorry. You'll have to go on working without me."

Physically I stayed present in the room, but emotionally I remained definitively not present until the two-hour session concluded. The group did continue its work. I was most grateful for the presence of my co-therapist. When the group disbanded, he asked me if he could do anything to help. "No, thanks," I told him. "I expect I'll have it figured out by morning. If not, I'll give you a call."

Not until I was in my car driving home through the night was I able to think clearly again. Knowing that depressions were usually kicked off by helpless rage, I began to wonder what had happened early in the evening's session to make me so angry. The answer came instantly: it was Bianca, one of the patients in the group; I was furious at her.

Bianca was a thirty-five-year-old woman who was not only a group member but also an individual therapy patient of mine. I had been seeing her for a year. Initially she had reminded me of a three-year-old: petulant, whining, and perpetually provocative. She blamed her husband for everything. Over the preceding four months, however, she had made great progress and had been acting her age— until that evening. The moment the group session began, Bianca had resumed her blaming and whining with a vengeance. It was as if she had regressed back to age three overnight, and I was enraged at her for it.

I knew it was common for such patients to regress temporarily in relatively early phases of therapy. Consequently I immediately realized there was something grossly inappropriate about the intensity of my anger at Bianca. So I sat on that anger, helplessly unable to express it. I was wise not to explode at her. The result, however, was my sudden and incapacitating depression.

By the time I reached home I had figured this much out. But my curiosity as well as my lingering depression propelled me to dig deeper. For some reason what should at most have been mild annoyance with Bianca had instead been inappropriate, almost explosive rage. Why? The answer again came quickly. There are times in the professional life of a psychotherapist when all of his patients seem to be getting better and he begins to think he has a golden touch. Then there are very different periods when nobody seems to be making any improvement, causing him to seriously question his competence as a healer. So it had been for me recently. Not one of my patients seemed to be progressing . . . except Bianca. Over the past month I had frequently consoled myself by thinking, "Well, at least Bianca is moving ahead like wildfire." Only now she wasn't; she was moving backwards.

I wondered if perhaps it would be appropriate for me to consider gradually giving up the practice of psychotherapy if things continued to go sour. I didn't know. What I did know, however, was that it was *not* appropriate for me to base the entirety of my professional self-esteem on a single patient, to become enraged because such a patient had let me down, or even to feel let down by any patient's behavior. It was not fair to Bianca. For that matter, it wasn't fair to me. I would not allow myself to fall into that trap again. Like it or not, I was going to have to learn to give up at least some of my need for self-esteem. When I retired that night I was no longer depressed. I had completed the work of depression—or at least the work of that particular depression.

When someone completes the work of depression, the story invariably has a happy ending. I began the next session by apologizing to the group for my depression the previous week. I explained its dynamics and what I had learned from it. I further apologized to Bianca for using her to bolster my self-esteem. Bianca, it turned out, was profoundly moved by the importance of her progress to me. She acknowledged her regression and doubted it would happen again. Indeed, the incident marked the beginning of another major psychospiritual growth spurt on her part. As for the other members of the group, they were actually pleased that their therapist was human enough to become depressed himself, smart enough to work it out, and brave enough to confess all the details. They proclaimed me to be a role model and, in the weeks that followed, seemed to use me as such.

———

Repeatedly I have used a phrase that is not in general parlance: "the work of depression." Most succinctly it is the work of existential suffering required for the healing of a depression. Since it is work of a psychospiritual sort and no one likes to suffer, most will try to avoid it by retreating from it. In doing so, they learn nothing and there can be no healing. But if they can hang in there with their depression long enough to deal with it thoroughly, they can work it through and emerge at the other end happier and wiser than they ever were before.

The work of depression is so critical to the betterment of individuals—and, as we shall soon see, to the betterment of society as a whole—that it deserves discussion in greater depth. The work can best be analyzed by dividing it into its four sequential phases.

The first phase is realizing that you are depressed and not running away from the fact. This is not as simple as it sounds. Just as people can deny that they are obviously dying, so they can also deny that they are seriously depressed. Perhaps half of the seriously depressed patients who come to psychiatrists do so with other complaints: insomnia, loss of libido, vague pains, restlessness, anxiety, marital problems, and so forth. Even to their friends they will look depressed, and the psychiatrist's first task will be to help her patient become aware that he is depressed.

Someone may also not be aware that he is depressed because the depression is relatively mild, gradual in onset, and complex in causation. During the summer of 1979 one of the early fans of *The Road Less Traveled*, a clergyman, came to visit me for several days. On his departure he commented, "I like you, Scotty, and I've enjoyed meeting you, but you're different from what I expected. On the basis of your book, I'd anticipated that you'd be a joyful, lighthearted man. Instead you seem to me heavy, almost depressed."

"I'm not depressed," I replied, "at least not that I'm aware of. Everything's going well for me."

Indeed the man's assessment seemed so strange, so off the mark, that it stuck with me. It wasn't until two years later, when my book was well on its way to fame and I'd become a somewhat accomplished public speaker, that I realized he'd sized me up accurately. Reflecting back on his visit, I remembered that I was waging an uphill struggle at the time just to keep the book in print, that I was facing my first speaking engagement with terror, and that my marriage was at its lowest point ever.

My depression of that time resolved itself with the improving circumstances of my writing and speaking career without my having to work myself out of it. One cannot do the work of depression unless he is aware that he is depressed. Six years later I was to enter a two-year period when I was profoundly aware of being moderately and continually depressed. Not surprisingly this lengthy depression centered on the time I turned fifty. It could very much be looked at as a midlife crisis. Part of that crisis was a complex of problems with our marriage. I had to do a great amount of the work of depression before I—and we—came out the other side. I have recounted several stories of the resolution of a depression over the course of a few hours, but one does not resolve the problems of a twenty-five-year marriage during a single evening.

Having completed the first phase of the work of depression by acknowledging that you are, in fact, depressed, the second phase is obvious: it is to ask yourself why. Why am I depressed? Obvious though the question might be, the answer usually isn't. For instance, the feeling of depression is frequently a concomitant of viral illnesses. Influenza and mononucleosis are notorious in this regard, but the phenomenon also occurs with lesser diseases. As a psychiatrist, I have been particularly bedeviled by this fact. Dozens of times I've felt mildly depressed and spent several hours wondering why before experiencing the onset of a low-grade fever and aching joints and coming to the realization: "I'm not really depressed; I've just got a little bug."

But that's a minor issue. The bigger issue arises when you've got an honest-to-God depression and day after day you ask yourself why, but you can't come up with an answer. If your depression persists in being inexplicable, it's time to get yourself off to a psychotherapist. The therapist will not be able to do the work of depression for you, but she can assist you in this phase of it. If you're willing to be honest, the gentle questioning of a therapist will commonly reveal quite quickly that you've got plenty of reason to be depressed.

But if you're a reasonably insightful person there's usually no necessity to pay for the services of a trained therapist to help you do what you're capable of doing for yourself. Remember my saying that a feeling of helpless anger—helpless rage—is almost invariably the cause of depression. Simply ask yourself, "What am I angry about?" For instance, as soon as I asked myself what it was about that group therapy session that had made me angry, I immediately realized I was furious at Bianca. It was a helpless anger, however, because I instinctively realized it was more my fault than hers.

My only warning in this regard is that depressions are often overdetermined—that is to say, they have more than one cause. Frequently it will not be something you are angry about but some things. The majority of my minor depressions are like this. I notice myself feeling depressed at two in the afternoon. Thinking about it I will realize that not one, not two, but five things have gone wrong that morning. Each thing in itself might constitute nothing more than a minor annoyance, but the last one will be like the proverbial straw that breaks the camel's back, and these incidents in combination have put me in a helplessly pissy mood.

Once you have discerned the thing or things you are angry about, you have discovered the cause of your problem and completed the second phase of the work of depression. The third phase is then to ask yourself, "What do I need to do to get rid of this helpless anger?" Occasionally this phase requires no work at all. For instance, if my depression is nothing more than the result of a buildup of minor frustrations, all I'll need to do is get a good night's sleep and I'll be fine in the morning. In the almost immortal words of Scarlett O'Hara, "Tomorrow is another day."

But when we're talking about a significant depression, sleep—if you can get it—isn't the answer. In fact, the work of depression now becomes more difficult, more laborious. For the answer to the question, "What do I have to do to get rid of this helpless anger?" is that I do have to get rid of something—something in *myself.* I have to give up a part of myself. In response to the failed chess game with my daughter, for example, I realized I needed to give up my excessive competitiveness. Similarly, my inappropriate rage at Bianca taught me that I needed to give up basing my self-esteem on my patients' progress or lack thereof.

What makes this phase of the work of depression so laborious is our instinctive resistance to giving up any part of ourselves. As soon as I've identified any part of myself that I need to give up, my first reaction will be: "I can't. It's impossible." How can one possibly not play chess competitively? How can one help but base his self-esteem upon the apparent results of his work? In Chapter 3 I spoke of how depressed people feel trapped, as if they were in a cage, but also how the bars of the cage are usually of their own making. The fact of the matter is that we can give up virtually anything if we want to badly enough. The problem is in the wanting. Many of us therapists have had the experience of our patients quitting the work of depression at this point and leaving our ministrations, preferring to stay depressed rather than relinquish a part of themselves, no matter how obviously self-destructive and unnecessary that part might be.

When I said we can give up virtually anything, I did not mean that we can or should give up anything that is constructive. We should not, for instance, give up our souls—although some people do. I am speaking of things of the ego, like an excessive competitiveness or need for self-esteem. The list of such "things of the ego" is almost endless: arrogance, unrealistic fantasies, a habit of sarcasm, and on and on. The list includes anything that isn't working for you anymore.

Once we have completed this third phase of the work of depression by identifying what it is that we need to give up and realizing that we *can* give it up, the fourth and final phase is to do it: give it up. Bump it off. Kill it. Excise it. Again, this is easier said than done. It does feel like death. Certainly it is a process of self (or ego) surgery and is usually motivated only by a sense of self-defeat. As I said earlier, the solution to certain problems is to accept that there is no solution.

So we are back to acceptance—the label Kübler-Ross used for the stage beyond depression, the place of spiritual peace we will reach if and when we complete the work of depression. Her focus was on the acceptance of death itself and the sense of self-defeat that must be worked through in coming to terms with the fact that death is one of those problems for which there is no solution—that we cannot beat it. Increasingly, as we specifically consider the issue of euthanasia, our focus is going to be on another kind of ego defeat that is central to the process of dying: learning how to give up control.

But make no mistake: the defeat of the ego is painful. I spoke of the work of depression as laborious; it is analogous to labor, as in the process of giving birth. The pain may start gradually, but in the later stages it can be excruciating. Yet the result is new life. Similarly, the work of depression is soul learning, and the result is a new life for the soul that is almost akin to resurrection.

———

I cannot overemphasize the importance of these stages of dying in the process of unlearning and new learning. Not only individuals but groups, as small as married couples and as large as nations, need to go through them. Consider, for instance, the behavior of the United States in Vietnam. When evidence first began to accumulate in 1963 and 1964 that our policies in Vietnam were not working, what was our nation's first reaction? Denial. Nothing was really wrong. All we needed was a few more special forces troops and a few more million dollars.

Then, in 1966 and 1967, as evidence continued to accumulate that our policies were not working and were obviously seriously flawed, what was the government's reaction? Anger. The day of the body count began. And My Lai. And torture. And bombing that seemed to be aimed at turning North Vietnam into an American parking lot. Yet by 1969 and 1970, when we had massive evidence that our policies in Vietnam were a failure, our next response was to attempt to bargain our way out of the war. We stopped bombing here as a carrot and started bombing there as a stick, thinking that we could somehow bring North Vietnam to the table. But that strategy also failed.

Although some of us as individuals at the time went through a significant depression over Vietnam, our government led the majority of Americans to believe that somehow we had succeeded in bargaining our way out. The truth is that we did not bargain our way out of Vietnam. Consistently in the wrong from the start, we were defeated, as we deserved to be. We fled with over half a million men. Because as a nation we generally failed at the time to do the work of depression involved in coming to terms with our collective guilt, there was little evidence that we learned any lesson as a result. Only recently, twenty-five years after the fact, does it look as if we may have done some portion of the work of that depression by learning to relinquish a shred of our arrogant desire to control the world and come to some modicum of humility in our international relations.

As for the smallest of groups, married couples, I believe that most successful long-term marriages go through these stages of death and dying in the same order that Kübler-Ross outlined. Certainly this has been true of Lily's and my marriage. For the first five years we devoted much energy to denying the painful reality that we were no longer romantically in love with each other. As this denial collapsed, we spent most of the next ten years angry at each other for not being the soul mate of our dreams. It was a time of criticism. Endlessly we specified the flaws we saw in each other, then tried to heal these deficiencies. Over and again I attempted to convert Lily to my way of thinking, and she tried to convert me to hers. Unconverted, we then went through a period of negotiating boundaries and rules that would allow us to work peacefully around each other. This activity was akin to bargaining—"I'll do this if you'll do that," we were both saying—but it brought us no joy. By the twenty-year mark both of us had become significantly depressed about the marriage. We were unsure that it could survive, indeed that it even should survive.

Yet, for reasons that seemed ephemeral at best, we hung in there in our depressing marriage for the next decade, and strange things started to happen. Gradually, almost without willing it, some of Lily's foibles began to amuse me. I slowly realized that each of her shortcomings was the flip side of a virtue that I very much admired and depended upon. Similarly, she observed that some of the things about me she used to curse were quite natural side effects of certain gifts of mine that she herself lacked. It slowly dawned on us that we meshed rather well. We became adept at consulting each other. What once had been cause for friction and rage now became a cause for celebration—celebration of our smooth interdependence. By the thirty-year mark our previously depressing marriage was mostly fun, and now, seven years later, when we are well embarked into retirement, it is a delight.

What I have been saying can be summed up by a generalization. In those marriages that successfully survive beyond twenty-five years, somewhere around the twenty-year mark the partners begin to learn how to *accept* each other. Isn't it amazing, I might add with a hint of irony, how rapidly we human beings learn?

Over the past fifteen years Lily and I and other leaders of the Foundation for Community Encouragement have taught approximately a thousand different groups, ranging in size from ten to four hundred members, throughout the world how to be learning communities. We have done this through two- to four-day experiential community-building workshops. The central aim of these workshops is to teach the group to do the work of depression. The period when the group is most deeply engaged in this work we refer to as "emptiness." During this phase the members of the group will empty themselves of whatever is standing in the way of their becoming an authentic community. Often someone will say about the process, "My God, this isn't what I expected. This feels like dying."

Major learning is always a bit like dying. To learn anything new of significance we must first unlearn that which is old and to which we are accustomed. We must give up a part of ourselves that has become anachronistic, and this process of self-emptying may initially feel like annihilation or a descent into nothingness. It can be terrifying.

The terror that may be involved was never more dramatically illustrated than in Martin's "rebirth." Martin was a slightly hard and depressed-appearing sixty-year-old man whose workaholism had made him extremely successful, even famous. During the stage of emptiness in a workshop he and his wife attended, and when the group was still attempting to deal with emptiness on the level of an intellectual concept, Martin suddenly began to tremble and shake. For a brief moment I thought he might be having a seizure. But then, almost as if he were in a trance, he began to moan: "I'm scared. I don't know what's happening to me. All this talk about emptiness. I don't know what it means. I feel I'm going to die. I'm terrified."

Several of us gathered around Martin, holding him for comfort, still uncertain whether he was in a physical or emotional crisis.

"It feels like dying," Martin continued to moan. "Emptiness. I don't know what emptiness is. All my life I've done things. You mean I don't have to do anything? I'm scared."

Martin's wife took his hand. "No, you don't have to do anything, Martin," she said.

"But I've always done things," Martin continued. "I don't know what it's like not to do anything. Emptiness. Is that what emptiness is? Giving up doing things? Could I really not do anything?"

"It's all right to do nothing, Martin," his wife responded. Martin stopped shaking. We held him for about five minutes. Then he let us know that his fear of emptiness, his terror of dying, had subsided. And within an hour his face began to radiate a soft serenity. He knew that he had been broken and had survived. He also knew that through his brokenness he had somehow helped the whole group toward community.

Many of the things the members of a group must empty themselves of to become a true community are almost human universals: expectations of what the experience will be like; prejudices; the need to heal, convert, or otherwise "fix" each other; argumenta-tiveness that precludes listening; a desire for formulas; passivity on the one hand and a tendency to dominate on the other; the need to control. I could go on and on. Other things that must be emptied may be exquisitely personal, like Martin's workaholism or some-one's preoccupation with a family situation that has nothing to do with the group.

In the earlier phases of emptiness not only do individual mem-bers often feel depressed but the entire group will look depressed to an observer. The leaders can do little except encourage the group to hang in and go deeper. The experience is perhaps even more painful for the leaders than for the participants. As the group goes deeper into its work of depression, into emptiness, it can be excruciating for the leader to sit helplessly by watching a whole group go through its death throes.

But "die" these groups do, metaphorically, and then they come out the other side into true community. It is not unlike Kübler-Ross's final stage of acceptance, but it's even more powerful because it is a group phenomenon. Again, it is like a resurrection. The group's sorrow has been turned into joy.

An important term in theology for this work of depression, of giving up or relinquishment, is *kenosis*—the process of the self emp-tying itself of self. It is a word of great power.

In the not-so-good old days many monks and nuns and other religious folks practiced the discipline of self-mortification. The word is derived from the Latin *mors* ("death")—as are "mortality" and "mortician"—and meant for them the "discipline of daily dying." It was often overdone with hair shirts and the like. But its basic purpose—kenosis—is essential to maintaining our vitality as individuals or as a civilized society.

The purpose of kenosis, or self-emptying, is not to have an empty mind or soul, but to make room for the new and ever more vibrant. The image of the kenotic individual in Christianity is that of an empty vessel. To live in the world we must retain enough of our ego to serve as the walls of the vessel, to be any kind of con-tainer at all. Beyond that, however, it is possible to empty ourselves sufficiently of ego that we can become truly Spirit-filled. The goal is not the obliteration of the soul but its expansion.

Dying individuals who complete the work of depression do arrive at acceptance. Groups who hang in there through the agonies of emptiness do arrive at true community. The learning is enormous, and the end result glorious. But I do not mean to whitewash the existential suffering involved. The relinquishments are gigantic.

The Kenosis of Dying

Just as most people deny their dying, so they also deny their aging. I know many in their sixties, even early seventies, who still think of themselves as middle-aged. Being who I am, I deny neither my aging nor my dying; instead I write about it.*

People are immensely different in many respects. They age, both physically and emotionally, at different rates. My father routinely played eighteen holes of golf until he was over eighty. At sixty I am generally doing well to get around nine, even with a cart and painkillers.

I am not middle-aged; I am old. What with flossing my teeth, doing abominable but lifesaving back exercises for the degenerative disease of my spine, using three types of eyedrops for my glaucoma, applying lotions and salves to my deteriorating skin, etc., etc., etc., it takes me well over an hour to get going in the morning and, with similar rituals, the same amount of time to prepare myself for bed in the evening. I don't sleep as soundly nowadays, so I must sleep longer. I have little physical stamina. Travel is exhausting. Concentration requires more effort. I write more slowly. Although I have not yet been given a specific fatal diagnosis, I don't have to be a wizard to realize that I am dying.

It also happens that, when I put my mind to it, I listen better. That's not a bad trade-off.

---

* Much of the material in this section is discussed in greater depth in my most autobiographical book, *In Search of Stones,* where whole chapters are devoted to dying and aging and related issues.

Being old now, I pay more attention these days to television ads addressed to the elderly. They generally infuriate me as much as those aimed at baby boomers, with their blatant use of sexual titillation. One such recent ad for an arthritis pain reliever depicted a woman supposedly in her sixties, though naturally she looked about forty, happily swinging her racquet on a tennis court. At its conclusion, a loud invisible voice joyfully proclaimed, "Live without limits!"

The notion that we can live without limits at any age is absurd. But what old age is more about than anything else is learning how to *accept* one's ever-increasing limits.

Acceptance is both a voluntary and an involuntary process. Each new limitation represents a loss, a little death. These losses are initially inflicted upon us involuntarily. It is not in our human nature to welcome limitations and losses any more than to welcome old age and dying in general. We grieve. The extent to which we are willing to do the work of grieving—the work of depression—is a voluntary matter, however. It is a matter of choice. The choice is not one that is generally encouraged in our pain-avoiding, death-and-old-age-denying culture that incessantly caters to our original sin and tells us to "live without limits."

No experience in my career as a psychiatrist was more painful than having to place several wealthy elderly patients in nursing homes against their will. They had lost the ability to add and subtract accurately and keep track of complex financial matters. Yet they refused to accept this limitation. When I visited them at home, at the request of their families, I found them surrounded by piles of balance sheets, unpaid bills, and checkbooks in disarray. They had been frantically working all day long and late into the evening to make sense of it all. My efforts to suggest that they could no longer make sense of it were to no avail. They had the wealth to hire competent and loving people to manage their affairs so that they could sit back and enjoy grandchildren, sunsets, and walks in the garden. But they would not give up control. So the control had to be wrested from them. They went to nursing homes not because of a failure of bodily function but because of their failure to accept less stringent limitations. It was terribly sad.

———

I have more or less equated limits with losses. The losses of aging are so numerous that they could fill books and so huge that they are incomprehensible to the young. We need every skill at our command to cope with them. One such skill is gallows humor. A particularly male variant of it goes: "At forty I would have settled for a beautiful woman. At fifty-five I would have settled for a great meal. Now that I'm seventy I'd settle for a good bowel movement."

Again without whitewashing, let me note that some of these losses may eventually come, for at least a few, to be experienced as liberation. Take the "beautiful woman" bit. In my fifty-fifth year I experienced a relatively sudden and dramatic loss of libido. It was not total, but along with it my capacity to attain and sustain erections became distinctly iffy. Such a loss of sexual potency would have sent many men, despite their embarrassment, running to their physicians in panic. Not me. Since I was a traveling man at the time, not infrequently subject to the attentions of beautiful women, this diminution of testosterone coursing through my veins felt as if I'd gotten a monkey off my back. It did take a while to accept, but when the while was done it seemed to me more like a healing than a disease.

I focused on this matter of sexual potency because potency—power, whether for women or for men—is what's most at stake. By power I do not mean just political power, as we ordinarily think of it. The loss of such power may be one of the great losses of aging. Mandatory retirement, for instance, can be devastating, particularly to those who enjoyed political stature because of their jobs. But most do not have much in the way of political stature. By power, as in willpower, I mean the capacity to do more or less what we want to do: simple things like having sexual intercourse, playing a game of tennis, riding a bike, driving a car, going downtown for a meal, even getting out of bed to go to the bathroom. Power can be equated with freedom, with choices and options and potentials, with at least a modicum of *control*.

I awoke this morning, for instance, with the potential (potency) of working on this book, writing on my yellow pad, and enjoying the view outside my rural office window whenever my attention wandered. There being no emergencies demanding that I do otherwise, I had the freedom to exercise this option, to choose the plan I most wanted. And so here I sit, in control. But what if my glaucoma were to get out of control and I were to become totally blind? Writing on my yellow pad would no longer be a potential choice. Enjoying the view would not be an option for me. Like my glaucoma, these pleasant, useful things—and many more—would be beyond my control.

Life whittles away at our sense of omnipotence almost from the start. You may recall that in Chapter 3 I spoke of how during our terrible twos we begin to get it rubbed in our faces that we are not kings and queens of the whole world. Despite this ongoing whittling, however, we tend to be remarkably tenacious in holding on to only mildly attenuated feelings of omnipotence. Indeed, in middle age we often feel more in control of our lives than ever before. But in old age the whittling speeds up. It can be so rapid that it seems violent, no longer a whittling away so much as a stripping away.

Aging need not all be agony, however. About five years ago, when I was just beginning to imagine retirement and the loss of power involved, I was encouraged by a *New Yorker* cartoon depicting a man approximately my age saying to his wife over the breakfast table, "I'm losing my grip on things, and it feels just wonderful." And, in fact, as I move ever deeper into retirement, my predominant emotion these days is one of relief.

But note this: I have it good. Lily also is in old age, and she too does not yet have a fatal diagnosis. We have each other to share our aches and pains with. Our marriage is better than at any time in its thirty-seven-year history. We also have plenty of money, a competent staff to support us, good friends, and trips to Europe. Ours is an unusually potent old age. Rejoicing over our enjoyment, I recently said, "These really are our golden years."

"Golden years, hell," Lily retorted. "They're our platinum years."

So I've been lucky, and it is important, I believe, for the reader to realize that my good fortune may color my assessment of these matters. Nonetheless, the stripping continues. There are ever more days when I would like to write or we would like to play nine holes but we can't because we've got doctors' appointments, and when we traipse off to Europe it is with ever more pills each trip. And we have escalated the frequency of these trips to get in as much as we can, precisely because we know our platinum years will not last much longer.

We know the stripping away of our options and our competence will soon become increasingly rapid and increasingly violent. What form will it take? Will we be like Victoria who, because of her stroke, couldn't dress herself anymore? Will we become incontinent where we don't even have control of our bowels and bladder? We cannot predict the details. What we can predict is that the day is not too far off when the stripping will be total, when it will be complete, and when, on this earth, we will have no choices left whatsoever.

———

Thus far I have been speaking of physical losses and limitations of the body. More painful to me over the years has been the loss of illusions. I have *really* had to go through the stages of death and dying and do the work of depression as I relinquished my treasured dreams, ideals, heroes, and fantasies.

Many such illusions are human universals. I can remember a professor telling us psychiatry residents when I was thirty, "Nobody can be truly mentally healthy or emotionally mature until he gives up the fantasy that he can cure his parents." I could connect with that in my work with patients, and I recall nodding sagely at the time. But it was to be a dozen years before I substantially relinquished that fantasy in relation to my own parents, and I even held on to shreds of it until they died.

As I said, I could connect with that fantasy in my work with patients, but I also learned early on the truth of the well-known lightbulb joke: How many psychiatrists does it take to change a lightbulb? Answer: Just one, but only if the lightbulb wants to change. More slowly I learned some of the ambiguities involved. I knew even Jesus couldn't heal anyone who didn't want to be healed, but I believed I could successfully take on all who were "well motivated." All I had to do was to love them enough. Yet I underestimated their biology and ambivalence and overestimated their capacities and mine, including my capacity to be all things to all people. In fact, I never healed any of my patients. I was merely fortunate enough to have a few with whom the mix was sufficiently right for them to use me as a catalyst in healing themselves before I burned out on my omnipotent idealism.

I could go on at inappropriate length about all the illusions I have learned to relinquish. But I will focus on only one more that is ubiquitous in our society and particularly germane to the subject at hand: the illusion of cure. This illusion is brutally exposed by Maggie Ross in *Pillars of Flame* (San Francisco: Harper & Row, 1988), a book about kenosis. Healing does occur, yes, and sometimes it may seem like cure, but in reality it is a very different process. My recovery from an almost fatal bout of pneumonia at age forty-seven is an almost simplistic example. After seventeen days in the hospital on three different types of intravenous antibiotics, I was released to recuperate at home, and within another six weeks I was back on the lecture circuit. But I was not the same man, either psychologically or physically. Psychologically, I realized that I had almost died because I'd been behaving like an iron man, lecturing all day in one city, only to get on a plane that evening so I could lecture all the next day in another city. As part of my healing I was forced, for the first time in my life, to accept and firmly set limits on my previously overdepleting schedule. I also, for the first time in my life, suffered from asthma, clearly as a result of what the pneumonia had done to my bronchial passages. Today, when we go off to Europe, some parts of the mountain of medicines we take with us are for asthma—to treat the effects of the disease of which I supposedly was cured more than a dozen years before.

As I've said, around the typical age of fifty I went through something of a midlife crisis and "healing depression." Among the things that sustained me through that difficult period was a little paperback of humorous quotes and drawings entitled *Who Needs Midlife at Your Age?** One of its quotes was: "Middle age is when you keep thinking in another couple of weeks you'll be back to normal." Ah, yes, the illusion of cure, the denial of aging.

All these delusions—perhaps all our illusions—are illusions of power. Of control and potency. Now let me point out that they are also all illusions of the ego. The soul does not care about power in the world's sense. Incontinence is often perceived as the worst thing that can happen to a person: the final lack of control, an utterly humiliating, total loss of dignity. But it is the ego that is humiliated. The soul does not concern itself with such niceties or with that dignity which is so superficial. Indeed, being immortal and pure spirit, the soul does not worry the least about the body, even the body's death.

———

It is the nature of the ego to cling to power, to chase restlessly the illusion of security, to deny loss, to refuse to accept limitations. Then how does a human being ever empty herself of these things? And why? How and why we do sometimes voluntarily relinquish power, choose to give up treasured illusions, overcome denial, and reach acceptance?

This happens because the ego is sometimes smart. After a while we can grow tired of butting our heads up against a stone wall. We can be clever enough to recognize that our illusions are killing us and that relinquishing them is the path toward healing. We may realize that our ego is getting in our own way and finally come to Buddha's and Jesus' understanding that the ego is its own worst enemy.

At this point, if we ever reach it, we embark upon the journey of kenosis, "the process of the self emptying itself of self," of

———

* Jack Roberts, Dick Gunther, and Stan Gortikov, *Who Needs Midlife at Your Age? A Survival Guide for Men* (New York: Avon Books, 1983).

purification, of the ego bumping itself off. Some engage in this journey of kenosis only halfheartedly, in fits and starts. That is to be expected. It is something of a miracle that we come to be engaged in it at all. A few eventually take up the journey wholeheartedly and come to see in it the very meaning of their existence.

The kenotic path is hardly encouraged in our "live without limits" culture. Take this matter of relinquishing illusions. In our culture we say, "Poor Joe, he's disillusioned." What we ought to say is "Lucky Joe, he's been disillusioned!" Instead, we commiserate: "Now he sees things the way they really are, poor guy."

As if it would somehow be better for him to deny that he is rapidly dying of a fatal disease and therefore unable to say his good-byes, as if it would be better for him to think he could still manage his finances when he can't count anymore, as if it would be better for him to have a heart attack while trying to prove a virility that no longer exists, as if he shouldn't realize that the research he is doing is being used by his company to manufacture weapons of mass destruction . . . and on and on.

But if the publishing industry is any indicator, there are some at least faint early signs of cultural change. Since the publication of Kübler-Ross's book *On Death and Dying* there has been a slow increase in the number of books on the subject of the *learning* of dying. Moreover, their quality seems to be improving. Two recent ones strike me as particularly sound and compelling, in part because of their spiritual yet nonsectarian nature. *Living Our Dying: A Way to the Sacred in Everyday Life* (New York: Hyperion, 1996) by Joseph Sharp, a long-term AIDS survivor, is the broader of the two. *Dying Well: The Prospect for Growth at the End of Life* (New York: Putnam, 1997) by Ira Byock is more rooted in details, including the mechanics of hospice care. I highly recommend both books and will mention them again.

The most commonly dreaded diseases in our society are probably AIDS and cancer, which cause an inexorable, gradual death where the afflicted have much time to watch themselves slowly deteriorate and waste away. Most people—if they had to die at all—would hope for a sudden death without even the consciousness of their dying.

Yet I once heard it reported that Dr. Kübler-Ross actually hoped she would die from cancer so that she would have the time and consciousness to learn from dying. I believe she was expressing a desire to learn kenosis.

But make no mistake: kenosis does not come easily or naturally. I am virtually certain that I myself could not follow a kenotic path, accepting without denial the stripping away of illusions and competencies that death and dying demand, nor could I welcome this stripping, were it not for my spiritual belief system. I couldn't do it unless I believed in a God who wanted me stripped away so that She could have me totally naked without any of the deceptive clothing of my ego . . . unless I had a personal relationship with God so that, among other things, I could complain to Him about His violence and possessiveness . . . unless I was convinced that I had a soul whose highest destiny was utterly and voluntarily to belong to Him . . . unless I knew with certainty that my only true power resided in my soul, that every effective and healing accomplishment of mine had been Her accomplishment emanating out of my real being, my soul, which She created, and that every stupid and wicked thing I have done originated in my ego and its self-preservative mechanisms . . . and unless I realized my ego to be but a temporary necessity, that it chose to cooperate with God as best it could and that I was forgiven from the day of my birth.

Chapter 8

EUTHANASIA:
A TYPICAL CASE

As the euthanasia debate heats up, literature on the subject is rapidly increasing. Of all that I have examined, the most compelling and succinctly informative is a lengthy piece in the May 22, 1995, issue of *The New Yorker* entitled "A Death of One's Own" (pp. 54–69). The author, Andrew Solomon, centers the piece on the suicide of his mother in the terminal stages of ovarian cancer during 1991. Mr. Solomon, his father, and his brother (apparently the entire nuclear family) were present at the time she took her fatal overdose of Seconal, making the event a passively assisted suicide. He makes it clear that he is a proponent of such euthanasia and more or less implies that he is a proponent of actively assisted suicide in appropriate cases as well.

Mr. Solomon has much to say not only about his own personal feelings concerning his mother's suicide but also about the euthanasia movement and the euthanasia debate in general. The article is remarkable for all that it includes. It is perhaps even more remarkable for what it leaves out. I am going to discuss these matters in that order: first, the particular personal details of the case; next, some of what the author includes; and finally, in greater depth, that which is missing.

Mr. Solomon's article is not only well written but personally courageous and, at times, intellectually penetrating. I believe he has done a real service in writing it. I therefore fervently hope he will forgive me for my criticisms of it and for what I myself may have unconsciously and inappropriately left out.

———

Judging from a 1984 portrait of her included in the article, Mr. Solomon's mother was a strikingly beautiful and dignified lady. She believed in euthanasia and, years before her cancer diagnosis, expressed to her family her desire eventually to die by that route. The article makes no mention of whether anyone in the nuclear family ever tried to talk her out of this in the abstract or later when the matter was not abstract.*

Mr. Solomon described his mother as "the center of the family"—and it appears to have been a loving, close-knit family indeed. He uses the word "rational" repeatedly in the article, and it seems clear that his mother was a particularly rational woman, very much given to planning, as was her husband and, we might assume, their two children. Typically, although there are exceptions, euthanasia tends to occur in a family culture of euthanasia, an upper-middle-class culture in which a high premium is placed upon rationality and good planning.

From practically the moment she was first diagnosed to have ovarian cancer, Mr. Solomon's mother spoke openly and more frequently about her desire for euthanasia if and when she became terminal. She made two things very clear from the start: she had no intention of committing suicide until she had exhausted every reasonable means of effecting a cure, and she wanted her family with

———

* In personal correspondence Andrew Solomon has told me that the family members did at times attempt to dissuade his mother from her intent upon euthanasia, but they ultimately accepted her decision.

Mr. Solomon is also the author of a novel centering on his mother's death, *A Stone Boat* (Winchester, Mass.: Faber and Faber, 1994), which is currently available in paperback (New York: Plume Penguin, 1996). Since it is fiction, the book cannot be used to verify his *New Yorker* article or my comments on it.

her when she did so. As Mr. Solomon notes, her desire to have her family with her at the time of her "final exit" is also generally typical of euthanasia as opposed to suicide in other circumstances.

His mother was true to her intent. It appears to have been approximately twenty-one months from the time of her diagnosis until her suicide. She went through four courses of chemotherapy during this period, suffering hair loss and allergies. Mr. Solomon mentioned nothing about severe physical pain but he describes the chemotherapy as "excruciating, humiliating."* She also had an exploratory surgery to assess the results of the first chemotherapy. He says she became emaciated and lost her earlier great beauty. But she also took "on a pale, illuminated, ethereal beauty" and "a radiance, both physical and profound . . . more powerful than her decay." This description suggests his mother had indeed reached the stage of acceptance.

It was during this period that she obtained at least three prescriptions for Seconal from different physicians, one of whom was a psychiatrist, under the thin guise of needing sleeping pills. Because of their potential lethality as compared with more modern sleeping medications, these pills were unlikely to have been prescribed by doctors antithetical to euthanasia or unwilling to be passive assistants to it. Indeed, the psychiatrist in talking to Mr. Solomon was quite explicit about his role in this regard. Although it would be months before she used these pills, the sense of control that the fatal cache symbolized seemed to give his mother great solace.

These things are also typical. The case does not suggest that physicians abound who are willing to prescribe Seconal, only that patients of intelligence and determination are usually able to seek out those who are willing under such circumstances. It is also typi-

---

* In the same personal correspondence, Andrew Solomon stated that his mother experienced episodes of considerable physical pain, which was not consistently well controlled by the medical professionals treating her. She was not, however, in physical pain at the time of her euthanasia. He imagines, nonetheless, that a fear of dying in severe, uncontrolled physical pain was probably her primary motive for choosing euthanasia.

cal that patients for whom euthanasia is an option do find enormous psychological relief from the sense of control, of the freedom of choice that a fatal supply of pills will give them—even if they die a natural death without ever exercising the option to use them.

Mr. Solomon's mother hoped to wait until after her other son's birthday to take her massive overdose of Seconal, but three weeks before that date her gastroenterologist recommended urgent surgery to prevent her tumors from quickly obstructing her intestines. The recommended procedure was clearly meant to be palliative—in other words, the surgery, if she survived it, would prolong her life somewhat, but not for long. If she delayed it, she realized, she might not be able to digest her pills. She immediately called her family together and explained why that very evening was the time.

Husband and sons assisted with the fine peripheral details of the plan: reminding her to take antiemetic medication to prevent vomiting and to eat a light meal, which they brought her and even joked about, and finally bringing her the water with which she herself swallowed the forty Seconal. It was quickly done. During the next half hour or so she and they, in turn, said the most loving of good-byes before she drifted into coma. Five hours later, without any vomiting, seizures, or other complications, her heart and breathing stopped. She was dead, and within another hour their physician had signed the death certificate stating the cause of death to be ovarian cancer. It was truly "a death of her own."

———

Mr. Solomon includes in his article a great deal of information about pro-euthanasia organizations and the subject of euthanasia in general. There is no need for me here to repeat most of it.

One part of his coverage, however, does deserve repetition: the passages in which he discusses rationality. He correctly notes that the more moderate euthanasia proponents "draw an obsessively careful distinction between 'rational' suicide and all others." A rational suicide is one that is not caused by depression or decided upon by a mind clouded with some other mental disorder. In contradistinction to those who assume that all suicide is inherently irrational and the result of a deranged mind, Mr. Solomon believes that some suicides may be rational.

I agree with him. Certainly his mother was a case in point. There is no evidence that she was mentally ill in any respect deserving such a diagnosis or that toward the end her mind was clouded by depression in the least. She had accepted the inevitability of her death, and the timing of her suicide was entirely reasonable under the circumstances.

Nonetheless, Mr. Solomon adds some notes of wise caution. He notes that there are different kinds of depression, not all of which are treatable, suggesting it may be impossible in certain instances to distinguish between depression and a reasonable response to adversity. Victoria, who deliberately starved herself to death and whom I described in Chapter 4, was just such a case. She was depressed at the time. She was also aged, crippled, and isolated in an unsatisfying marriage. Antidepressant medications were ineffective. She might well have benefited from psychotherapy had she been willing to engage in it, but she was not willing. And though depressed, she was not psychotic; she was, in fact, quite rational.

Solomon also points out that the less moderate euthanasia advocates, such as Dr. Kevorkian, "seem to think that 'rational' means 'straightforward.'" He compellingly challenges this simplistic attitude. Rational decision making he accurately describes as a "slow, tangled, peculiar process, whose convolutions are . . . madly individual."

But what makes Mr. Solomon's article so truly powerful for me is the mention of his own personal ambivalence. "The fact is that a suicide is a suicide," he discerningly says, "overdetermined, sad, somewhat toxic to everyone it touches." He goes on to describe how at its conclusion his mother's death felt like a letdown; how he, his brother, and their father hardly talk or even miscommunicate about it; and how they seem to be in a kind of denial of their own. Yet near the end of the article he clearly states his intention to choose euthanasia himself when and if he has a terminal illness or is in an isolated and debilitated old age. "Having seen the simple logic of euthanasia in action," he writes, "and witnessed the comfort of that control, what astonishes me is how many people die by other means."

I find it remarkable that Mr. Solomon should so clearly see the downside of euthanasia and then end up so clear about his own death scenario. I do not find it astonishing, however.

Dealing well with ambivalence is one of the largest psychospiritual challenges we humans need to face throughout our lives.

The word "valence" is customarily used to denote the electrical charge of an atomic or subatomic particle. A proton, for instance, has a positive charge, or valence, and an electron a negative one. This is fine for such little particles. As with magnets, opposites attract, and the different valences of these particles play a crucial role in keeping them together. Not so with the human psyche. The prefix "ambi" means "both," as in the word "ambidextrous," used to describe someone who is equally proficient in using both his left and his right hand. But when we use the word "ambivalent" in psychology we are referring to feelings, and we mean that an individual has both positive and negative feelings about some issue in his or her life. In this instance, "ambivalence" means to feel torn apart.

It is usually normal for us humans to be ambivalent about some situation on an almost daily basis. Such situations may be quite minor. For example, during the seventh year of our marriage, Lily and I struggled mightily together over whether or not to buy a dishwasher. On the one hand, we clearly needed it, and all of our young physician peers had one. On the other hand, we were paying for my psychoanalysis at the time and had chosen to send both of our children to a private nursery school. We had no savings. Yes, it was a small issue, but with our money spread so thin each of us felt torn apart over it.

On a larger scale we are often profoundly ambivalent about the people who are closest to us. I've recounted how Lily and I felt ambivalent about each other and about our marriage for two decades. From childhood into advanced adulthood it is common for us to be ambivalent about our parents. At one and the same time we are likely to feel angry toward them for not being all that we want them to be and feel grateful to them for all that they have given us.

I cannot think of any situation more guaranteed to create colossal ambivalence than the one Andrew Solomon was placed in by his mother. Who among us could feel anything but torn apart when requested to assist in the suicide of a dying parent or spouse?

Although ambivalence is normal, the way we deal with it may be healthy or unhealthy. I think most ambivalence can be looked upon as part of the existential suffering of life. Because it is suffering— because it is painful to feel continually torn apart—our natural tendency is to want to escape from it as quickly as possible. Often we do this too quickly by what I have been taught to call "running with one side of your ambivalence." This means exaggerating one side while repressing the other side. The result is not a healthy resolution of the ambivalence but a simplistic, often destructive, black or white kind of certainty. We might, for example, hear a young adult say, "I hate my father totally; he has no redeeming features whatsoever," or "I love my father so much I'd do anything for him; he's been everything to me." Whenever I hear such certainty I suspect that there is some repressed, unresolved ambivalence lurking underneath. This is my suspicion about Andrew Solomon's clear-cut advocacy of euthanasia at the conclusion of his article.

An entire book could be filled with examples of how people pathologically escape from their ambivalence by running with only one side of it. Suffice it to say that the healthiest response is usually to live with it—to live with the existential suffering of uncertainty and conflictual feelings. I am not saying that ambivalence never can or should be resolved. I am saying, however, that the healthy resolution of deep ambivalence requires facing it over an extended period of time and with a great deal of psychospiritual work, including often the work of depression.

Still, it is painful to live in ambivalence, and on the whole I sense that Andrew Solomon has done rather well with it. It is particularly painful, however, to have to take major action out of deep ambivalence without having to justify your action forever thereafter. One must continue year after year to question the rightness of one's own inherently ambiguous decision. This is partly why I think Mr. Solomon is devastatingly correct when he states that "Euthanasia breeds euthanasia." Assisting a suicide, even passively, is such a dramatic choice of behavior that it seems to me human nature to develop a certain investment in that behavior.

It worries me that euthanasia breeds euthanasia. Indeed, one of my principal reasons for writing this book is to help prevent the breeding, or at least the overbreeding, of euthanasia. While it is true that goodness breeds goodness, it is also true that sin breeds sin.

I am not saying that what Mr. Solomon did was a sin. Had I been in his shoes, particularly given his mother's personality, I might well have felt compelled to make the same choice. Nonetheless, as will increasingly be made clear, the situation was at best highly ambiguous. Moreover, as I have agonized over his situation and his brave article, I have come to like Andrew Solomon. It therefore makes me all the more sorrowful that he should feel so locked in to a narrow vision for his own demise.

————

The most remarkable feature of Mr. Solomon's brilliant article is not all that he has included but all that he has left out. Particularly striking, but not necessarily surprising, is the absence of a discussion of God and the learning of dying.

The absence of God is glaring, at least to a believer. Mr. Solomon does superficially mention existence of some liberal Protestant support for euthanasia on the one hand and adamant Roman Catholic opposition on the other. He comments that the "sacred value of life" may be used either in support of or in opposition to euthanasia in this "secular era." But nowhere in the fifteen thousand words of his article does the word "God" appear. We are given no idea of the personal religious beliefs of the author, his mother, or the rest of the family. From this omission we might assume theirs was a secular family culture in which God was considered irrelevant to the euthanasia debate.

Speaking of the debate, Mr. Solomon writes: "Talk of euthanasia provokes sometimes irrational responses on both sides, and these responses center on the emotional issue of who should control a life. The person whose life it is? The person's doctors? The State?

Some elaborately negotiated balance of these?" The possibility that God might have some role to play in the control of a life is not raised. God is missing from the list of potential stakeholders. Possibly Mr. Solomon would categorize the inclusion of God as one of those "sometimes irrational responses."

In a convoluted way, Mr. Solomon may have inadvertently addressed his exclusion of God in the concluding words of his article: "Why we die, the question from which religion springs, we will never understand, and so we leave that matter in the capable hands of the philosophers. But *when* we die—this is a powerful business, and it is here that, at last, we are beginning to discover our heady dominion."

I both agree and disagree with these words and what they imply. I agree that why we die is the question from which religion springs, but to say we will never understand it offhandedly dismisses all religion. While we will never *fully* understand why we die, the religious quest—in conjunction with the science of biology—can give us some great glimpses of truth not only about death but also about life. I don't understand why, having designated the matter as a religious one, Mr. Solomon doesn't refer it to theologians or priests and rabbis and other clergy as well as to the philosophers, who are generally more secular.

I also agree that Mr. Solomon has put his finger on *the* issue in the final sentence of the article: the issue of power even to the point of dominion. To choose euthanasia—to choose when to die—is indeed a matter of power and dominion. I am much more uneasy about this, however, than the author.

The record of human beings exercising power without restraint, exercising dominion in any sphere, is not impressive. Mind you, as will become ever more clear, I am not advocating a total abdication of power by those who are dying. I do advocate sharing the power, however, not only with doctors and family but also with God. In Chapter 6, where I suggested that since we are not our own creators we do not necessarily have the moral right to be our own destroyers, I proposed that our highest destiny can be to become co-creators with God in life . . . and in death. In determining when to die this does not mean handing everything over to God. But it does mean allowing God at least some portion of the dominion in the matter. It is a more paradoxical path of which I shall soon be giving examples. What it means is that if we can allow God into this decision making about timing, then we can be co-creators of our dying.

The issue of power brings us to the other major matter that Mr. Solomon totally neglects in his article: the learning of dying. I don't know whether his mother learned anything—whether her soul developed—during the twenty-one months of her dying. The whole question is left out.

What could she have learned from such a difficult business?

Maybe I have misread the portrait-in-words that Mr. Solomon has drawn of his mother. The omission of religion suggests she was secular-minded. She was the center of the family and given to planning; she designed her own tombstone; when she first spoke of her intention to choose euthanasia, after the diagnosis of cancer, her son inferred that she "was expressing a sense of outrage at the indignity of what lay ahead and a profound fear of losing control of her own life. . . . It was as though she wanted vengeance for the snub she had received from nature." Her wishes were to be carried out to the letter. Indeed, just before she took her fatal overdose, she remarked to her family, "I got my wishes so often."

The picture I get of Mr. Solomon's mother is that she was an unusually powerful lady who was indeed accustomed to getting her own way, controlling herself and others. I found myself wondering whether the author ever felt manipulated by her. The closest he came to answering that question was in saying, "You tend to accommodate the very, very sick. There was no answer to my mother's rage and despair after her surgery except to say yes to whatever she demanded."

I am very familiar with powerful people in business, even more familiar with the powerful people in my family, and most familiar with myself. We powerful women and men are invariably strong-willed, which is potentially good. Usually we could be described as controlling, which is not necessarily bad. But often we could

properly be termed "overcontrolling." It may well be that I am pro-
jecting my own character onto Mr. Solomon's mother, but I very
much suspect she was either overtly or subtly overcontrolling. Certainly I am. And the biggest struggle of my soul in my old age is to
become less so. The older I get, the more that battle heats up. It is
obvious to me that when and if I develop a lingering fatal illness—
with all the panic and self-centeredness such an illness inevitably
encourages—the battle will become very hot indeed.

So what kind of soul-making might Mr. Solomon's mother have
learned in the final months and days of her life on earth? She could
have learned how to give up a little power—a little control. Not
total control; that would have been stupid, even soul-defeating. But
just a little. It is said that "God is in the details," so it is necessary to
look briefly at the details of dying to consider how she might have
done it differently. What might I—an overcontrolling person but
one with a sense that his soul is always at stake—have done differently were I in her shoes? I don't know.

No one human being can ever put himself totally in another person's shoes. It is conceivable to me that when my time comes—and
if it comes in the same sort of way—I might do exactly what
Andrew Solomon's mother did. It is also conceivable I might accept
the kind of palliative surgery she evaded to buy myself a few weeks
of poor-quality time.

I find it easier, however, to conceive for myself a middle course.
Like Mr. Solomon's mother, I would recognize that the jig was up
and would see no point to such surgery. But instead of euthanasia, I
would ask my family to bring hospice care into my home. As long
as the hospice authorities could assure me of adequate relief of
physical pain while dying at home, I would surrender to them. I'd
lie back and wonder: "Well, God, what's in store for me next? Will
it be intestinal obstruction and slow starvation as predicted? Or will
it be something more unexpected? They've agreed to IV fluids as long
as I'm still conscious, but they have also agreed to withhold nutritional supplements while giving me all the IV morphine I need. I'm
in their hands. How long will it take, Lord? I don't know. It's in Your
hands. I'm not very good at putting myself in Your hands, am I?

Teach me how. Teach me everything I need to learn here at the end. What is it that I still need to learn? Teach me. Teach me."

In my fantasy I would say my loving good-byes to my family, just as Andrew Solomon's mother did, and give them plenty of space to say theirs to me—including all the space necessary for previously unspoken forgiveness and reconciliation. But I would not lay upon them the burden of participation in the precise timing of my death. That I would leave up to physiology and to God, all the while praying: "Lord, all real power belongs to You. Teach me how to give up, to give up control . . . to give it all up to You . . . to let it go. Teach me, Lord. Thank you. It's been a wonderful trip. Will it go on? I don't know. But thank you. And teach me. What do I still have to learn? Teach me."

And all the time there will be terror that the reality may be messier than my fantasy.

Euthanasia as Denial

No two people are totally alike, but the suicide of Andrew Solomon's mother was remarkably similar to the majority of cases of euthanasia about which I have read. Indeed, the similarity is so striking that I can dare to draw a "typical" profile of a person who has committed euthanasia in recent years. It is atypical only in that it is a profile of a man; for reasons I do not yet fully understand, the majority of reported cases of euthanasia are those of women. I use the bland, dehumanizing "name" of X and put the account in quotes because this is a generalization.

"X has a fatal disease. He sought and accepted unpleasant treatment for his disease as long as there was a chance for a cure. Now there is no longer such a chance—he is clearly terminal—and he has decided upon euthanasia, an option he believed was rational and perfectly moral even before the diagnosis of his disease.

"X has a powerful personality. During his life he has overcome considerable obstacles and, given those obstacles, has been remarkably successful. Although he has the social sensibility not to label himself as such, he wouldn't attempt to rebut the assessment of

others that he is a self-made man. He gives some superficial credence to the possible value of religion, but has never himself had
any personal relationship with God.

"During the course of this final illness, X has gone through the
typical emotional stages of death and dying: denial, anger, bargaining, depression, and acceptance. Although sad that it is now the end
of a rich life, he is not at this point depressed. Indeed, at times he
almost glows with light. He has clearly accepted that he is dying.

"If he has any fear about this, he doesn't talk about it. What he
does speak about is the rationality of his decision for euthanasia.
Now! He doesn't want strangers—hospice personnel or others—in
his home. He feels he's suffered more than enough indignity. His
time is up, he's ready to go, and he has the right to refuse any more
treatment of any kind and to refuse to watch his body further decay.
He wants this much control. There is no reasonable point to any
more mess.

"The pills are at hand. For him a neat death requires his family's
knowledge and acquiescence to the fact that euthanasia is a good
death and not an irrational suicide. But as far as he is concerned, it
is not a matter for family debate. He does not seem to consider the
possibility that his family might feel any ambivalence about his decision. He assumes, correctly, that they will respect his wishes in this
final decision, which is, after all, his alone to make. He says loving
good-byes to them, and as he requested, they watch him take a massive overdose and are prepared to tie a plastic bag over his head if the
pills don't seem to work."

Having actually chosen to hasten it somewhat, X would clearly
seem to have no denial about his own death, yet why doesn't he
invite hospice services with their assurance that he can die at home
without physical pain?

The most radical answer, I believe, is that no one can assure him
that his dying will be *emotionally* painless.

Without euthanasia he would indeed be likely to have to watch
his body further decay. He might have to suffer the indignity of
incontinence and mental confusion. He would probably become
more and more helpless, forced to rely increasingly upon the assis-

tance of others. Ultimately he would have to give up all power and control. It could be quite messy. And he would have no idea just how and when the end would come. All of this would involve emotional suffering. With euthanasia, however, he can avoid any such existential emotional suffering.

I call such suffering existential because it is inherent in the process of dying a natural death from a lingering disease, and such a death is so often a natural part of existence. Dying is likely to be inherently messy and characterized by progressive helplessness and loss of control.

I wonder if those who opt for euthanasia, in insisting upon a neat death at a time of their own choosing and totally under their own control, are not still on some level denying death by denying the natural processes of dying. I wonder if they aren't still trying to beat death by meeting it wholly on their own terms and not on death's terms. Or God's terms. I have railed against the medical professionals for using heroic measures and withholding pain relief in terminal cases out of their desire to beat death. But is the answer to go to the other extreme of euthanasia, where a dying person can beat death in the sense of abruptly circumventing the entire dying process?

Why not? What's wrong with such an answer? Why shouldn't someone circumvent a few weeks of existential suffering by orchestrating his demise so as to make it neat? Indeed, to do so seems completely rational, considering the fact that hospice care is still not cheap. The reality is that euthanasia, among other things, is cost-effective.

Cost-effective, that is, without any reference to the meaning of life, which is that we are here for our learning. Had X (or Andrew Solomon's mother) chosen hospice comfort care over euthanasia, he might have had two to six weeks of physically comfortable existence. From those weeks he might not have learned a blessed thing. On the other hand, he might have learned how to negotiate a middle path between total control and total passivity, about how to welcome the responsible care of strangers, about how to be dependent once again, about the paradoxical potential power of helplessness and emptiness, about how superficial the dignity of the body or ego is in comparison to the dignity of the soul, about how to trust and maybe even, out of his existential suffering, at least a little bit about how to pray or talk with God.

It might have cost a few thousand dollars for the opportunity to acquire such learning. Since there is no guarantee that he would have arrived at any such learning, it would have been a gamble—from a purely rational, secular standpoint, one that was hardly worth the trouble. From the standpoint of the soul, however, the choice of such a death could well have been the most cost-effective thing he ever did in his life.

Part III

INTO THE FUTURE

—◆—

SOCIETAL
CONSIDERATIONS

Chapter 9

ASSISTED SUICIDE

The euthanasia debate is much more than a legal issue. It is a debate for the entire society. Nevertheless, society's norms, values, and mores—and its changes—eventually end up as laws. Moreover, the complex and painstaking legal process of discernment is one ideally suited to bring societal debates into focus. That focus is currently on the issue of physician-assisted suicide.

The seeds of the issue were sown more than two thousand years ago by the great Greek physician Hippocrates. Through the centuries until this day, physicians-in-training customarily take his Hippocratic Oath, which imposes upon them two primary duties: to prolong life and to relieve suffering. The issue arises because these two duties are sometimes in conflict. Usually, but not always, the conflict between them can be resolved with a balanced approach (see Chapters 1 and 2) upon which the medical community and society at large generally agree. Nonetheless, given all the technology of modern medicine, it remains unclear to a substantial number of physicians when prolonging life should take precedence over relieving suffering. In the past few years an increasing number of patients have insisted that the relief of their suffering at the expense of a rapid death should be their choice and their right. Many physicians are agreeing with them. Dr. Kevorkian has become a household name through obliging patients within the glare of publicity. Others have obliged without any apparent desire to become political figures. Still, I suspect that the vast majority of physicians—myself among them—have extremely serious qualms about the whole matter. We see that a distinction is still to be made between suicide and natural death—and hence between relieving the suffering of a natural death and accommodating a patient's desire to die painlessly at a time of his own choosing.

In 1994 a federal district judge found a Washington State law banning physician-assisted suicide to be "partly unconstitutional." Her judgment was reversed in a 2–1 decision by the federal court of appeals in March 1995, but the case was sent on to a larger panel of the court for another hearing. On March 6, 1996, that panel reversed the appellate court's decision 8 to 3, finding in essence that terminally ill patients who are mentally competent have a constitutional right to determine the time and manner of their death. At this point it is certain that the issue will be passed on to the U.S. Supreme Court.

That will not be the end of the matter. The wheels of justice grind exceedingly fine and slow, and judicial opinions tend to be case-specific and precisely limited. They can also be reversed. Although the law plays a powerful role in defining society, society ultimately plays a more powerful role in defining the law. As Lee LaTour of the Hemlock Society has said, "Euthanasia is the abortion debate of the next century."*

———

Two recent books represent the moderate position in favoring physician-assisted suicide under strict guidelines.

Dr. Timothy E. Quill, a former hospice medical director, wrote an account of the suicide he assisted of a leukemia patient; it was published in the prestigious *New England Journal of Medicine*.† He was astonished by the resulting furor which, among other things,

———

* Quoted in Solomon, "A Death of One's Own," p. 67.
† *NEJM* 324 (March 7, 1991): 691–94.

resulted in his being brought before a grand jury. The jury decided not to charge him. He also apparently received considerable support from the medical community. Out of this experience he went on to write *Death and Dignity: Making Choices and Taking Charge* (New York: Norton, 1993). The influence of this book can clearly be seen in the March 6, 1996, majority opinion of the federal appeals court panel.

Dr. Lonny Shavelson, a reporter and physician, also personally assisted a suicide of a terminally ill patient. Out of this experience, the death of relatives, and reportorial investigation he has written *A Chosen Death: The Dying Confront Assisted Suicide* (New York: Simon & Schuster, 1995). This strikes me as the more profound book because of the ambiguity of the cases he describes in the greater depth. Nonetheless, he echoes Quill in his belief that terminally ill patients not only have the right to refuse further treatment and die relieved of great pain but specifically have the right to determine the exact time and manner of their death.

In this shared belief, the two books (and Andrew Solomon's lengthy article) are remarkably similar. They all leave the issues of God and the learning of dying out of the equation. Like Solomon, Quill and Shavelson are obviously decent people but say nothing about their own spiritual beliefs or the absence thereof. I would guess that the authors are probably secular humanists to whom God and soul-learning constitute a significant blind spot.

―――

Or perhaps these physician-authors simply felt that these issues of God and soul-learning were too hot to handle. For me, these issues are too hot *not* to handle.

They are hot because of the First Amendment to the Constitution, part of which guarantees freedom of religion. Over the past fifty years or so this guarantee has been interpreted by the courts to include the freedom not to be religious—to be an atheist, an agnostic, or another type of secularist without suffering any persecution therefor. No one could support the First Amendment more heartily than I, but I have grave reservations about the latitude with which it has been interpreted by the courts. It has led, for example, to the total secularization of public education and to a state of affairs in which values cannot be taught adequately in our public schools. It is as if there can be no middle ground. We have jumped from the frying pan of bigoted religious teaching into the fire of implicitly teaching a secularism that is in its own way equally bigoted. This is a book about euthanasia and not about the huge contemporary problems of public school education, but euthanasia is a predominantly secular phenomenon. How we deal with it cannot be divorced from the subject of education.

I have explained secularism as a stage of psychospiritual development—a stage well beyond primitive religiosity but still short of a fully mature spirituality. One does not simply yank another out of a stage. When and if secularists convert to a more advanced stage they usually do so gradually and of their own accord. Vigorous attempts by others to convert them are often invasive and can do a kind of violence. But does this mean secularists should be deprived of all information that might even gently challenge them? I do not think so.

Being humane physicians, both Shavelson and Quill are vigorous proponents of informed consent—the concept that patients should be fully informed of their condition and of all possible treatments so they can share the decision making with their doctor even to the point of choosing to reject their doctor's recommendations. In cases of euthanasia this seems to Quill and Shavelson to be solely a matter of providing medical facts, such as side effects and the likelihood of cure or remission. This does not mean that the physician will inevitably acquiesce to the patient's request for euthanasia. He may say, for instance, "I believe you're too depressed right now to make a decision. Let's consider it again when you're not so down," or "I'm not at all sure your condition is terminal. Let's get some tests in a few more weeks and then see where we stand."

Neither Shavelson nor Quill, however, considers the possibility that the patient has a right to be informed of psychological and spiritual matters that might have a bearing upon her or his decision. If they inform the patient of reasons not to opt for euthanasia, they restrict themselves to providing purely technical and medical reasons. In one sense this is understandable, since most physicians receive little training in clinical psychology and none at all in theology. Understandable though it might be, however, I do not think they are in fact fully informing their patients.*

Who is trained to provide such psychospiritual information? The answer is pastoral counselors, of whom there is an abundance. Unfortunately, they are not all equally well trained or, by reason of their own denial and personal development, suited to do so. If they are to be used for the job, they need to be carefully selected. The provision of psychospiritual information is often challenging. Patients should not be clobbered with it. Candidates for counseling the dying ought to have the capacity to be simultaneously involved and detached, simultaneously tough and gentle.

How might I personally provide relevant psychospiritual information to a patient requesting euthanasia? Since each patient is unique, I can offer no formula, but I would probably do so mostly or entirely by asking questions roughly in the following order:

- Questions about their illness, its history, progression, and prognosis; their feelings toward it and any fantasies they have about it; their feelings and fantasies about death and dying.
- Their reasons for requesting euthanasia.
- Their families and support system; conflicts that might be reconciled; good-byes they want to say.
- Their religious beliefs: Have they had any mystical experiences? Is their relationship with God personal? Do they believe in and have fantasies of an afterlife? How might euthanasia be consonant or dissonant with their beliefs?
- If their belief system is secular, I would be accepting but I would ask about their notions of the soul and their awareness of why some religious people support euthanasia and others decry it.

---

* Quill does suggest that "spiritual counseling should be offered, depending on the patient's background and beliefs"—in other words, nonconfrontational spiritual counseling should be provided for those who are already spiritual and are less likely to request euthanasia.

- What might their regrets be? Can they imagine there is anything they might learn by dying a natural death? Is there anything else at all that they'd like to learn?
- Have they had any experience with hospice care, and what do they know about it?
- Are there any questions they'd like to ask me? Do they want to think about some of the things we've talked about? How do they feel about our meeting?
- Would they like to see me again?

I'm sure that Quill and Shavelson would themselves ask some of these questions, but I doubt they would feel comfortable about the more religious ones. Possibly they have never even asked them of themselves. I imagine they'd feel such questions to represent a violation of the patient's privacy or freedom of religion. Indeed, it is even conceivable to me that the courts might agree with them. Since secularism is itself a religion of sorts, shouldn't the secularist be free to make a secular decision about his own life without challenge, however gentle?

Yet I come back to this matter of informed consent. Can we say that a patient who opts for euthanasia has been well informed if she has never been asked to consider psychospiritual reasons for rejecting it? Do we simply assume she has thoughtfully considered them already? That is not an assumption that I could justify. Moreover, I do not see how a decision for euthanasia could be thoughtful—full of thought—without such consideration. Yes, we may be a secular society, but I wonder how the courts will deal with the fact that "thoughtless informed consent" and "partially informed consent" are contradictions in terms.

––––––

Both Dr. Shavelson and Dr. Quill are knowledgeable supporters of hospice and the comfort care it provides. At the same time they justify their support of euthanasia by contending that the relief of suffering is inadequate in up to 25 percent of hospice cases. To my mind, they utterly fail to document this contention. To understand this critical flaw in their work, it is necessary that we reexamine Hospice—and its problems—in greater depth.

In terms of culture and history, Hospice is a remarkably recent organization. As more briefly noted in Chapter 2, it was founded in London in 1967 by Dr. Cicely Saunders (Dame Saunders now that she has been knighted for her contribution) at Saint Christopher's Hospice and imported to the United States the next year by Florena Wald, then dean of Yale University's School of Nursing. Its rapid growth in both nations can be attributed to its successful response to the increasing problem of using medical technology to keep dying patients alive as opposed to easing their dying. Being a relatively new organization, however, neither it nor its philosophy of comfort care for the dying has yet been fully integrated into the social fabric. Local hospices are largely independent of state and national Hospice organizations. I receive reports that the availability and the quality of hospice care vary from community to community. A lot of people simply don't know about it. It is heavily dependent upon local volunteers. Some insurance companies, willing to reimburse more expensive, unnecessarily heroic traditional medical treatment, may be unwilling to reimburse the comfort care of hospice. Many physicians are still resistant to it.

The problem of physician resistance is so strange—almost bizarre—that it deserves discussion. It is an overdetermined phenomenon. Hospice is new, and people, even physicians, often resist that which is new. To this day our medical students are given little or no training in either death and dying or advanced techniques of pain management. Physicians feel great satisfaction when they beat death but are often profoundly uncomfortable with the notion of assisting dying. In particular, they are uncomfortable with giving pain-relieving medications that may hasten death, resulting in what is called the double effect. Although it is not usually required, hospice does sanction the double effect as a frequently necessary element of comfort care. Many physicians wonder about the morality of this. When I talk to them about the subject, they are astonished to learn that the Roman Catholic Church, which is in the forefront of opposition to euthanasia, actually sanctions the double effect.

Dr. Robert I. Misbin writes about this:

> For example, a patient with lung cancer and widespread
> metastases would be permitted to reject the extraordinary
> means represented by a mechanical respirator. But what, then,
> should the patient's doctor do to combat the patient's pain and
> anxiety in the face of impending respiratory failure? According
> to Roman Catholic teaching, the physician would be permit-
> ted to give the patient morphine, even though such treatment
> would hasten the patient's death. This is based on the principle
> of double effect, according to which it is permissible to take an
> action that has some bad effects, provided that a good effect is
> intended. That bad effect, however, cannot be used as a means
> to achieve the good. Thus, the patient with cancer could be
> given increasing doses of morphine to control the pain and
> anxiety, even though this treatment may ultimately shorten the
> patient's life. To start with, a lethal dose would not be permit-
> ted, because in that case the intention would be to cause death
> rather than relieve suffering. Thus, the Roman Catholic posi-
> tion allows physicians to use effective means to alleviate the suf-
> fering of dying patients, but it does not sanction direct killing.*

The principle of the double effect is of such significance it is necessary to look very briefly at a specific case of hospice care. Let me
take the one most recently reported to me, that of a patient I'll call
Mary, a case remarkably similar to Dr. Misbin's hypothetical one.

Mary was diagnosed two years ago, when she was in her late forties, to have a malignant tumor metastatic to her bones. She was
treated with several courses of chemotherapy by an oncologist in a
chemotherapy center somewhat distant from her home. Neither the
oncologist nor the hospital was hospice-friendly. The chemotherapy

---

* Jonathan D. Moreno, ed., *Arguing Euthanasia: The Controversy over Mercy Killing,
Assisted Suicide, and the "Right to Die"* (New York: Simon & Schuster, 1995),
p. 129.

initially retarded the cancer growth, and save for its discomfort, Mary was free of serious pain. Nonetheless, her oncologist five months ago informed her that the tumors were growing again and she likely had no more than six months to live. Mary blandly reported this prognosis to her friends, one of whom happened to be deeply involved in hospice. Although clearly still in denial, Mary agreed to be enrolled in the local hospice program, and home visits by hospice volunteers were begun.

Two months after this rather passive enrollment, Mary began to experience moderate pain that was well controlled for the next three weeks by modest doses of oral opiates. Her denial continued. Suddenly one night, however, her pain escalated from moderate to extremely severe. Panicked, she called not hospice but her oncologist, with whom she'd had the longer relationship. He admitted her by ambulance to his hospital and started her on doses of IV morphine whenever she asked the nurse for them, but she was not on a morphine pump or PCA (patient-controlled analgesia) machine. He informed her that the X rays demonstrated she now had metastases to her lungs as well as to her bones. He also advised further chemotherapy, not because it would give her any significant remission but because it might allow her to get by on lower doses of morphine.

At this point, confronted by the excruciating reality of physical pain, Mary was no longer in denial. Although given the opportunity, she demonstrated no inclination to discuss the psychospiritual aspects of her dying with her hospice friend and visitors, but she was quite willing to discuss the technical aspects. She never mentioned euthanasia, but she could not see the point of further uncomfortable chemotherapy merely for partial and temporary pain relief. She also was distressed that although she reported the recurrence of pain to the nurse immediately, by the time the nurse got back to her with her shot she was in agony again. Her hospice friend and volunteers told her that her local hospital had just that week opened an inpatient hospice unit and advised her to request that she be transferred there. She accepted the advice.

Upon transfer to the new unit and into one of its homey rooms, she was immediately started on a PCA machine. She was grateful for the virtually total relief of physical pain. She seemed for the next four days to enjoy the visits from her family, her hospice friend and volunteers, and the medical director of the new unit. Then, however, she became gradually but inexorably short of breath due to the spreading tumor in her lungs. This phenomenon is like slowly drowning, and Mary became duly terrified. The unit medical director looked her straight in the eye. "Mary, this is one of the most frightening ways to die. I can give you more sedation to relieve you of this terror, but it will likely cut short your life by a couple of days and I need it to be your decision."

"Give me the sedation," Mary answered. "I'm ready to die."

Further sedation was added to her morphine, and twenty-four hours later Mary peacefully died while asleep, without any apparent pain or terror.

How was this different from euthanasia or physician–assisted suicide? The physician at the hospice unit administered fatal doses of narcotics to hasten the patient's death at her own request and did so to relieve the terror of being breathless—a type of suffering that might be considered as much emotional as physical. There are two differences. They are differences in timing and the nature of suffering.

———

To both Quill and Shavelson these differences seem like such fine points that they are inconsequential and do not merit mention. To me, however, they strike at the very essence of the issue. I am not alone in this opinion. Ira Byock's book *Dying Well* is not about the euthanasia debate but does consistently report the adequacy of hospice care, with which he has been deeply involved for many years. He refers to the issue of euthanasia fleetingly when he comments, "People unfamiliar with the purposes of palliative care may see little difference between sedation to control persistent physical distress and euthanasia. What philosophically appears to be a fine line is, in practice, a chasm." I might add that the courts also have yet to recognize this chasm in the matters of timing and the variety of suffering.

Once again in Shavelson's and Quill's moderately pro–euthanasia books we find important discussion missing. While both books proclaim the physician's Hippocratic responsibility to relieve suffering, neither makes any distinction whatsoever between physical and emotional suffering. Nor do they distinguish between that emotional suffering which is useless and unnecessary and that which might be existential and productive of spiritual growth.

One has to read between the lines to realize that in contending that hospice care is inadequate for a quarter of its patients, Shavelson and Quill are not speaking of inadequate relief of physical pain. Nor are they speaking of the utterly useless emotional suffering that may accompany the dying process, such as Mary's terror as she was beginning slowly to asphyxiate. They would seem to agree that hospice care, when done well, is in fact fully adequate in these regards. Then to what *are* they referring as inadequate?

Although I believe the authors vastly overestimate their current prevalence, their cases of true euthanasia represent a tiny minority of terminally ill hospice patients who want somewhere toward the end to control totally their dying. They are patients who would rather kill themselves than be killed by their disease. Indeed, one of Shavelson's patients, Mary Hall, delayed her planned euthanasia for weeks so as first to achieve a reconciliation with one of her sons. Once it was achieved, she proceeded to take a fatal dose of Seconal even though she'd been assured she would die painlessly in no more than another day or two. The patients described, like Mary Hall, are strong-willed, seemingly secular people who want to orchestrate their dying and who, to achieve that end, will choose suicide over natural death, no matter how comfortable that death is made. And both Dr. Quill and Dr. Shavelson believe that frustration of the patients' self-determination in this regard causes them such intolerable suffering that it is a physician's duty to facilitate their suicide and acquiesce to their desire for such control.

I do not have the authors' certainty about the matter. At the risk of seeming inhumane, I still feel I must state that their true euthanasia patients, as recounted, struck me as control freaks. It did not seem to occur to the authors to call in a psychiatrist or other psychotherapist to attempt to deal with these patients' control issues.

It only seemed that a failure to accede to the patients' desire for control would be to abet rather than relieve "perfectly rational" and "intolerable" suffering.

As Andrew Solomon pointed out in relation to his mother, it is very difficult to say no to those suffering severe physical disease, but that doesn't mean it shouldn't be done. As a control freak myself, I have resonated to two quotations: "Life is not a problem to be solved but a mystery to be lived," and "Life is what happens to us while we are making other plans." I find I need remind myself of these quotations on a daily basis. Among other things, they point out to me that the loss of control, the irrationality, the mystery, and the insecurity inherent in dying are also inherent to living. The suffering involved in dealing with these realities strikes me as a very important segment of what I call existential suffering. It seems to me that the "true euthanasia" patients of Shavelson and Quill were suffering not so much from a problem of death as from a problem of life. I think they might have had a lot to learn from being assisted to face this problem rather than being assisted to kill themselves in order to conquer it. This is not to say that they would have learned . . . only that they might have. And even if they didn't, I would still find it hard to construe the frustration of their desire for euthanasia as "intolerable suffering."

———

The fact that I would vote against physician assistance in the suicide of such patients should not be taken to mean I am against euthanasia under any circumstances whatsoever.

First of all, in this unpredictable business of living and dying, there are always exceptions. The true euthanasia patients of Quill and Shavelson were potent and competent people who could have obtained good hospice care had they so desired. But what about those who are not so competent? Quoting Quill, Andrew Solomon succinctly raises this concern. Referring to the Hemlock Society as something of a "social club," he writes of euthanasia: " 'It's still an upper-middle-class concern,' Quill says, 'because Americans who are worried about getting *any* care aren't distracting themselves with this.' And yet it is for people without much privilege that legislative change is most urgent; whereas rich people with private doctors and good connections can almost always find the means to kill themselves quietly at home, most others are subject to the philosophies of random overworked physicians" (p. 60).

My immediate concern with those dying in poverty is not that they should be unable to obtain a fatal cache of pills but that they should be unable to obtain good hospice care. Were hospice simply not at all available, I would be an avid supporter of the right to euthanasia for others as well as for myself. But given what comfort care by hospice can do, the answer to the problem of assisted suicide is not more euthanasia but more hospice. Society and the courts seem to me to be jumping the gun on this matter. We seem to have it backwards. The first order of business should be to establish that dying patients have a constitutional right to competent hospice care. Only *after* this right has been established does it make sense for the courts to turn their attention to the question of whether terminally ill patients should have an additional constitutional right to physician-assisted euthanasia.

Be that as it may, society does not always move logically, and I cannot state without equivocation that physician-assisted suicide should be utterly illegal. From what I have read, I would personally have denied it to all the hospice-eligible patients whom Shavelson and Quill have written about. Yet I did not meet those patients. Nor can I be certain that I might not find somewhat similar patients more deserving. I would be unwilling to deny euthanasia to anyone without a hearing. But here I am talking about decision making on a case-by-case basis. This is very different from saying simplistically that the terminally ill have a constitutional right to euthanasia. I am saying only that they should have a right to a hearing. The knotty question of who should conduct the hearing is one to which I will shortly return.

––––––

There is a rule that hospice services can be offered only to those patients who have been medically assessed to have no more than six months to live. Since such assessments may not be accurate, many hospice providers question this rule and certainly bend it upon occasion. Nevertheless, there is no question that hospice exists solely to serve the terminally ill and their families.

But what about the chronically ill whose condition has not been diagnosed as terminal? I speak of them not because their medical care is necessarily inadequate but to make clear that euthanasia is not solely an issue for hospice-eligible patients. I am speaking here of quasi-euthanasia as opposed to true euthanasia: namely, suicide to avoid or escape the existential suffering of severe and unremitting incapacitation that is unlikely to be relieved shortly by death.

In reporting the case of Kelly, a quadriplegic whose suicide was finally assisted by his mother after Kelly had made two failed attempts at suicidal starvation, Dr. Shavelson raised this issue. But it seemed to get lost in the greater focus on true euthanasia.

In reaction to the horror of the Euthanasia Program of Nazi Germany, I believe we developed an absolutist rule in our collective conscience or unconscious: "Thou shalt not put to death anyone not already dying." I am glad that we were revolted by the nightmare "efficiency" of the Nazi regime, but I wonder how clearly we are thinking when our primary concern is with the existential emotional suffering of those who have but a week or a month to live and not with those who endure much the same sort of suffering but have years and years to live. It hardly seems fair to me to call physician-assisted suicide of the terminally ill a "right" before we offer such a right to those with the greater and probably even more intolerable suffering. Here again it seems to me that we have our societal priorities reversed.

I am not stating a clear belief that the chronically ill should have a right to physician-assisted suicide. In Chapter 7 I told of having dinner with a monk who was in the later stages of Lou Gehrig's disease but was not quite yet terminal, a man who had become saintly perhaps as a result of his chronic suffering. I am grateful he had not opted for euthanasia. In my experience with nursing homes, I have noticed that a few chronically crippled patients give more care to their caregivers than they themselves receive. These patients serve as an uplifting presence and spiritual center for the institution and in their supposed impotence play a more powerful role in life than those of us who are blatantly functional.

I am also not suggesting that the chronically disabled who want euthanasia are not suffering from control issues or other forms of psychopathology that are potentially treatable. Shavelson's quadriplegic patient, Kelly, struck me as remarkably self-centered and domineering. Self-centeredness is quite natural in anyone so helpless, but it is not inevitable, and I'm not sure Kelly received any even gently confrontational psychotherapy or spiritual counseling over all the years he sought euthanasia.

What I am saying is that these patients worry me. I think about Kelly who was so paralyzed he couldn't have taken a fatal overdose of pills by himself even if he'd had them. I think about Victoria who could no longer dress herself, who was stuck with a distant, uninvolved alcoholic husband, and who felt she had to starve herself to death rather than accept around-the-clock care. I think about the Van Dusens. It was their case that first worried me about euthanasia, but I also worry about Dr. Van Dusen, who was no longer able to preach, and his elderly wife, who was crippled with arthritis. And I worry about all the people like them: the victims of ALS and strokes and Alzheimer's and multiple sclerosis and on and on. And I think of the shut-ins, the homeless, those whose spouses have died and whose families are distant, the terribly lonely.

I am not saying these people should want euthanasia. What I am saying is that if physician-assisted suicide is to be a right of any rapidly dying patient, the chronically ill also deserve a hearing when they seek it. Indeed, in order of precedence, I believe they deserve it even before the hospice-eligible terminally ill, who have less time left to suffer the vicissitudes of their condition.

––––

For the past few pages I have been waffling, but what if I were backed into a corner and could no longe waffle? What if I were a jurist sitting on a court that had to decide *today* on the legality of physician-assisted suicide? What would be my judicial opinion?

My judgment would be to keep physician-assisted suicide illegal. I would make this judgment knowing full well that back-alley euthanasia would continue to occur as it had in the past and would continue to be a source of anguish and tragedy. This would be my decision for three reasons:

- The other extreme—making assisted suicide so fully legal that it is considered a right—has, I believe, profound negative implications for society as a whole. My concern is not simply, as Andrew Solomon put it, that "euthanasia breeds euthanasia" or that the floodgates would be opened. My primary concern is the message that would be given to society. It would be yet another secular message that we need not wrestle with God, another message denying the soul and telling us that this is solely our life to do with as we please. It would be a most discouraging message. It would not encourage us to face the natural existential suffering of life, to learn how to overcome it, to learn how to face hardship— the kind of hardship that calls forth our courage. Instead it would be a message that we are entitled to take the easy way out. It would be a message pushing our society further along the worst of the directions it has already been taking. I shudder at the results.
- A decision for the middle ground legalizing assisted suicide under certain circumstances and not others would lead us into a legal quagmire. Despite their enormous expense and frustration, such quagmires might be all to the good if we were prepared to wallow in them. I do not believe that we are currently so prepared.
- As a society, we are not yet ready to grapple with the euthanasia issue in a meaningful way. There are just too many even more important issues that need to be decided first: the right to physical pain relief, the right to hospice comfort care, the right to public education that is not wholly secular, the right to free discourse about the soul and human meaning, the right to education about the nature of existential suffering, the right to medical care in general, and the right to quasi-euthanasia for the

chronically ill. Only when we are clear about these matters, among others, will we be in a position to tackle the issue of legalizing physician-assisted suicide for the terminally ill.

———

Suppose, however, that society chooses not to follow my guidance. Suppose the Supreme Court decides to declare unconstitutional any blanket state law making physician-assisted suicide illegal, thereby compelling the states to enter the middle ground of establishing some kind of code that will set criteria for legal assisted suicide? And suppose I am still a jurist, bound to uphold the law of the land? What kind of opinions might I render to guide the states in the establishment of such criteria?

Here the reader would quite naturally want me to draw up a model code, but, for several critical reasons, I am not going to oblige.

The most critical reason is that I would not want to diminish the responsibility of the reader in this regard . . . not one iota. I began this chapter by stating that euthanasia is a debate for the entire society. My purpose in writing this book is not to relieve citizens of this burden but to clarify it . . . not to enjoin citizens to stay on the sidelines but to encourage them to enter the debate as educated participants. Such participation is the only route toward social sanity in matters of such great importance. I suspect the courts will behave accordingly, refraining from setting clear codes but pushing states and local communities to create their own codes, which the courts can then at great leisure review for constitutionality.

Then, as I said, the middle ground will be a legal quagmire. Any code I might propose would inevitably be imperfect and subject to immediate criticism. Indeed, Dr. Quill has already proposed criteria, which his own ally, Dr. Shavelson, has already called into some question.

Actually, I believe that if we are to enter this middle ground, Dr. Quill's criteria would be a good place to start. They are quite thoughtful, and Quill is fully aware that they are "less than ideal." I also very much appreciate his intent that his criteria—which are very different from euthanasia on demand—should not create a process that is either "easy or impersonal." In their abbreviated form, Dr. Quill's seven "Potential Clinical Criteria for Physician-Assisted Suicide" are as follows:

1. The patient must, of his own free will and at his own initiative, clearly and repeatedly request to die rather than continue suffering.
2. The patient's judgment must not be distorted.
3. The patient must have a condition that is incurable and associated with severe, unrelenting, intolerable suffering.
4. The physician must ensure that the patient's suffering and the request are not the result of inadequate comfort care.
5. Physician-assisted suicide should only be carried out in the context of a meaningful doctor-patient relationship.
6. Consultation with another experienced physician is required.
7. Clear documentation to support each condition above is required.*

Dr. Quill elaborates upon each of these criteria, but, to my mind, his elaborations fail to answer the key questions. Criteria 1, 3, and 4, for instance, have to do with suffering. Yet, as I have pointed out, nowhere in any of these elaborations or in the rest of his writing does he define suffering, make a distinction between physical and emotional suffering, or attempt to distinguish between that emotional suffering which is unconstructive and that which is existential and therefore potentially productive of psychospiritual growth.

To further demonstrate the complexity of the matter, let me quote Dr. Quill's sixth criterion in its entirety: "*Consultation with another experienced physician is required* to ensure the voluntariness and rationality of the patient's request, the accuracy of the diagnosis and prognosis, and the full exploration of comfort-oriented alternatives. The consulting physician should review the supporting materials, and personally interview and examine the patient" (p. 163).

---

* Quill, *Death and Dignity,* pp. 161–64.

This is hardly a *bad* criterion, but is it enough?

It assumes that the physician requesting the consultation already finds merit in the patient's desire for euthanasia. Then how does he choose *his* consultant? Certainly he will not go to a physician he knows is antipathetic to euthanasia, and probably not to one who, like me, is deeply torn over the issue and leery of it; he will naturally go to the most like-minded colleague of his acquaintance—one he knows will almost undoubtedly confirm him in his judgment supporting euthanasia. Although better than nothing, such consultation is not a democratic process. Moreover, I imagine it would lead to the development of a distinct subculture of physicians: a subgroup known to support euthanasia but not representative of the profession as a whole. (Quill doubts this would occur but offers no rationale for his belief.) I am not sure we want the practice of euthanasia to become such a medical subspecialty.

There are several alternatives, but each one raises its own questions. For instance, most hospitals now have ethics committees, and it would seem quite natural to refer cases of requested euthanasia to them. But these committees usually meet infrequently. Members may or may not show up. No standards generally govern the composition of these committees: in some hospitals all the members are volunteers; in others they are elected; in still others the members are appointed. Generally, all the members are physicians with little or no training for this type of work. Should such committees always include a psychiatrist? How about a pastoral counselor? A nurse or two? A member of the clergy? A lay member from the local community? To what degree should they be representative if they are to make euthanasia decisions? How do the politics of such representation work? What would the introduction of such politics and changes do to the culture of the hospital? Perhaps an alternative lies in a county-appointed committee of two physicians, a lay psychotherapist, a member of the clergy, and a political representative from the city council. But I can foresee this group running into all the same sorts of problems.

I use the word "problems." I am reminded of a wise retired corporation president with whom I once served on the board of directors of a not-for-profit foundation. On a certain issue the board had recently voted to move from a clear-cut absolutist position to a middle ground. The result was rapidly escalating contentiousness throughout the organization. In considering how to deal with the contentiousness, this experienced businessman pronounced, "It is not a problem; it is a dilemma."

"What do you mean?" we other directors inquired.

"A problem is something that has an adequate, if imperfect, solution," he answered. "A dilemma has no adequate solution."

Maintaining the illegality of assisted suicide strikes me as an adequate, albeit imperfect, solution to the problem of euthanasia. Going to the other extreme of legitimizing euthanasia on demand would also be an adequate solution, although one I strongly believe would prove to be far more seriously flawed. All my usual instincts are to search for a middle ground. In this instance and *at this time,* however, my experience suggests that choosing the option of a middle ground would move the issue of euthanasia from the status of a problem to that of a dilemma. Please be forewarned.

———

Among the many things I respect about Quill, with which I imagine Shavelson and Solomon would agree, is his clear insistence that the final decision about assisting a suicide should be *personal.* By this he means that whoever assists the suicide of a patient should be personally involved with that patient. Never should the final decision be made by someone who does not even know the patient, who has never even spoken with him or her, who has not taken upon himself the emotional agony of an individualized, case-by-case determination. Although never fully stated, this insistence arises, I believe, from the fact that these authors are so deeply humanistic that they have a sense of how inhumane impersonal bureaucracies can become. Yet I also think they underestimate this potential.

At the moment, when physician-assisted suicide is generally illegal, physicians may be called to account for assisting at all. Yet the accounting thus far has been soft indeed. I do not envy what Dr.

Quill went through in being hauled before a grand jury, but the jury did decide not to indict. The public climate is currently gentle.

What might things look like if society went to the other extreme of legalizing physician-assisted suicide—in other words, euthanasia on demand—as a right? There would be no requirement for any personal doctor-patient relationship in the matter, no room for any negotiation. Physicians would be automatically obliged to terminate the lives of requesters who met only limited, almost mathematical diagnostic and prognostic criteria.

But that would be the least of it. Over the past twenty years U.S. society has been moving with increasing rapidity toward managed care—medical care impersonally managed not by physicians but by insurance company or government bureaucrats whose sole bottom line is the dollar. To such managers, euthanasia will look so cost-effective that they will be hard put not to encourage it. Think of the possibilities! Premium refunds or tax rebates, for instance, could be offered to euthanasia volunteers. Or particularly high reimbursements to physicians for euthanasia procedures. Or euthanasia franchises. A Brave New World could be right around the corner.

This potential scenario has been given a name: "the slippery slope." By this, critics of euthanasia suggest that establishing a right to physician-assisted suicide will start society on a rapid slide into ever greater disrespect for the value of human life. Proponents of euthanasia doubt any such result and often point to the Netherlands to support their argument. They claim that although euthanasia has been legalized in Holland it has not led to any societal deterioration in that nation. This is, however, a very shaky claim.

In fact, euthanasia has not been legalized in the Netherlands. It remains illegal, but over the course of more than a decade, a rapidly changing system has been developed for establishing guidelines and reporting cases to the coroner. This system, if followed, guarantees that the physician concerned will not be prosecuted. Thus far the reporting to the coroner has been poor. Research has been difficult, but some obvious abuses have surfaced, leading euthanasia critics to suggest that the Dutch experience, rather than disproving the slippery slope scenario, actually supports it. Margaret Pabst Battin, a professor of philosophy at the University of Utah who has deeply studied the subject, argues that neither claim is justified. Additionally, she points to profound differences between the American and Dutch legal and medical systems. In particular, the Dutch medical system is socialized in such a manner that physicians can in no way profit from the practice of assisted suicide. She concludes that at this point in time it would be unwise for either opponents or proponents of euthanasia to use the Dutch experience to support their claims. The controversy over euthanasia continues in the Netherlands in its unique manner, and I suspect that Dr. Battin hopes, as do I, that it will continue in the United States in its own different way.* In any case, the slippery slope hypothesis will remain potentially very real for me until proven otherwise.

The euthanasia debate was initiated in part by a somewhat mechanistic society in which the technology of modern medicine played a leading role. In the case of many hopelessly ill patients kept alive by painful heroic measures, it has been a technology run amok. Dying people quite properly do not want to be put at the mercy of machines. But now that this situation has begun to improve significantly, moving to the other extreme of making assisted suicide a right strikes me as a most destructive example of reaction formation, of throwing out the proverbial baby with the bathwater. Among other things that advocates of euthanasia on demand fail to realize is that the achievement of their ends would quite possibly create a society even more soulless and mechanistic than the one we have now. It would be a society where there is no potential glory in dying, an utterly rational society where people are simply put to sleep upon request without any reference to the irrational mystery of their souls or to God who is their source and that of all true glory.

---

* Battin, "A Dozen Caveats Concerning Discussion of Euthanasia in the Netherlands," in Moreno, ed., *Arguing Euthanasia,* pp. 88–109.

Chapter 10

THE HOPE OF THE EUTHANASIA DEBATE

I have expressed my hope that the euthanasia debate will heat up and become ever more passionate. Conversely, my fear is that the courts will continue their strange rush to judgment in legalizing physician-assisted suicide, and that the public will passively accept such judicial opinion, and that the matter will then cease to stimulate the deep attention of the entire society.

It might seem odd to encourage broad societal debate and intellectual struggle. My concern, however, arises from the understanding that the current acceptance of euthanasia is a symptom of two serious societal diseases. If the symptom is relieved by a facile judicial decision, it is probable that the diseases will proceed unchecked. On the other hand, the more heated the euthanasia debate becomes, the more likely it is that society will constructively and rapidly address the two underlying problems. One of these problems is the spotty, unpredictable quality of medical care in the United States, particularly in regard to pain management and the assistance of natural death. The other is our rampant secularism. If it can stimulate society to heal these two disorders, then the euthanasia debate is a cause for great hope.

———

"Spotty" is an almost euphemistic description for our medical system. U.S. medical care is frequently the best in the world. With equal frequency, however, it is so poor as to be inexcusable. What this means, among other things, is that it is unpredictable. Consider the medical insurance system. Some Americans can count on care by physicians or hospitals of their choosing; some can count on care, but not by physicians and hospitals of their choosing; and some cannot count on any care at all.

Diseased though our medical insurance system may be, the euthanasia issue is rooted more primarily in other unpredictabilities. Since quality pain management and care of the dying are generally not taught in medical schools, the expertise of physicians in such matters is spotty indeed. The average patient has no idea whether she is going to be the beneficiary of good pain management or poor pain management. If she's dying, she cannot predict whether her physician believes in hospice and comfort care or whether he is antagonistic to both. Indeed, she cannot even count on her physician being willing to talk with her about dying. Given the impotence—the lack of control—attendant upon such unpredictability, it is no wonder to me that many would want the power of management offered by the right to physician-assisted suicide.

Nevertheless, their desire is symptomatic of a diseased medical system. A right to physician-assisted suicide is like an antidote to a poison. It would be far better to get rid of the poison than to have to administer the antidote all the time, especially when this particular antidote is itself dangerous and counteracts only a part of the poison.

In personal communication Andrew Solomon has told me he believes his mother would have allowed herself to die a natural death if she had been certain that it would be physically painless, if she could have counted on her physicians not to hesitate to employ the double effect were it necessary. But at the time, rightly or wrongly, she felt she could not count on it. So Seconal—suicide— was her antidote to her not unrealistic fear that she would fall into the hands of one or more physicians with no understanding of comfort care. It is a serious poison indeed when suicide has to be its antidote. Let's get rid of this poison.

If the euthanasia debate can be not only kept alive but heated up, I believe physicians and nurses will respond by removing the poison. Public opinion as well as their own consciences will lead them to establish mandatory nursing and medical school courses in sophisticated pain management, death and dying, hospice care, and the double effect. Not only will those who are dying be the beneficiaries, but so will all patients in pain and, surprisingly, the physicians and nurses themselves. In my experience, most medical professionals find their lives enriched by such education.

As long as the euthanasia debate doesn't die too early a death, I am almost certain the medical profession is capable of this self-reformation without any government interference. Doctors abhor any prospect of regulation from outside their profession. This doesn't mean that the government can't subtly encourage them to change. And there is one area where the courts could with a single sentence offer extraordinary encouragement: not by legitimizing physician–assisted suicide but by legitimizing the double effect.

Critical though it is to the euthanasia issue, the double effect has never to my knowledge been tested in court. Probably there has never been reason to. No one has ever sued because a relative died without pain, and the government has not seen fit to interfere in what it has regarded as a purely professional medical judgment. Yet it is my sense that, because of their oath to prolong life and their dread of being sued for malpractice, a vast number of physicians are unnecessarily afraid of the double effect, as if it's something they shouldn't touch. The matter need not require test by lawsuit. Indeed, in my best-case fantasy the Supreme Court issues a majority opinion holding that physician–assisted suicide is not a constitutional right for a variety of reasons, including the perfect legitimacy of the double effect, which may be used to ensure that a natural death need not be a painful one.

Government acknowledgment that the double effect is in no way illegal would be a giant step forward in solving the problem of euthanasia—the symptom—by giving physicians and nurses a giant dose of encouragement in healing this underlying disease of medicine. Medical professionals would feel liberated—liberated from a groundless fear, liberated to talk openly about the double effect, liberated to teach the care of the dying, liberated to accept hospice, liberated to practice comfort care . . . I could go on and on. If this change was the only result of the euthanasia debate, U.S. medicine would look back upon the debate with gratitude for centuries to come.

———

But this will not be the only change as long as the euthanasia debate becomes increasingly vibrant. Assuming such vibrancy, I can barely imagine the number and the magnitude of societal improvements that could result. Again, it is quite conceivable to me that historians of the future will mark the debate as *the* turning point in U.S. history, on a par with the Declaration of Independence. They will see it as a watershed time when a possibly moribund society almost magically became revitalized. It may seem paradoxical that the serious consideration of death and dying would be revitalizing, but the world is full of paradox and it is both my experience and that of others that whenever we are willing fully to engage ourselves in the mystery of death, the experience is usually enlivening. Indeed, this is the central message of Joseph Sharp's book *Living Our Dying: A Way to the Sacred in Everyday Life.*

I suggested that our society is possibly moribund. We can see many symptoms of its potentially fatal disease, ranging from our confused health care system to our dysfunctional federal government. I believe the major underlying disease is the secularism of U.S. society as manifested in its denial of the soul. The greatest hope I can see on the horizon for the healing of this disease lies in the euthanasia debate. If many are willing to think deeply about the issues of the debate, then many will encounter their own souls, often for the first time.

Please understand that I am not worried about the tiny number of outright atheists or about the larger number of thoughtful agnostics. The secularism that alarms me is that of the vast number of titularly religious people. How is it that a nation primarily composed of supposedly religious believers, many of whom are fond of public prayer breakfasts, can have a thoroughly secular society? The answer, as I suggested in the chapter on secularism, goes deeper than the First Amendment's separation of church and state. The problem lies in a pallid religion. The fact of the matter is that most people in the United States do not take their religion, their God, or their souls very seriously.

Whole books can be and have been written about this phenomenon. The best I have read recently is *The Trivialization of God: The Dangerous Illusion of a Manageable Deity* by Donald W. McCullough.* If, as McCullough suggests, we are generally so arrogant as to think we can manage God, then it is hardly surprising that we should have a secular society where there is not yet dramatic opposition to the notion that we have the right to manage the time and means of our death. The fact is that we are terrified of a *real* God. Naturally, then, we are terrified of the time of our death, the time when our souls will actually meet the real God. Could it be that our generally bland response to the euthanasia issue is symptomatic of a subconscious wish that we could euthanize God from our lives?

Since this issue is spiritual as well as medical, it would be entirely appropriate for the euthanasia debate to be waged most vigorously in our churches, synagogues, mosques, and temples. I am not, however, optimistic that this will happen. My overwhelming experience with religious congregations is that they will do almost anything to avoid open debate. Just as the members tend to want a manageable deity, so they want a smoothly managed religious life without conflict. Still, I can hope. Huge numbers of clergy for years have spoken yearningly of the need for revitalization of the church and of their congregations. The euthanasia debate offers the ideal means for this to occur. I suspect, however, that it will occur only to the degree that clergy are willing to take the risk of forcing the issue. I

---

* Donald W. McCullough, *The Trivialization of God: The Dangerous Illusion of a Manageable Deity* (Colorado Springs: NavPress, 1995).

pray for those who do, for they are likely to meet with much resistance. Yet if they can succeed, there will be revitalization, and they will have congregations renewed by wrestling with the mystery of death and hence with the real God.

———

In saying that the secularization of our society goes deeper than the separation of church and state, I didn't mean to imply that this separation hasn't had some ill as well as benign effects. I am particularly concerned about the secularization of public education, which has made it virtually impossible to teach values in our public schools. The First Amendment has been interpreted in such a way as not only to make mandatory public school prayer illegal but also essentially to outlaw the very mention of God. I do not know how to teach values to our children without reference to theories about the meaning of human existence. I do not know how to teach about meaning without reference to theories of the soul. And I do not know how to teach about the soul without reference to theories of God.

The result of outlawing discussion of these matters has been far more devastating, I believe, than a mere deficiency of spiritual education. Marshall McLuhan became famous through his thesis that "The medium is the message."* What message are we giving our children through the medium of an educational system sanitized to be unrelievedly secular? It seems to me that by implication we are teaching them that values are unimportant, that the issues of meaning are irrelevant, that God is not a proper subject of discussion, and that as far as our government is concerned, the children are soulless beings. Certainly the message is that the soul is of no consequence. In other words, without meaning to do so, we are indirectly teaching our children nihilism—a diabolic philosophy that there is no meaning and consequently anything goes.

The answer to this dreadful condition is one I raised in the pre-

———

* Marshall McLuhan, Kathryn Hutchon, and Eric McLuhan, *Media Messages and Language: The World as Your Classroom* (New York: Simon & Schuster, 1980).

ceding chapter in relation to counseling applicants for physician-assisted suicide: the notion of informed consent, or informed choice. The secularist is entitled not to believe in either God or the soul, but is he entitled not even to be exposed to these concepts? He seems in his public schooling to be entitled to education about Darwinian theory, about atomic theory, about the Big Bang theory of the origin of the universe—all of which are indeed theories rather than proven facts. Why should he not also be entitled to education about "soul theory"?

The only problem, as far as I can see, is one of *how* he is exposed. If soul theory is crammed down his throat by fundamentalist teachers as a fact in which he had better believe or else, then I think he should have recourse to the Constitution. If it is presented to him as a widely accepted and inherently important concept that is considered highly debatable by many, then I don't see why he should need to seek recourse in the law. He is free to accept or reject the concept—in other words, to make an informed choice.

But specifically how might soul theory be taught? There are dozens of potential ways, and I challenge educators of all stripes—in college and graduate school, in medicine and business—to flesh out the most creative ones possible. I would use them all. As the one that would reach the widest possible audience at the earliest appropriate time, I would dearly like to see a mandatory and credited course on death and dying taught in every senior high school across the land.

Twenty years ago in my local New England community, after one of their number had died from leukemia and another in a car crash, the local high school juniors and seniors petitioned to have an elective noncredit course on death and dying. A liberal Protestant minister stepped forward with his offer to manage the course and provide a wide variety of instructors—all free. It so happened, however, that in this township the local school board had to approve any new course, whether elective or not, whether it cost anything or not. The school board met and voted 8–1 to deny the course on the grounds that it was "morbid."

There was some hue and cry over their decision: letters to the editor protesting its wisdom and even an editorial doing likewise. Indeed, the turmoil was sufficient to compel the school board to meet for a second time so as to reconsider its decision. Once again it voted 8–1 to deny the course for the same reason.

So society may not be ready to teach its young people—or anyone else—about death and dying. But that was twenty years ago, before pulling the plug became an open issue, before PCA (patient-controlled analgesia) machines came into use, and above all, before the euthanasia debate. Wouldn't it be fascinating and wonderful if the major end result of the euthanasia debate was the institution of such a curriculum change in our public education system!

How might I myself teach such a curriculum?

"Your own death may seem far off at the moment," I would begin by telling the students, "but this course is being taught now because one of the characteristics of thoughtful people is that they begin in adolescence to think about their mortality. What does 'mortality' mean? What does it imply when we say we humans are mortals?"

From there I would cover the denial of death in general and the Kübler-Ross stages of dying in particular, but I would speak also of the exceptions. Then I would relate the stages to the process of major psychological learning in general. "Have any of you gone through these stages already at some time in learning something difficult about yourself or about life?" I would ask. "I want you to think about this, so I'm assigning you to write a one-page story about such a learning." As a textbook for the course I would probably use *Living Our Dying*, a brief, well-written book already mentioned centering on the thesis that we are all dying and have a great deal to learn from living this reality rather than trying to avoid it.

Then I would ask them if they believed in an afterlife and elicit from them their differing visions of it. In response to terrifying medieval notions of hell and purgatory, I'd inform them of more modern Christian notions (C. S. Lewis's view of hell as a place where people—not God—put themselves and my own vision of purgatory as a time of gentle learning and healing). I'd also explore the beliefs of other religions, including karma and reincarnation.

Following this I would solicit their ideas about the soul and how it might differ from the ego as well as how it might relate to learning and maturation. We'd consider secular as well as religious ideas about meaning, such as nihilism and existentialism. From there we'd move on to the various ethical theories with particular emphasis upon ideal observer theory. Among philosophers it is not only the most recent of such theories, but also the only one I know that subtly encourages prayer. We would wonder about distinctions between natural and human evil as well as distinctions between evil, death, and how a supposedly loving God might permit these painful things.

And finally we would conclude the euthanasia debate in all of its ramifications, among them the different types of suffering. It would not be my purpose to urge the students to accept one position or another; it would be purely to inform them so that they would and could engage in the debate with the utmost personal vigor. I suspect it would be vigorous indeed. I suspect it would be a lively course. I suspect the opinions of the students at sixteen would not be the same as at twenty-six, forty-six, or sixty-six, but I also suspect that some worthwhile seeds would have been planted merely by the serious consideration of such deep matters.

―――――

The euthanasia debate is complex and multifaceted. It deserves to call forth the best thinking not only of jurists and ethicists but also of physicians and nurses, theologians and sociologists. Among other things, before the courts rush to judgment, we deserve more plain scholarship and hard scientific research, ranging from more about the situation in the Netherlands to psychological profiles of those seeking euthanasia in the United States.

Nonetheless, it has seemed to me that the most essential issue of the debate is already discernible. I am referring to the concept of the soul. This book is entitled *Denial of the Soul* because, correctly or not, I have seen the euthanasia movement as a predominantly secular phenomenon, and I have spied certain dangers in it. Conversely, in the debate about euthanasia I have envisioned great hope for the potential correction of certain societal imbalances through renewed attention to the soul.

The soul is a larger subject than euthanasia. The truly big question is not so much what society is going to do with the euthanasia issue, but whether we want a society that encourages the soul and its development. Almost all the complexity of the euthanasia debate can ultimately be resolved if it can be put in the context of that one simple question: do we want a society that encourages the soul and its development?

All who wish to explore FCE's services or support its mission are
welcome to write or call
The Foundation for Community Encouragement
P. O. Box 449
Ridgefield, Connecticut 06877
(203) 431-9484
(203) 431-9349 (fax)

INDEX